WHEN MONEY
IS KING

WHEN MONEY

How Revlon's Ron Perelman Mastered the
World of Finance to Create One of
America's Greatest Business Empires,
and Found Glamour, Beauty, and the
High Life in the Bargain

IS KING

RICHARD HACK

DOVE
BOOKS

ISBN 0-7871-1033-7

Printed in the United States of America

Dove Books
8955 Beverly Boulevard
Los Angeles, CA 90048

Distributed by Penguin USA

Text and insert designed and typeset by Folio Graphics Co. Inc.

First Printing: October 1996

10   9   8   7   6   5   4   3   2   1

To Anne Jordan
Always

CONTENTS

Contents

ACKNOWLEDGMENTS

All writers would like to think their work is their own. But such is not the case. Any book, but particularly a biography, is the sum of research, inspiration, and judgment, with input from a variety of sources as well as a technical support team. Their contribution to this book is equally as important as my own, and I would like to recognize them here.

Beth Lieberman, my editor, was both a joy and a taskmaster with whom to work. I look forward to many more books with this talented woman. Les Whitten, who did my tedious line editing, was part-savior, part-teacher. Thank you Les for sharing your wisdom. And a thank you as well to Michael Viner, my publisher, for continuing to inspire me with ever-growing challenges.

Marilyn Richards, who continually opens her home and heart, and provides me a base over which to spread my mess in Los Angeles, you deserve a reward. You have my love.

Ronald Kimani Saleh, my contact within the White House, deserves special mention for his unique personality and attention to detail. Stephen Waudby provided me with my introduction to the Library of Congress, allowing me to master its inner workings with speed and ease. Sterling Richardson and Craig Bowman were my superb hosts in Washington, D.C., permitting me to take over their home during the blizzard of '96.

Thanks for keeping the heat on high. And for all the folks at the Securities and Exchange Commission, my appreciation for access to filings and documents. I've kept my word and your identities secret.

To my hosts in Manhattan, Molly O'Connell and Dave Anderson, you were the best. I still have the key, so expect me back. In Delaware, my sister Joan Anne Henn, as always, warmed the welcome mat. Special thanks to Cassandra Estepp and Richard Henn for guiding me through the research facilities at the University of Delaware, Newark.

Robert Elias Deaton, once again, provided feedback and encouragement during the proofreading process. Thank you, Robert. D. E. Eastman fed the dogs, cats, and Weezie the bird through long periods of incommunicado. You've got the job forever. Thanks as well to the former executives, secretaries, and personnel of Perelman-owned companies. Your input proved invaluable and your insights essential to this biography.

And, finally, to Ronald Owen Perelman, my appreciation for living a life that combines humor, suspense, joy, disappointment, glamour, drama, intrigue, and success in such grand quantities. You gave me a story worth telling.

RICHARD HACK
Maui, Hawaii
September 1996

PROLOGUE

Sun Valley, Idaho, 1996. Ronald Perelman's private jet circled the Friedman Municipal Airport as the pilot waited for final clearance to approach the far runway. Waiting was not one of Ron Perelman's more practiced traits, and it showed. In the posh cabin of the Gulfstream jet, his foot tapped the carpeted floor, as if *that* might make things happen more quickly. The billionaire clutched an unlit H. Uppman cigar in the fingers of his right hand. It was his trademark, handmade for him by the foremost roller at his Consolidated Cigar Company's La Romana factory in the Dominican Republic.

When the plane finally rolled to a stop next to a lineup of no less than a dozen other private planes, Perelman was anxious to step into the Idaho sun; then, just as quickly, pushed into a waiting limousine and disappeared behind the tinted glass. He was far from his Manhattan home base, where his houseman and servants, secretaries and assistants, served to buffer him from the more mundane aspects of everyday life.

He was, after all, extremely wealthy. He owned or controlled over twenty companies, including cosmetics giant Revlon Corporation. *Forbes* magazine last estimated his worth at nearly $4 billion, and that figure was generally conceded as conservative. Without a doubt one of the top five richest men in the United States, he was a few billion behind Microsoft

Corporation's Bill Gates and financier Warren Buffett. Ask Perelman himself about his worth and he would be the first to plead ignorance. It wasn't about the money, in any case. For Ronald Perelman, it was about being a successful businessman. He thought of himself as a builder of companies. And he had come to Sun Valley to be among his own kind.

More than a dozen years had passed since investment banker Herbert A. Allen began assembling some business friends for what he liked to call a "little outing." It was designed as a family affair where corporate executives and their spouses and children could play in the clean Idaho air. Over the years, the event had grown in importance as well as size, and now over 200 chief executive officers from some of America's most influential media giants received Allen's coveted invitation.

Allen & Company had turned the function into a week-long summit where business leaders could share their thoughts about the future of their companies and the nation's economy. It was a hush-hush affair where the press were not invited, and publicity of any kind was shunned. Given the secret guest list, there was little doubt why.

In addition to Gates and Buffett, Allen's guests included Alex J. Madl, then president of AT&T Corporation; Steve Case, the chairman of America Online; M. Douglas Ivester, president of Coca-Cola Company; and John Malone, chairman of Tele-Communications. There was Edgar Bronfman, Jr., president and chief executive officer of The Seagram Company and acting chairman of recently bought MCA-Universal, and Viacom's Sumner Redstone, whose company had won a bidding war for Paramount Studios. In fact, amid the lure of golf and tennis tournaments, rollerblading, skeet shoots, massage therapy, white-water rafting, horseback riding, and personally guided fly-fishing expeditions, a veritable Who's Who of Hollywood was assembled here as well—from Walt Disney Company heads Michael Eisner and Michael Ovitz to MCA's Frank Biondi and DreamWorks SKG chiefs David Geffen and Jeffrey Katzenberg; Silver King Communications' Barry Diller; movie producer Ray Stark; Warner Bros. chairman Terry Semel; Saban Entertainment's Haim Saban; plus News Corporation's chairman Rupert Murdoch. And Ronald Perelman, whose own entertainment credentials hinged on his controlling interest in New World Communications, a group of television stations with production and syndication divisions.

Ironically, months earlier, Murdoch had tried unsuccessfully to buy New World from Perelman, but the two never came close to agreeing on a price for the corporation. Now in the unlikely setting of Sun Valley, Idaho, in the shadow of Mount Baldy, the two billionaires met once again.

While the official morning presentations were well attended, it was at Allen's private evening dinners in his own condominium where dealmakers had an opportunity to quietly discuss potential agreements. Quiet was the way Herbert Allen liked things. His own easy laughter, cynical sense of humor, and gentle guidance had long been hallmarks of his business technique at Allen & Co., and so it was here as well. Surrounded by traditional furniture, American impressionist art, and family photos, this was obviously a home, not an office. But where businessmen move, business moves with them.

At the prodding of Peter Chernin, chairman and CEO of Murdoch's Fox Film Entertainment, the media mogul approached Ron Perelman and suggested the two strike a deal. It mattered little that the agreement could be worth upwards of $3 billion. There weren't lawyers, advisors, and analysts struggling to be heard. Just two billionaires meeting over an early dinner so both could be in bed by 10. Perelman said he would listen; Murdoch said he would call.

Three days later, on Sunday afternoon, the phone rang in Perelman's Beaux Arts townhouse on Manhattan's East 63rd Street. Rupert Murdoch made an offer. Ronald Perelman gave him an answer. The resulting fallout would alter the face of broadcasting across America, affecting millions of viewers as well as thousands of employees. When the final deal was made public, it amazed many. Yet, to Perelman, it was business as usual.

His entire life had been orchestrated in the privacy of boardrooms and executive suites. From childhood onward, he had learned to demand respect through accomplishment. Brilliant in business, energetic and enthusiastic, his sport of choice was the making of money and the running of corporations, and he excelled to the point where he had little competition among his fellow businessmen.

While many financiers leapt to share in the bonanza that was sired by junk bond mania in the 1980s, less than a handful emerged with profit intact when, a decade later, government intervention brought a crashing end to that form of leveraged buyout. Ronald Perelman stood virtually alone as an insider with the money, power, and desire to attack, conquer, and devour any publicly held company that showed vulnerability.

Perelman knew the rules of the corporate jungle better than anyone. Survival of the fittest was the way to maintain prosperity, the way Perelman had learned to fight, long before he had become a favorite of Wall Street, even before he had moved to Manhattan. It was the way of business in a world where power and deals and money became his family, his heritage, his life.

WHEN MONEY
IS KING

ONE

The Early Years

Ronald Owen Perelman wasn't born with a silver spoon in his mouth. More like a sterling place setting for eight. His parents, Raymond and Ruth Caplan Perelman, were themselves born into wealth, and his father's business sense and negotiating skill had made them millionaires by the time Ruth gave birth to Ronnie, her first child, in 1943.

They were living in Greensboro, North Carolina, where Raymond Perelman was stationed in the Air Force. A graduate of the University of Pennsylvania, Raymond was one of two sons of a Jewish Lithuanian immigrant, Morris Perelman, who had made a modest fortune with his firm American Paper Products.

Raymond and his brother Leon joined the family business. Upon their father's death, the siblings took control of the company and began an expansion campaign just as he had apprenticed them to do. For Morris, hard work and long hours were the essential ingredients of success. Raymond and Leon applied those principles and added a few of their own: no-nonsense negotiating and an arrogance built on the foundation of experience.

Based in the north Philadelphia suburb of Elkins Park, Raymond developed a reputation as an elegant, but brutal, businessman whose main concern was the bottom line. Wanting to expand into more lucrative and far-flung enterprises, Raymond left the paper-products business in his brother Leon's capable hands in the early fifties, and went on his own. His first major acquisition was Belmont Iron Works, a fabricator and erector of structural steel. At work, he was critical of the slightest sign of weakness in others, and he brought the same unbending expectations home at the end of the day.

Young Ronnie's father was demanding and relentless in his desire to motivate. There was no time for sandlot baseball or Saturday matinees. Other than attending services together at the nearby Frank Lloyd Wright–designed Beth Shalom Temple, Raymond Perelman's relationship with his oldest son was based on business. Just as his own father had done, Raymond raised his boy to understand the intricacies of balance sheets and cash flow.

Any suggestion of vulnerability or sensitivity was crushed beneath the father's drive for family success. Raymond didn't hesitate to ridicule or lambast the child any more than he would his business associates. His behavior in the boardroom was legendary. Even as late as 1993, the elder Perelman, at age seventy-five and then chairman of RGP Holding Company, made a move to resuscitate auto parts maker Champion Parts' stock. Using his seat on Champion's board of directors, he bruskly dumped that firm's chief executive officer and assumed the position himself. He lasted a month before the verbally abused board removed him from the post.

"He's a rough customer," another member of the Champion board told *Crain's Chicago Business* in 1993. "A month of him as CEO was all the board could take."

Rather than rebel, Ronnie Perelman became determined

to match his father's toughness. He plowed into the increasingly familiar world of business ledgers and stock reports. By the time he was eleven, he was sitting in on board meetings at his father's company. While other teenagers were reading comic books and forming friendships, young Perelman was spending solitary hours after school poring over profit and loss statements and annual reports.

As his father's business grew, Ronald's knowledge grew with it. Each new acquisition became a learning experience. Not content with merely telling his son about takeover prospects, Raymond Perelman would bring Ronald along in the family car to inspect the various sites. On their way home, the two would analyze the potential of the company in question.

By the time Ronald Perelman began attending The Haverford School, a private boys' academy on Philadelphia's posh Main Line, he was a short, thin, and impatient go-getter. Around the school's campus on Lancaster Avenue, he was known as a loner who had little tolerance for the practical jokes of other youths.

Nicknamed "Ginsy" by his classmates on account of a girl he was dating named Ginsburg, his pet expression was "You guys ain't got no right," a response to being teased for his no-nonsense approach to life. Dressed in the requisite uniform of coat and tie, Perelman seemed a yuppie before the word was even coined. Conservative, arrogant, and self-assured, he moved through his high school years uneventfully, graduating in 1960 and sharing the honor of being voted "Most Handsome" with two other classmates. (Ironically, he was not picked "Most Likely to Succeed.")

His thick dark hair, angular features, and inherent wealth were not lost on the local female population, who considered Perelman to be quite a catch. He moved easily among a handful of girlfriends, and escorted them to local dances at the Ashbourne Country Club, the most elegant and exclusive in Elkins Park.

His family's two-story colonial home at 8311 Fairview Road was small by comparison to some of the estates of his Haverford classmates, but in the Perelmans' conservative, predominantly Jewish neighborhood in north Philadelphia, it was a palace. With its second-floor ironwork balconies, the home was more showy than the others on its block, just a short distance from a major highway called Township Line Road.

In the fall of 1960, following his father again, Perelman enrolled at the University of Pennsylvania, located in downtown Philadelphia. Not surprisingly, his major was business. Thrusting himself into the rigors of college life with the same determination he displayed in his father's company, he excelled in his coursework and regularly challenged his professors when he disagreed with their opinions.

If it were not for his combative behavior with his instructors, Perelman would have remained rather anonymous among his Penn classmates. He had little involvement in campus activities, joining only the Hillel Foundation. In fact, Perelman was a racehorse, tethered at the starting gate, eager to return to the realities of the business world. Just as he had done through high school, he continued to work with his father, reviewing spreadsheets, improving productivity, and evaluating potential acquisitions.

In 1961, at the end of his freshman year in college, Ronald Perelman had the opportunity to prove his worth to his father in a tangible way. The elder Perelman had set his sights on acquiring the Esslinger Brewery, a small family-owned beer producer with a strong following in Pennsylvania. Crunching the numbers on the $800,000 purchase, the college student focused on the unrealized potential of the firm, while analyzing the weakest elements in its production line. Projecting substantial profits with limited investment and subtle inventory changes, Ronald laid out a plan for his father which did more than merely suggest a money-making opportunity. It hit the mark—dead center.

Three years after the company's purchase, during Ronald's senior year at Penn, he helped his father sell Esslinger for a profit of $1 million. Equally as important, the deal carried with it a $200,000 tax-loss write-off which could be carried forward and applied against other Perelman businesses.

The coup did far more than make his father a generous return on his investment. It provided the young businessman with his first taste of that unique adrenaline rush on which entrepreneurs thrive. Like a hard-won athletic triumph, the victory was sweet—and highly addicting. Ronald Perelman was hooked.

That summer, flushed with his success and a diploma from the University of Pennsylvania's undergraduate Wharton School of Economics and Finance, the twenty-one-year-old took a vacation cruise to Israel. He visited the holy cities of Jerusalem and Bethlehem, touched the Wailing Wall, and attended services. When he returned to America, he found that he had been moved in profound ways. He intensified his religious commitment, and resolved to keep a kosher home and unfailingly observe the Sabbath. He also fell in love.

Faith Golding was a shy seventeen-year-old student when she and Ronald first met on the cruise to Israel. She was the granddaughter of a New York real estate mogul with numerous holdings in the Bronx and Manhattan, including the Central Park South property on which the famed Essex Hotel was built. Her family also controlled Sterling National Bank.

Faith was attractive, polite, rich, and Jewish—the four elements which Perelman found essential. The fact that she was also quiet only added to her appeal. Faith saw in Perelman a man who was mature beyond his years and who could spoil her much as her family had always done. She found Perelman handsome, attentive, and a source of boundless energy. He was also someone she felt wasn't attracted to her for her money. And she had plenty—some $100 million. After they were married in 1965, Faith Golding Perelman moved to Pennsylvania and Elkins Park, into a home which Ronald had purchased on Meeting House Land, just around the corner from his parents.

By that point, Perelman had started attending the University of Pennsylvania's graduate Wharton School of Finance and Business, earning his master's degree in 1966. He wasted no time in applying his education. Hired by his father as a vice-president of the family's Belmont Iron Works, Perelman traveled between the company's plants in Eddystone and Royersford, Pennsylvania.

Even though he held no equity position in the company, the younger Perelman worked tirelessly for his father, hopeful of impressing the man. The father and son team were successful, even by Perelman standards. In 1967 alone, the pair analyzed and then acquired five different companies—all within Pennsylvania and all operating below their potential.

Schiller-Pfeiffer Company produced garden tools, while General Machine Corporation manufactured industrial equipment. Later in the year, Ronald personally oversaw the $3 million acquisition of P&C Holding Corporation, a privately held company which controlled three additional firms: Penn Galvanizing Company, a metal-coating operation in Philadelphia; Reliance Steel products, which produced bridge flooring, steel and aluminum gratings, and stair treads from their plant in McKeesport; and Hopenn Corporation, a gray-iron foundry in Fairview Village.

The following year, Belmont changed its name to Belmont

Industries while adding Newton Tool and Manufacturing Company plus Edwards Shoes to its growing collection of businesses. In each case, the formula for success remained the same: sell off extraneous divisions of the various companies to lower debt and return them to their core business. The concept worked so well for the father-son team that in late 1968, Belmont announced a three-for-one stock split and increased dividends per share.

With her husband spending all of his days and many of his nights working, Faith found herself rather isolated in her new surroundings. While eager to start a family, she was having little success in becoming pregnant, and eventually she and her husband decided to adopt a child. With the arrival of their son Steven, Faith willingly became a full-time mom. Later, they would adopt a second son Josh, and a daughter Hope. Soon after, Mother Nature intervened and Faith became pregnant with their daughter Deborah.

Coinciding with the adoption of Steven, Ron Perelman began smoking cigars. Even though cigars and babies are a classic duet, in this case the events weren't associated. Perelman's initiation into the circle of cigar aficionados came during a long, drawn-out meeting. As the hours passed, a Belmont Industries attorney, Laddie Montegue, removed a cigar from his pocket and lighted it.

Of the twelve businessmen in the meeting, only Montegue seemed to be enjoying himself. Although he had never previously smoked, Perelman asked the lawyer for a cigar. The flavor and satisfaction he claims to have received upon lighting up were strong enough to keep him smoking between one and five cigars every day since.

The Perelmans were outwardly content. Yet, between Ronald's obsession with work and Faith's devotion to the children, there was little available time for socializing. As a result, the pair developed few close friendships. One major exception was Ronald's introduction in the mid-seventies to a powerful Philadelphia attorney named Howard Gittis. Nearly ten years older than Perelman, Gittis was a partner in the law firm of Wolf, Block, Shorr & Solis-Cohen, and was recognized in the business community as a brilliant negotiator, a man whose diplomacy and tact were at odds with Perelman's harsh and abrupt style. Together, however, they made a winning team, and one which was destined to last a lifetime.

At first, Gittis found Perelman's sheer energy extraordinary. Helping him to harness it proved next to impossible. "I tried to get Ronald to slow down, be more patient," Gittis would later say about those early years in their relationship. "But it was tough getting him to slow down."

He began to make regular trips to New York in an effort to reorganize Faith's business affairs, which had severely deteriorated due to mismanagement. "Ron did a brilliant job in reorganizing Faith's affairs," Gittis later said. "He literally saved her fortune." He also introduced himself to Manhattan and Wall Street—two elements which would play important roles in his life ahead.

If anything, Perelman was more impatient than ever. Though he was surrounded by the trappings of success, there was a major void in his life—one which neither Faith nor his family could fill. Working long hours under his father's watchful eye denied him any real decision-making power within the company. He was essentially a businessman without a business to call his own.

In 1978, Raymond Perelman turned sixty years old. It had been twelve years since his son had joined Belmont Industries. During that time, their core business, Belmont Iron Works, had been liquidated through a sale to Ingalis Iron Works Company of Birmingham, Alabama.

The remaining companies were strong, achieving record levels of sales and profits, and Ronald was anxious to capitalize on their potential by expanding even more dramatically. At age thirty-five, the younger Perelman felt he was ready to take over the reins at Belmont and asked his father about his plans for retirement.

When Raymond informed his son that he had no foreseeable desire to retire, Raymond immediately began making plans to leave the family concern. He would later comment that during his time with Belmont, his position was "vice-president of learning." Within months after his talk with his father about retirement, he concluded that his education at Raymond's knee was complete, and he struck out on his own for New York City.

"It wasn't enough," Perelman said about his decision to leave the family nest. "I wanted to create an entity on my own, without the constraints of the familial relationship."

His father didn't understand his son's need to become independent, didn't approve of the way he left Belmont Industries, and essentially turned his back on his oldest child. For the next six years, they barely spoke.

If the elder Perelman ever respected the risk his son was taking in cutting his ties with Pennsylvania and his family's cash flow, he never admitted it. From his point of view, Ronald had jumped ship without preparation and with characteristic impatience and haste. Although he had considerable exposure to financial statements and boardrooms, Ronald Perelman arrived in Manhattan without important connections or a game plan.

He had money, however, and plenty of it. He had amassed considerable savings and, combined with the financial security of his wife's revitalized estate, hit Manhattan looking less at the bottom line than his own future. He moved with Faith and their four children into the sumptuous Sherry Netherland Hotel, and from there he launched his life, walking a financial high wire with no net in sight.

Impetuous, caustic, and demanding, Perelman didn't finesse his way into the financial community. In the late seventies, the "Old Boys Club of Wall Street" was faced with a rash of upstarts attempting to make their own names in the stock market. Most established bankers at the time saw Perelman as one of those upstarts, a man whose pushy demeanor and cigar smoke gave them more reason for irritation than for confidence.

Not so, however, with Don Engel at the investment banking house of Drexel Burnham Lambert. The high-octane financial type was a close ally of Michael Milken, whose own exploits on the West Coast had jarred the investment world with his theories of creating vast amounts of capital based on illusion rather than collateral. Engel recognized a kindred spirit in Perelman and befriended the newcomer.

Engel and several of his business broker buddies began to feed Perelman likely candidates for his takeover strategies. Assisted by the continual advice—and restraint—of Howard Gittis, who remained in Philadelphia, Perelman single-handedly did what he had always done so effectively for his father. He crunched numbers and projected profits, and after several flurries of selection, analysis, and rejection, this process led to a target: Cohen-Hatfield Industries.

Melvin S. Cohen and Glen J. Hatfield, Jr., were the chairman and president of a family-run chain of nineteen retail jewelry stores in California, Kentucky, and Michigan which operated under the name of Hatfield Jewelers. In addition to these nineteen, the corporation operated jewelry counters inside 218 Wal-Mart, Zayre, and Sky City discount stores. Hatfield Jewelers were heavily into the gold chains, small diamonds, and inexpensive gemstones that appealed to the mass consumers of the late seventies. They were also in financial chaos.

The company was publicly traded on the American Stock Exchange and, despite its estimated book value of $7 per share, was selling at just $3.75. It was a bargain that Ronald Perelman could not let pass. He knew nothing about diamonds, emeralds, or pearls. His knowledge of gold chains was negligible. But he knew about assets. Cohen-Hatfield was sitting—literally—on a gold hoard of sellable goods that could be liquidated rapidly, easily, and at an enormous profit. The gold alone was worth three times the selling price of the stock.

When Perelman approached Melvin Cohen with an offer to buy 40 percent of the company's 1.4 million outstanding shares at a price of $1.9 million, the seasoned jewelry executive welcomed the newcomer and his capital. With the principal shares coming from members of the Hatfield family, it seemed a safe enough transaction.

On May 24, 1978, Cohen concluded the deal. The following day's late issue of the *Wall Street Journal* reported the sale. It would be the first time that "private investor" Ronald Perelman was mentioned in the publication. And although Mr. Cohen could hardly have known it at the time, he was launching an American financial empire.

With additional stock pulled from two outside holders and a few non-active members of the Cohen family, Ronald Perelman was appointed vice-chairman of the corporation under Melvin Cohen. He had consummated the deal by floating a $1.9 million bank loan, secured by his own personal funds.

Ronald's first stop after buying into Cohen-Hatfield was the Arkansas office of Sam Walton, chairman of Wal-Mart Stores. "Ron had never met the man," recalled Gittis, "but made an appointment and went to see the billionaire to talk him into buying Cohen-Hatfield–owned jewelry counters in all the

Wal-Mart Stores." Walton jumped at the opportunity. It was a process which Perelman would repeat across the country. By the following year, all Cohen-Hatfield's jewelry stores had been sold, while their most valuable diamond and gold pieces were disposed of independently. Helping him complete the deal: Howard Gittis, who had been added to Cohen-Hatfield's board of directors. After repaying his bank loan, Ron Perelman netted a quick $15 million profit—seed money for his company buy.

With Cohen-Hatfield Industries now reduced to its most profitable operation, the wholesale jewelry division run by Melvin Cohen, Perelman called once more on business brokers to find him another ripe asset. Perelman was not alone, by any means, in the takeover arena. The national financial centers were swarming with overzealous entrepreneurs eager to make a quick profit where they could. They were abetted by a consumer recession that had taken a heavy toll on many businesses.

Making the financial markets even more skittish, and thus open to leveraged buyouts, was the unrest that prevailed around the globe. Oil prices had soared, causing massive lines at fuel pumps, and the Middle East was plunged into scattered yet continuous wars between religiously opposed factions. Looking on this unstable climate as an untapped opportunity, Perelman walked where most others feared to even glance.

Armed with a new assortment of potential takeover prospects, Perelman spent his characteristic long hours reworking the numbers, specifically targeting corporations with unprofitable divisions that might be liquidated to his advantage. Along the way, he picked up several new assets. One was a spacious apartment that Perelman and his wife Faith bought at 740 Park Avenue. The other: an important ally, Barry Slovin, then a highly paid executive of Sir Gordon White's Hanson

Industries. Studious and refined, Slovin had established an impeccable reputation by acquiring businesses for Hanson. On meeting Perelman, Slovin was impressed with the young financier's remarkable energy and drive as well as his enthusiasm for acquisitions.

Perelman, for his part, was eager to keep up his momentum. And now he had attracted the attention of the entrenched and established financial houses. As his reputation grew and his connections strengthened, Perelman increased the pressure on himself to perform. There must be no false steps, no obvious mistakes, on his second move. For that reason, he returned to familiar ground: a small New Jersey company called MacAndrews & Forbes, whose name was to figure mightily in his future.

Almost ten years before, when a younger Perelman was learning the business from his father, the elder Perelman had made a run for MacAndrews & Forbes Company, a supplier of licorice extract and bulk chocolate which had been started a century before. At the time, Raymond Perelman was rebuffed. Instead, MacAndrews & Forbes ended up being purchased by a Polish immigrant named Samuel Rosenblum and his partner Lawrence Katz.

Katz and Rosenblum, well known in Philadelphia for their twice weekly late-night games of gin at the famed Locust Club, were cigar-smoking buddies straight out of Damon Runyon. Together with their wives, the pair regularly traveled to Iran in search of licorice root, dined with the Shah at his palace, and hunted for trinkets of jade and ivory.

By the late seventies, however, Katz was ailing and Rosenblum was tiring of the business, which had become quite unpredictable, in large part due to the instability in Iran and the overthrow of its royal leader. When Ronald Perelman learned

of the partners' desire to liquidate their share of the operation, he moved.

Rosenblum and Katz retained Michael Tarnopol at the
brokerage house of Bear Stearns & Company to sell their 25
percent of the business. Despite repeated overtures from
Perelman, Tarnopol was unable to convince the partners to
sell to the financier. Tarnopol would later remember that the
pair were simply unpredictable. "These guys refused to sell to
Ronald," he was quoted in *Institutional Investor.* "They didn't
think his money was green." In reality, Rosenblum and Katz
remembered quite well the elder Perelman's rush for the business a decade before and refused Ronald Perelman's overture
because of it.

Tarnopol, instead, sold the shares in April 1979 for $8.6
million to a pair of investors from Binghamton, New York—
Richard and Burton Koffman. Then, as now, Perelman did not
like to lose, and he kept watching the firm, biding his time.
Meanwhile, he looked at other potential acquisitions—a paper
manufacturer, not unlike his grandfather's, and a small publisher in Philadelphia. But neither offered the profit potential
that MacAndrews & Forbes Company did. By October 1979,
interest rates were skyrocketing, and the Koffman brothers
elected to liquidate their newly acquired MacAndrews &
Forbes stock. They planned to use the resulting cash to make
high-interest loans with a guaranteed return.

With Tarnopol acting as intermediary, Perelman was introduced to the Koffmans and quickly negotiated the purchase.
Just before Halloween, Cohen-Hatfield announced that it had
purchased 394,591 shares of MacAndrews & Forbes stock from
Commonwealth Life Insurance Company and the Koffmans.
The selling price was $25 a share for a total of nearly $10
million. Perelman's sole purpose in buying the stock, which

amounted to a 22 percent ownership, was to position himself to wholly acquire the business in the months ahead. It was to be an arduous task.

The revolution taking place in Iran, as well as its war with neighboring Iraq, made the supply of licorice root inconsistent at best. An alternative supplier, Afghanistan, was also feeling the effects of an internal war, and the stability of MacAndrews & Forbes was in question. The price of the stock fell 20 percent in two months, leaving analysts questioning Perelman's continued interest in the company. Their wonder heightened when, just before the close of the year, Cohen-Hatfield offered to acquire all of MacAndrews & Forbes for $24 a share, substantially more than it was currently trading for.

Despite what many analysts viewed as a generous offer, the board of MacAndrews & Forbes attempted to negotiate the price higher. Melvin Cohen, still chairman of Cohen-Hatfield Industries, responded by stating: "We've told them that's the price. We feel it's been accepted." It would be the last time Cohen spoke on the record in Ronald Perelman's behalf.

Although the MacAndrews board would officially approve the merger several weeks later, a group of angry investors filed suit to block the $34 million sale. They called the melding of jewelry and licorice an unsuitable blend, while alleging that it "lacked any bona fide business purpose." Had they taken the time to analyze Perelman's past business dealings, the purpose would have been clear. It was to make a huge profit for Ronald Owen Perelman.

By filing suit in New York court on February 24, 1980 for unspecified damages, the dissident stockholders hoped to forestall what proved to be inevitable. Despite their claims that Perelman's offer of $24 a share was "grossly unfair," the court refused to stop the takeover, and two months later the financier added licorice and chocolate to his growing empire.

15

If the stockholders had any question about Perelman's serious intentions when he bought the company, he didn't leave them wondering for long. Moving swiftly into action, he consolidated his holdings under the new company banner of MacAndrews & Forbes Group, and appointed the licorice firm's former senior vice-president and treasurer, Robert T. Carlton, his chief financial officer. At the same time, Melvin Cohen found his former firm, Cohen-Hatfield, absorbed into the holding company, and he became chairman of MacAndrews's jewelry division.

Confident of his salesmanship, Perelman traveled to North Carolina and personally met with executives from various cigarette manufacturers. Licorice extract is commonly used to heighten tobacco's flavor, and soon cigarette makers became a major new outlet for the company. Uncomfortable relying on Iran and Afghanistan for his supply of licorice root, Perelman sent buyers to Russia, Iraq, Eastern Turkey, and the Xinjiang Uygur province of China to develop relationships. In addition, he extended MacAndrews's wholesale market to Europe by buying a licorice-extract supplier in France with its established continental distribution network.

At the same time, he held meetings with Bear Stearns and Drexel Burnham Lambert. His goal: to convince investment bankers they should handle the sale of $35 million in low-grade, high-yield debt for the purchase of MacAndrews. It required big talk, bright concepts, and intense energy. As Perelman was buying he was selling himself, and Wall Street was only too happy to go right along for the payoff. It was a precursor of the legendary junk bond, and Perelman was positioning himself on the second floor before most of the rest of Wall Street was even in the elevator.

He used the proceeds to repay the consortium of banks that, led by Chase Manhattan Corporation, had floated the loans for his MacAndrews stock buyout.

On a roll, and flush with cash (as well as ever-increasing debt), Perelman returned to his profit and loss sheets, searching for his next takeover target. He increased his work hours, stealing them from the few moments he was currently spending with his family. Ronald Perelman had made a choice: his work was his life, and his family, including his wife Faith, was slowly realizing that this commitment was getting stronger.

For months, he had been following the activities of Richardson Company, an Illinois manufacturer of specialty chemicals and battery parts, incorporated in Ohio. He had even quietly bought a minority shareholder position in the firm through MacAndrews & Forbes Group. In November 1981, he decided the time was ripe to buy up the remainder of the company. It was just over two years since he had done the same maneuver with MacAndrews & Forbes Company. This time, however, he was using his own funds.

"Ronald's confidence was his strongest feature and his weakest," a Wall Street analyst was later quoted. "He believed he was a financial genius. The Richardson experience proved he was more like a lucky opportunist."

In early November, the board of directors of the Richardson Company rejected the takeover bid of MacAndrews & Forbes Group. They based their decision on a written opinion of the investment banking house First Boston Corporation, which had found MacAndrews's bid "inadequate as to price." First Boston advised that Richardson would be "better served by remaining independent."

Perelman had offered the company $24 a share, or $44.8 million, for the 81 percent of the company he didn't own already. Leaving little room for compromise, Richardson's board notified its shareholders that it "strongly urged that the offer be rejected."

In an effort to make certain that the company remained unraided, Richardson's board filed in a federal court in Ohio for a temporary restraining order to block MacAndrews & Forbes's tender offer. Judge Arthur S. Spiegel denied the request, but scheduled a preliminary hearing on the matter for November 23. He cited Richardson's contention that Mac-Andrews was violating Ohio state law, and instructed the state to detail its position.

While the lawyers were busy preparing their cases, the board of Richardson Co. took behind-the-scenes action and approached Witco Chemical Company to rescue them from the grasp of what they privately labeled "some candy company." Witco responded firmly and positively. Three days before the preliminary hearing, Witco offered $27.50 a share, or $60.4 million, for its Des Plaines, Illinois, competitor in a friendly buyout. It was not only a $3.50 per share increase over Perelman's offer, it was substantially more than the going price of the stock. Smith Barney, Harris Upham and Company, and Goldman Sachs & Company were brought in to handle the Witco tender offer, while First Boston continued to advise Richardson.

Ronald Perelman had been publicly slapped down. Several weeks later, the MacAndrews & Forbes Group returned all the Richardson Co. shares it had tendered under its offer, while turning a small profit on the few Richardson shares it had held before its raid. Wall Street was smugly relishing the slip, but failed to realize that Perelman didn't regard it as a failure. Like his time spent serving under his father, this, too, was a learning experience. His profit was in the form of knowledge rather than big bucks. But he profited nonetheless.

During the Richardson gambit, Perelman was being counseled by Joseph Flom, the inspired attorney who was instrumental in turning the legal firm of Skadden, Arps, Slate, Meagher & Flom into a Wall Street powerhouse. And while Flom's advice hadn't helped Perelman capture Richardson Co., it had provided an introduction with a far more lasting impact on the financier's life.

For several years, Flom had been mentoring a smart legal cookie named Donald Drapkin, who joined Skadden, Arps in 1978. Educated at Brandeis University, the cocky and streetwise Queens native went on to study at Columbia Law School, where he was a Harlan Fiske Stone Scholar.

The flashy Drapkin began his law career at the top-notch firm Cravath, Swaine & Moore, where he so distinguished himself that Skadden, Arps and Joseph Flom lured him away with the promise of ever-larger takeover wars. The short, bald, cigar-smoking attorney could have been mistaken for Perelman's brother in appearance, taste, and mannerisms.

Despite their similarities, their backgrounds were quite different. While Perelman had been raised in luxury, Drapkin was from a middle-class family (his father George owned a taxi company). And while Perelman inherited much of his business sense and drive, Drapkin learned his skills through arduous study and thoroughness.

Yet, so naturally did Drapkin and Perelman bond that the young attorney soon was providing the fledgling financier with regular legal advice. More than merely an advisor, "The Drapper" became Perelman's best friend in New York, much the same way the older Howard Gittis had been in Philadelphia.

Eager to brighten his tarnished Midas touch, Perelman

plunged into discussions with Gulf + Western Industries about a friendly acquisition of its Consolidated Cigar Company division, the largest producer of cigars in the United States. Perelman pledged $30 million in long-term notes in addition to $75 million in cash for the company. Charlie Bluhdorn and Martin Davis of Gulf + Western were anxious to remove the capital-intensive cigar company from their books. At the time, Gulf + Western was involved with entertainment, financial services, consumer products (among them cigars), manufacturing, automotive and building products, and natural resources and foodstuffs, and was in radical need of streamlining its operation.

While the two firms agreed in principle to a sale, and even signed an agreement in April 1982, there were unresolved conditions such as certain warranties that Perelman wanted and Gulf + Western refused to give. As the months passed with no resolution in sight, Perelman began to weary of the delay. He dropped out of the deal in August.

Within weeks, Consolidated Cigar was sold to a management consortium that negotiated an internal buyout. While the deal was broken at Perelman's instigation, to many on Wall Street it looked like another miss for the high-flying financier.

Although he had not annexed a new firm in two years, Perelman's financial picture was stronger than ever. MacAndrews & Forbes was increasing its share of the licorice business, and the wholesale jewelry division was operating profitably. With his enlarged cash flow, it was only a matter of time before he found another target for acquisition.

Technicolor had been a prominent component of the movie industry since the advent of color technology in the 1930s. Long known for its panoplies of reds and blues, the Technicolor stamp added cachet to a production. In the late seventies, the company decided to diversify into one-hour retail color processing labs, capitalizing on the Technicolor name. The start-up costs were a financial drain on the corporation and the consumer outlets never attracted the customer attention for which Technicolor executives had hoped. This Hollywood legend had been on the sales block for a while with nary a taker until Ronald Perelman came to town.

He happened upon the company quite by accident one day while conducting business on an upper floor in the building housing Technicolor's corporate offices. As he was riding down in the elevator, the car happened to stop on Technicolor's floor, offering Perelman a brief glimpse of its lobby and reception area backed by a large Technicolor logo.

"That's a good company," Perelman remarked to a stranger in the elevator, indicating Technicolor. "It's a *great* company," the man replied. The innocent exchange was enough to whet Perelman's curiosity, for when the elevator reached the ground floor, Perelman pushed the button to head back to Technicolor's floor. Walking into the firm's lobby, he asked the receptionist for the company's annual report. That night he spent the evening crunching numbers and decided to buy the film-processing house.

Bear Stearns & Co.'s Michael Tarnopol would be Perelman's Dolly Levi in his love affair with Technicolor. Only weeks later, at Perelman's request, Tarnopol interceded with Technicolor board member Fred Sullivan to arrange an introduction with the company's chief executive officer, Morton Kamerman. Sullivan was only too happy to fly to Hollywood with Perelman to set up the meeting. After all, he had the promise from Perelman of $150,000 for his effort.

Since Kamerman was already looking for a buyer, and Perelman was eager to pay what was viewed by many as a premium price, it took little salesmanship from the financier. He promised to purchase Technicolor for $102 million, or $23 a share, and to assume $17 million of its debt. As recently as a month earlier, Technicolor stock had been languishing at $9 a share. The slam dunk of the Technicolor deal was accomplished within months, with MacAndrews & Forbes taking control in January 1983.

Fred Sullivan benefited substantially from the takeover deal. And Mort Kamerman also came up a winner. He renegotiated his contract so as to be phased out of the operation after two years, with his $426,215 a year salary continuing until 1988. He then would serve as a consultant to the firm for five years, at an additional salary of $150,000 per year plus expenses.

Yet, not everyone was happy about the transfer of ownership—among them investor Michael Forman. Forman's family owned Cinerama Corporation, which in turn owned 4.5 percent of Technicolor stock. Forman thought the purchase price of $23 a share was grossly inadequate, and sued Perelman in order to have a court decide the matter. It would be years before the suit would be heard; and, at the moment, Ronald Perelman's attention was focused on restoring Technicolor's leadership position in Hollywood.

Almost immediately upon taking control of the business, Perelman started to micromanage it. He sold off five extraneous divisions, including the one-hour film labs and some assorted real estate, reducing his debt by $68 million. He then moved himself onto the board of directors as its chairman, and hit the ground running.

Taking his dog-and-pony show on the road, Perelman begged meetings with Hollywood's studio elite, including MCA-Universal's Lew Wasserman and Warner Bros.' Terry Semel. He pitched Technicolor's low-cost processing at a time when others were asking top dollar. Morning, noon, and night, he labored far from his familiar Northeast surroundings in an effort to convince Hollywood's filmmakers to stick with Technicolor or give the company another chance to prove its worth. His pitch was as effective as it was timely. Technicolor began a turnaround, aided by the advent of multiplex theaters. Six, eight, or twelve theaters in one facility became the norm, and movies thus opened in 1,700–2,000 theaters on a single day. It was a boom period for all film processors, Technicolor among them.

As the months passed, not only did Technicolor's worth in Hollywood rise, but so did Ronald Perelman's. The show business community was taken with his zesty arrogance and fed off his energy. He developed friendships among studio executives and stars alike, and was invited to parties where names like Schwarzenegger and Stallone were in attendance.

Returning to New York, buoyed by his renewed success, Ronald Perelman turned forty. He was rich; he was famous; he was pals with celebrities and political power figures alike. Yet, he remained a man without love in his own heart. His relationship with his wife deteriorated through a series of chilly altercations to a remote coexistence. His parents also remained distant.

It was during this period of commerce at mental highs and emotional family lows that Ron Perelman began an affair with a woman who was both attractive and attentive. She worked as a florist on the East Side of Manhattan. He whisked her off for romantic interludes in the United States and abroad, and showered her with presents. One such trinket: a gold bracelet from Bulgari Jewelers.

Bulgari mistakenly sent the bill for the bracelet to his home instead of his office. Faith Perelman opened the envelope. She immediately hired a private detective, who followed her husband, allegedly witnessing the lovers kissing in the back of his limousine on their way to secret rendezvous at hotels like the Algonquin and the United Nations Plaza.

Faith swiftly contacted well-known attorney Stanley Arkin. He agreed to handle her divorce suit filed on the grounds of adultery. For eighteen years, Faith Golding Perelman had been the quiet wife. She was about to be quiet no longer.

TWO

The Land of Milken Money

H iring a private investigator and an attorney were just the beginning of Faith's moves. She also went through bank records, searching for additional proof of her husband's extramarital affair. She didn't have to look far. In an affidavit filed with her divorce papers, she stated that her husband's mistress had received "at least $100,000 worth of merchandise and services purchased by Mr. Perelman including Bulgari jewelry, a 1982 Mercedes-Benz, expensive clothing, and air transportation to London, Amsterdam, Rome, Geneva, Paris, Zagreb, and various other exotic locales."

More important, as far as Faith Perelman was concerned, was her claim that her husband didn't even use his own money to purchase the gifts. As alleged in her affidavit, the items and services were bought with money which Perelman "wrongfully diverted from First Sterling Corporation—[a real estate holding company] whose shares are beneficially owned in their entirety" by her.

Her husband immediately denied her assertions through his attorney, Roy Cohn. The legendary Mr. Cohn, who had made his own multitudes of fans and enemies as sidekick to

Senator Joseph McCarthy during the famous McCarthy Hearings in the 1950s, began negotiating with Faith's attorney Stanley Arkin to resolve the matter quickly.

When the two first married, Perelman was merely wealthy. Eighteen years later he was *enormously* rich, with a main tent full of corporations and companies over which he ruled supreme. Faith Perelman claimed part ownership of everything, thereby attacking the very heart of her husband's power base.

With Cohn at his side, Perelman moved rapidly to protect his investments. The magnate announced in May 1983 that he intended to take MacAndrews & Forbes Group private by creating a new company, MacAndrews & Forbes Holdings. The new firm would borrow funds against the company's assets to buy the 65 percent of MacAndrews & Forbes that Perelman didn't already own.

MacAndrews & Forbes Group's fortunes had skyrocketed with the addition of Technicolor on the books. In the first quarter of 1983 alone, sales had more than doubled to $83.4 million—although net profit amounted to only $1.9 million. It would have been higher had not Perelman settled former Technicolor chairman Mort Kamerman's contract for a $1.8 million pretax charge.

With Perelman's announcement that MacAndrews was "going private," the corporation's stock plummeted on the American Stock Exchange to $44.75 a share. The reaction was due in part to the news that the company was going deeper in debt. Prior to the purchase of Technicolor, Standard & Poor's had given MacAndrews & Forbes a "B-minus" debt rating. With the Technicolor deal adding $102 million of additional debt, Standard & Poor's dropped the Perelman corporation to a "triple-C," citing "increased financial risk."

If Wall Street was frowning after Perelman's announcement, they were smiling wryly after Faith Perelman made one of her own. *She,* not her husband, she alleged, owned his stock in MacAndrews & Forbes Group. In a statement filed with the Securities and Exchange Commission, Faith said the 33.9 percent controlling block of stock in the corporation was held in his name for her.

According to Stanley Arkin, money for 480,242 shares came from a loan from the Bankers Trust Company granted in both their names but "predicated on Mrs. Perelman's credit." A further source of funds was a joint account whose mainstay was her independent income, Arkin stated.

Roy Cohn attempted to defuse the explosive situation. "Her claim to that stock is a joke," he said, laughing. "Every filing for the last six years lists Ronald O. Perelman as the owner, and not once has she ever claimed any kind of interest in the stock." As for the bank loan, Cohn called Faith's assertions "a lot of nonsense. It was an unsecured loan and there was no collateral. She has no interest in it whatsoever."

Faith Perelman was not about to be dismissed so easily. The SEC took her filing seriously and began its own investigation. Now on a roll, Faith gave her estranged husband another slap by filing an additional suit through her attorney. In this separate claim, she alleged that her husband defrauded First Sterling Corporation of $9,000 for a Mercedes-Benz automobile he had bought for her, as well as $25,000 in travel expenses. Despite Perelman's general denial of all her allegations, $18,000 was suddenly repaid to First Sterling Corp. by a New Jersey travel agent.

"It's baloney," Cohn tried to explain. "First Sterling is not her company. It's *his* company. He built it by his own efforts and had full authority to draw travel expenses." Cohn filed a countersuit to have the court establish ownership of the firm.

The world of business had watched Ronald Perelman's rise to financial power with mild interest. Now, they were glued to their local morning news for the next installment of "As Perelman Turns." For weeks, the divorce titillated the mighty and hoi polloi alike. Roy Cohn never missed an opportunity for publicity, and Faith Perelman supplied him with ample statements to refute.

His private life made public in this way was Perelman's most shattering nightmare come true. His affair with the florist was doomed. One couldn't very well be sneaking into the Algonquin while all of New York watched and told. Rather, Perelman moved quickly to clamp a lid on the entire issue by giving Faith what he knew she understood. Money. And lots of it.

While the details of their divorce settlement have widely been reported in the neighborhood of $3.8 million, the actual figures are far more substantial. To get Faith off his back and out of his life, Ronald Perelman is said to have handed her $8 million in cash and assets. Additionally, she received the apartment on Park Avenue, all her jewelry and her Mercedes, plus the uncontested ownership of First Sterling, child support for their four children, and repayment of a $3.5 million bank loan.

For his effort, Ron Perelman got to keep what he wanted: MacAndrews & Forbes, and all the other firms that now found themselves under its sovereignty. By the end of September 1983, the terms of the divorce were settled and signed, and business at hand returned more to his liking.

At the time, Technicolor was reaping the benefits of Ron Perelman's salesmanship and his negotiating talent. Its processing plants operating at capacity, it looked eagerly for major expansion opportunities in the growing video duplication market. Technicolor already owned a subsidiary called Vidtronics, and now Perelman bought a 20 percent stake in a company called Compact Video, and named Howard Gittis and Don Engel to its board.

Business was booming, but such could not be said for his private life. He was lonely (his affair with the florist had crashed and burned) and was in need of an ego boost. Despite escorting a number of available women on the town, he had lost a bit of himself when he lost Faith Golding. She was not only the mother of his children, she represented his youth and his dreams. Now she was gone, and her disappearance had been bitter and public.

Still, as one of the most desirable bachelors in town, Perelman did not remain lonely. On January 11, 1984, he was having lunch at the fashionable Le Cirque restaurant at his usual front table when he noticed an attractive, animated woman across the room. Dennis Stein, Perelman's resident factotum and frequent lunch partner, happened to know the woman and introduced the billionaire to Claudia Cohen.

Claudia had come to Le Cirque with her mother, and her chance meeting with Perelman satisfied a near lifelong quest. As columnist Liz Smith told *Spy* magazine, "I had never seen an attractive woman who was so anxious to meet Mr. Right. I would say, 'How are you?' and she would say, 'Still looking for Mr. Right.'" If the events that followed were any indication, Ron Perelman qualified, and then some.

Claudia was a gamine—an outspoken and tough one-time gossip queen who had risen to new heights on the local ABC "Morning Show" starring Regis Philbin, where she delivered "entertainment news."

While they were rarely the freshest or the most exclusive items, Claudia nevertheless managed to deliver her lines with a breathlessness that convinced the listener she had overheard her juicy revelations only seconds before. She was fun, she was pretty, and she was rich.

A native of the well-to-do bedroom community of Englewood, New Jersey, Claudia grew up destined for greatness. Her father was the influential and wealthy president of the Hudson County News Company, a major national distributor of books, magazines, and newspapers. After having attended the University of Pennsylvania, Cohen plunged into the world of scandal journalism, rising to the peak of her talent in 1978 through 1980 when she edited the famed Page Six column for the *New York Post.*

Cohen was no mere giddy gossipeuse. Her writing was laced with wit and quite fun to read, and she had a sharp eye for her kind of news. There seemed to be an endless parade of stars floating through New York's Studio 54 disco and doing all sorts of illegal things in the private VIP rooms. As a prime media fixture, Cohen met them all.

A famous story that made the rounds in New York in those days is said to have occurred at the venerable Russian Tea Room. Kirk Douglas was eating lunch with his publicist Bobby Zarem. Because she had met Douglas previously (albeit briefly) in Cannes during the Film Festival, Cohen sent Zarem a note asking to be reintroduced.

The protective Zarem continued with his meal, mentioning nothing about the note to his client. Cohen, who had a well-deserved reputation for getting what she wanted, sent Zarem note number two, this time adding a threat. "If you don't give my note to Kirk Douglas, your name won't see its way onto Page Six for six months!" With high dudgeon, Zarem lifted the note well above his head and dramatically ripped it to pieces, allowing the bits to flutter to the floor. True to her word, Zarem wasn't heard about on Page Six for the rest of the year.

In 1980, Cohen had moved over to the *Daily News* where she penned the equally clever but not equally well-read "I, Claudia" column, which lasted less than a year. Her appearances on New York's "Morning Show" began in earnest in

1983 and were still featured on "Live with Regis & Kathie Lee" in 1996.

When Ron Perelman asked Dennis Stein, "Who is that beautiful girl?" that afternoon at Le Cirque, he had no way of knowing he would be taking a shortcut to romance. Word has it that when the two were introduced, it was love at first sight. In any case, Claudia and Ron became New York's most seen new couple.

While Perelman continued to be media shy, refusing to give interviews, he didn't seem to mind making public appearances on an ever-increasing basis with his new love. The darlings of the party and film premiere circuit, they cut a dramatic picture: Claudia always flawless in presentation from jewels to clothes; Ron in an extravagantly priced $3,000 tuxedo tailored to show off his trim physique while drawing attention away from his polished dome.

On one such occasion, the Perelman-Cohens attended the celebrity-glittering opening of Brian DePalma's *Body Double*. Those present said the rich-rich couple drew up in a taxi to curbside where Ronald began to bowl through the crowd who were patiently waiting in line.

"These were hardly street people," said one guest. "We were entertainment professionals who had been invited just like he was. There was some snafu in getting in, but none of us minded. It was even fun standing outside and waiting. Or at least until there was this stirring in the crowd as somebody started to shove their way through." Enter Ron Perelman and Claudia Cohen.

New York Magazine reported the incident from another spectator's standpoint. "Suddenly, there's this guy holding a ticket in the air and pushing people out of his way. He's yelling, 'Claudia Cohen! Claudia Cohen!' Then he comes up to us and pushes my wife over so he can get past. I grab his shoulder and says, 'Hey buddy, don't push my wife.' At which point he turns to me and says, 'Who are you? Who do you work for? Who do you work for?' He must have asked me that five times. It seemed like a strange question. Anyway, he kept pushing his way through the crowd, yelling Claudia Cohen's name the whole way, until he got to the front of the crowd and inside."

The friendship of a new woman in his life served Perelman well. He was rejuvenated at work, redoubling his efforts to take MacAndrews & Forbes private.

To do so he proposed a transaction that would prove controversial. Stockholders in MacAndrews & Forbes Group would receive $5 in cash for each of their shares plus MacAndrews & Forbes Holdings debentures, due the following year, with a market value of $48.25 plus interest.

Nine separate lawsuits were filed against the plan by shareholders. Entered in the state courts of New York and Delaware, the suits had a single message: the only person profiting from this deal was Ronald Owen Perelman. According to a suit filed by attorney William Klein II for a holder of 18,000 shares of MacAndrews & Forbes, the worth of the stock was more accurately $150 a share. Sequoia Fund, an open-end mutual fund which controlled another 60,000 shares, agreed. Customers of Sequoia's parent company, Ruane, Cunnif Co., owned an additional 90,000 shares of stock, and joined the case as a plaintiff.

Additionally, AM Investment Corporation, a St. Louis–based firm which owned 3,000 MacAndrews & Forbes shares, filed an independent suit in Delaware. And Lindner Fund, a St. Louis–based mutual fund controlling 60,000 additional shares, did likewise in the New York State Supreme Court in Westchester County.

Inside word around Wall Street was that investors were hoping for a white knight to hear their pleas and pluck MacAndrews & Forbes from Perelman with an offer in the $65 a share range. While the swirl of lawsuits and countersuits kept the firm's name in play, it didn't serve to produce any other bidders. What it did do, however, was force Perelman to up the ante. When the dust finally settled in March 1984, Ron Perelman owned MacAndrews for $56 a share. To accomplish the feat, he assumed $52.7 million in debt. The inner workings of how he accomplished it, however, would forever change the face of financing.

During his frequent trips to Los Angeles to pitch Technicolor to the studio heads, Ron Perelman was not alone. More often than not, Drexel's Don Engel joined him for the trip, and not without good reason. With Engel in tow, Perelman was assured entrée into the offices of Drexel's junk bond czar Michael Milken. Until now, the two men had been passing associates in a position to help one another, but when Engel opened the door, the Milken-Perelman marriage was consummated.

Because Milken was to play such an important role in Perelman's life, his own history is worth exploring. Despite his youth, Milken was something of a marvel to Perelman, who shared many facets of Milken's work ethic, including a workday that lasted at least twelve hours. They both loved what they were doing; both believed they were making American business work better.

It was a driving concept for Milken since his school days in California. The son of an accountant, he became a business major at UC Berkeley, and was president of his fraternity in his senior year. As one classmate recalled: "It wasn't charisma or because he was so popular. He campaigned for the position. Very hard. He worked at it. Even then he was driven to succeed."

While he followed Perelman into the University of Pennsylvania, their circumstances were considerably different. While

Ronald Perelman studied full time and left campus to work for his father at night, Michael Milken became a part-time student while working in Philadelphia at Drexel Firestone, the forerunner of Drexel Burnham Lambert. He wouldn't receive his MBA from Wharton until 1978.

But, like Perelman, Milken's expertise was in crunching numbers, attacking profit and loss sheets. An operations research major at Wharton, Milken loved nothing better than using mathematics to analyze organizational problems that plagued businesses. He also had a devotion to the subject of low-grade, high-yield corporate bonds—junk bonds in the vernacular—and it was a devotion which would eventually lead him to California in 1978, when he opened Drexel's Beverly Hills office, arriving at work at 5 A.M.

When Milken began to work with Perelman, the investment counselor was overflowing with activity and wealth, putting into action a system that would revolutionize—for a time—the way American business was bought and sold. The way Milken explained it, low-grade, high-yield bonds were the eighties version of free money. And the way he explained it passed close enough to common sense to convince a lot of people—Ron Perelman among them.

The idea had come to Milken years before, while he was a student at UC Berkeley. It was simple enough. Forget the notion that debt was bad and cash was good. Replace it, instead, with the real truth: There are points in corporate life when debt is good. So good, in fact, that if a corporation had no debt, it was in deep trouble by Milken's theory. Debtless corporations were prime targets for takeovers. Fat sitting ducks.

Money, Milken the prophet announced, needed to circulate to keep the economy healthy. If spending all that you had was good, spending *more* than you had was even better. While at the University of Pennsylvania's Wharton School, his favorite book was W. Braddock Hickman's *Corporate Bond Quality and Investor Experience*. Slow reading for some; akin to the Bible for Milken.

At the time he had moved from Wharton into the real world of investment banking at the Beverly Hills office of Drexel Burnham Lambert, the conventional thinking was what working folk have heard all their lives. Those with plenty of cash could easily qualify for loans they didn't need, while those who needed loans hadn't a prayer of qualifying for them. They weren't rich enough. Everyone knew that. Everyone except Michael Milken.

He was only too happy to accommodate cash-strapped businesses through the issuance of high-rate bonds. Getting the loan was simple. Paying the loan off—well, that could be arranged. By using the loans to buy businesses that could be broken up and sold in pieces, debt could be neutralized as it came due, while the remaining portions of the business generated operating capital.

It was a concept that Ron Perelman understood. He had already employed it on a small scale with Cohen-Hatfield and Technicolor—well before he had met Michael Milken. Was it any wonder that the two became allies in the New Order of Corporate Finance?

Initially, what Perelman needed from Drexel Burnham Lambert was cash. The stockholders of MacAndrews & Forbes were a contentious lot, as his recent swarm of lawsuits attested. They were not subject to appeasement with bonds in exchange for their stock—even high-yield bonds. But Donald Drapkin suggested another remedy. What if Drexel sold MacAndrews & Forbes junk bonds to Drexel clients for cash, and Perelman gave solid, viable cash to his stockholders? Drexel clients would get a high return on their investment and MacAndrews's stockholders could take their money and allow Perelman to run the company however he wanted.

As ingenious as the concept sounds, it was something that had seldom, if ever, been efficiently attempted on a corporate level. Even Milken was impressed by the simplicity of the MacAndrews deal, and he eventually bought into the process to such an extent that it ended up becoming an integral element of his junk bond business. It also served to solidify the friendship between the two men, as well as to ratify Drapkin's continued value to Perelman.

By successfully taking MacAndrews & Forbes private, Perelman could march back into the business spotlight with renewed enthusiasm. Freed of the constraints of stockholders, he felt liberated to pursue deals without having to explain his behavior to anyone. He didn't have to search for his next acquisition. It came looking for him.

The managers who had taken control of Consolidated Cigar never formed a working relationship with each other after they assumed control from Gulf+Western Industries. Internal fighting and back-stabbing had reduced the operation to a legal battleground from which there could be no winners.

"I reached out to one of the management groups to see whether they'd be interested in selling," Perelman would later say in *Cigar Aficionado*. "Of course they were and we very quickly negotiated a transaction." The agreed-upon price was slightly more than he had attempted two years earlier—$124 million, with $15 million in cash and $109 million in additional debt.

Not wanting to keep the feuding management in place, Perelman turned his efforts to finding the senior executive best able to run his new company. He placed calls to tobacco distributors, cigarette conglomerates, even the publisher of *U.S. Tobacco and Candy Journal*. They proffered a near-unanimous nominee—the executive vice-president of Bayuk Cigar, a man named Theo Folz.

But as he pursued his quarry with typical nonstop verve, Perelman was discouraged to find that Folz was happy with his current job and with his life in laid-back Fort Lauderdale, Florida. Perelman offered cash and stock incentives, making some eighteen overtures during the next two years. Folz's answer was always the same.

It was not until Perelman took his message to Folz personally one Saturday morning in New York that he managed to persuade the reluctant cigar chief. A formal business meeting on Saturday, the Jewish Sabbath, was impossible for the observant Perelman. But so intent was he on convincing Folz to head up his team at Consolidated that he offered to join him for a social breakfast—even though Perelman was unshaven, carried no money, and would not talk business. Only after Folz learned the significance of the meeting in the context of Perelman's religious life did he finally understand the extent of the businessman's obsession with Consolidated Cigar.

The conversion of Theo Folz wasn't Perelman's only challenge. In mid-1984, he made a bid to buy Milton Bradley Company as well. Although he only owned 5 percent of the New England toy and game board manufacturer, the firm's consistent earnings and its brand name appeal fell neatly within Perelman's prerequisites for potential acquisition. He approached Eric Gleacher, then working with Morgan Stanley & Company investment bankers, and discussed the deal.

Gleacher proposed a preemptive buy of Milton Bradley Co., which he represented, at a price of $45 a share—take it or leave it. Perelman left it. He wanted to negotiate. He *always* wanted to negotiate. And when Gleacher balked at this course, Perelman walked. At the time, Milton Bradley was trading for

$32–$34 a share, so Gleacher was offering no bargain, at least as Perelman saw it.

Unfortunately for Ronald Perelman, he wasn't the only buyer looking at Milton Bradley. Rival Hasbro Toys also was into the acquisition game and offered to come up with $50 a share—part cash/part stock swap—for Milton Bradley. Gleacher jumped at the opportunity. By the time Perelman attempted to save his deal by raising the ante to $49 a share, all cash, he found that he was too late. Perelman had been outmaneuvered at his own game, and spent several months planning his next move.

The quiet of summer, 1984, was finally broken by the bustle of fall when, in early October, MacAndrews & Forbes Holdings opened discussions with Video Corporation of America, a tape duplication and stage rental house located on the East Coast. MacAndrews & Forbes offered $33.3 million to acquire the firm, intending to place it under its Technicolor division. But Perelman was met with immediate opposition by a group of investors who held 22 percent of Video Corporation's stock. In a suit in Delaware's Chancery Court, the brokerage firm of Reich & Tang, representing stockholders, called the bid "grossly inadequate" based on projected sales and the current stock price.

While Perelman's attorneys were able to eventually squash the opposition, the financier turned his attention away from the stock market and concentrated on romance—his and that of jocular yes-man Dennis Stein. Stein had been deemed the "man of the moment" in Elizabeth Taylor's life. She had just finished shooting the TV gossip biopic "Malice in Wonderful," cast as a slightly more glamorous than real-life Louella Parsons to Jane Alexander's Hedda Hopper.

With Stein on her arm, Taylor was the talk of Le Cirque, Perelman's regular lunch spot. Much of the drama, of course, was just that—fodder for publicity—and despite Perelman's efforts to encourage the romance (even to the point of promising the happy couple a new Rolls-Royce as a wedding present), the Taylor-Stein affair ended up being much ado about nothing.

Like so many of Taylor's romantic flings, Stein's involvement seemed to center around dinner parties and celebrity events. For months they made the rounds of New York's top eateries. Often along for the evening: Ron Perelman and Claudia Cohen. For Perelman, the coupling fitted perfectly into his growing ease with public appearances. While still press-shy to the extent that he wouldn't grant interviews, he seemed to love the kind of insulated publicity which periodic photo opportunities provided.

With Elizabeth around, marriage was never far from the conversation, and it was only a matter of time before Ronald Perelman picked up the message, proposing to Claudia Cohen over dinner late in the fall of 1984. Taylor would be an honored guest at the wedding, of course. Since she was due to spend Christmas in Gstaad with Stein, the wedding date was set for January 11—one year to the day after Ron and Claudia first met. The New York tabloids gushed over the engagement, incited by Cohen's own celebrity gossip column status.

When Ronald Perelman married Claudia Cohen, the ceremony took place at the MacAndrews & Forbes Holding Company townhouse on East 63rd Street. Orthodox cantor Joseph Malovany assisted Judge Marie M. Lambert as thirty people looked on, among them Elizabeth Taylor, her hair frosted for the occasion and wearing a tight yellow suit trimmed in black velvet.

As important as Taylor's attendance at the wedding was, for the groom it took second billing to the appearance of Mr. and Mrs. Raymond Perelman. Son had buried the hatchet with father, and the appearance of his parents (as well as Ronald's younger brother Jeffrey) made the moment complete. Other guests at the ceremony included Palladium and Studio 54 impresario Steve Rubell; Cohen's friends and fellow journalists Jack Martin and Cyndi Stivers; former *Interview* editor Bob Colacello; and attorneys Howard Gittis and Roy Cohn.

"It knocks me out that God made a couple that compatible," Cohn was said to have mentioned to all who would listen. (He could have used a little divine intervention himself. Within months, Cohn would be disbarred. Then, eventually, he died, a victim of AIDS.)

The couple were married under a dogwood *chuppa*, while a snow shower dusted 63rd Street. Post ceremony, the lucky few guests were invited to a private lunch at Le Cirque, which had closed for the day; then the honeymoon couple flew in Ron Perelman's private jet to St. Moritz. There they stayed in the bridal suite of the Palace Hotel and took lessons in skiing. (Claudia loved to be coached in sports. As a teenager, she took tennis lessons, not from the local pro, but from Jimmy Evert— Chris's father.)

For those who knew Ron Perelman only as an executive power broker, his marriage to Claudia Cohen seemed unlikely. He was, after all, a man who outwardly claimed to be concerned with his privacy. She was, bottom line, a woman who made her entire career by telling tales out of school. For those who knew Perelman well, however, the romance was made to order.

As with all the women who had entered Perelman's life before and have been through it since, this one served a purpose. Her world was one of glamour, not business. She could open doors for Ronald Perelman which his money alone could not. As one friend later put it, "Elizabeth Taylor never attended any wedding for Sam Walton's children."

In addition to his new wife's show business connections, she was well known in New York society. Always available to attend charitable events, Claudia also had impeccable credentials among the "ladies who lunch." She not only was one of them; she knew where all their skeletons were buried.

She was as loved, criticized, and feared in her own world as Ronald Perelman was in his. "They were loved in public, scorned in private, and lived a fairytale life," one longtime Perelman associate observed. They also seemed to be genuinely in love.

The normally vitriolic and outspoken Perelman thought nothing of publicly showing his affection for his new wife, even in front of his office staff. Since the Perelmans' Manhattan townhouse doubled as MacAndrews & Forbes corporate headquarters, Claudia was at work even when she was at home, gliding down hallways and calling out to her husband, who obliged her by tossing kisses like a lovesick teen.

She became known as Princess Perelman, and for good reason. She wielded her husband's power as if it were her own; and in a large part of New York society, it was. In addition to national TV exposure, she now had expensive jewels, limousines, estates, and was—or so it seemed—intelligent, charming, and passionate. Who else in the world had that? Only Princess Di, and she was hardly ever in New York.

If Perelman was uncomfortable in his newfound spotlight, he didn't show it. While the details of his life and business remained private, he developed the public persona of a smiling, successful, cigar-smoking tycoon, regularly captured by the paparazzi en route to glamorous events.

Seemingly recharged by his romance, Perelman returned from his honeymoon and immediately set his acquisition pack on the scent of takeover possibilities. At the top of their list was a small grocery store chain that had operated for years under the name Food Fair, and had emerged from bankruptcy in 1981 as Pantry Pride.

Faced with a decreasing cash flow but nevertheless rich in store assets, the company was a willing mark for a Perelman takeover bid. Unlike Consolidated Cigar, which manufactured a product in which Perelman believed, Pantry Pride was a corporation whose main attraction was the fact that it had been so poorly run. Because of its losses, the company had tax-loss carryovers totaling $330 million. By taking over the company, Perelman could use the tax write-offs to shelter income produced by his divisions making big bucks.

For its part, the board of directors of Pantry Pride had been laboring to achieve success after pulling themselves from bankruptcy protection. Their supermarkets, as Food Fair, had long fought the reputation of being old-fashioned and out of touch with the consumer marketplace. They had relied heavily on neighborhood locations to attract shopper interest.

The heavy price competition in the late seventies and early eighties had forced the chain to give itself a long-overdue facelift—including the name change to Pantry Pride. Unfortunately, it hadn't attracted enough consumer response to continue growing. In addition to its chain of Pantry Pride stores, the firm owned a string of barely profitable Devon retail stores and Adams Drugs.

In late February 1985, Perelman made his move, offering to absorb Pantry Pride by buying up to $50 million in preferred stock which could later be converted to common stock worth $5.63 a share. Involved in the purchase was MacAndrews & Forbes Group's newest executive—its chief financial officer Fred Tepperman.

Tepperman, who had been executive vice-president and chief financial officer of Warner Communications, was hired by Perelman to replace Richard T. Carlton in June 1984. The new financial officer, ten years later, would prove to be a large stone in Perelman's craw.

Not only had Perelman managed to take over Pantry Pride in a friendly fashion; the structure of the takeover benefited him in several ways. In addition to gaining the tax shelter from the tax-loss carryovers, Perelman was able to deduct the interest on the funds he had borrowed to buy out the grocery store chain and pocket the handsome dividends on the stock.

Perelman's world indeed seemed to have come together in the seven years he had been in Manhattan. Richer than ever, in charge of seven separate companies, and with Claudia Cohen as his new wife, he began to enjoy being away from his desk for the first time in his life. Despite having commented to a reporter from the *New York Times* that his idea of a fun evening was "being in bed by 10 o'clock at night," Perelman and Cohen became the newest darlings of the very gossip columns Cohen herself once wrote.

This more "with-it" Perelman was typified by a wedding reception held months after the actual ceremony, a no-expense-spared gift from Cohen's generous parents. The evening for 400 guests began with a reception in the Mike Todd Room of New York's trendy Palladium. Later in the evening, the group was led down to the main dance floor for a black-tie, sit-down dinner, complete with a ten-minute, $80,000 performance by the Pointer Sisters.

The evening was described as "an incredible event" by one of the guests, who added, "There was nothing like being there having the Pointer Sisters singing 'Jump.' At least if you were under sixty."

The business side of Perelman's life was jumping as well. Now installed as chairman of Pantry Pride, and with

MacAndrews & Forbes Group president Bruce Slovin doing double time as Pantry Pride president, Perelman began to sell anything and everything Pantry Pride called an asset. Within months, all of Pantry Pride, Devon, and Adams Drugs stores would be liquidated, leaving Pantry Pride a corporate shell with cash to spend.

While Perelman had millions in ready cash, he still didn't have the kind of capital he really wanted. Ronald Perelman was ready for the *big* time. To fund his next acquisition, he again turned to Drexel Burnham Lambert and Michael Milken. When Milken asked how much the investor needed, Perelman's answer was immediate: "$700 million."

In the land of Milken money, such a figure was not extreme. He had arranged $1 billion in junk bond funding for MCI to start up the company in 1983. He had also set up the bonds that allowed Carl Icahn to make his successful run on TWA. Given Ron Perelman's success in the past, raising the funds would pose little problem.

Ron Perelman took to the road to help drum up enthusiasm for his junk bond issue, with Don Engel opening the doors to Drexel investors. Milken personally supported the drive, and Drexel Burnham Lambert surpassed itself, delivering $761 million into Perelman's war chest.

Perelman's staff had assembled a new list of potential takeover targets, and with customary attention to detail Perelman began the arduous task of sifting through the candidates. With $761 million in high-interest bonds gathered over his head (he was paying in the neighborhood of 14.5 percent for the money), he had to move quickly to avoid taking a financial bath.

After days, then weeks, rejecting one possibility after another, Perelman returned to Milken and Drexel Burnham

Lambert and came up with a plan that many found astounding. He invested nearly 40 percent of the $761 million in an assortment of high-yield junk bonds himself, going not only to Drexel but also to First Boston, Merrill Lynch, and Goldman Sachs.

While his money made money, Perelman went back to his cost breakouts and profit and loss sheets, mulling over more than twenty-five different company takeover options. In the end, none of them was to his liking. There wasn't a knockout in the group; a company so unique, so famous, that owning it would bring not only the wealth but also the respect and credibility he now desired.

It was then that Perelman received a call from Eric Gleacher. The investment banker with Morgan Stanley, aware of both the financier's predicament and his vast potential, had his own suggestion for Perelman's next acquisition: Revlon, the cosmetics colossus. It was a stroke of genius.

Perelman listened eagerly as the veteran broker suggested how Revlon might be converted to show a gigantic profit. At that time, in mid-1985, Revlon Corporation was a slumbering Titan. It had reached its peak in popularity and profitability a decade before under the leadership of founder Charles Revson. Since his death, Revlon had drifted aimlessly into unrelated fields: health, pharmaceuticals, eye care. Its cosmetics division was faltering amid the cutthroat pricing of other high-visibility fashion brands.

Profits had fallen from a high of $229 million in 1980 to $141 million in 1985, and the stock had slid to half its 1979 price despite a bullish market. Turning the company around would be a challenge, sure to demand hands-on attention and a total commitment of Perelman's time and energy.

Still, Perelman reasoned, the Revlon moniker remained the most famous brand name in cosmetics. While tarnished, it was extremely well respected, an element vital to Perelman's ego. Revlon: Ronald Perelman rolled the name over in his mind, and came to a decision. Revlon would be his.

Its corporate offices were on top of the General Motors building overlooking Central Park just a few blocks from Perelman's townhouse headquarters. The financier requested and was granted a meeting with Michael Bergerac, onetime head of ITT Corporation and Revson's handpicked heir. Perelman's hope was that his acquisition of Revlon, like that of Pantry Pride, would be a friendly merger. Bergerac could make out handsomely on the deal; Perelman would make out even better.

Michael Bergerac saw things differently. Others had already tried to take over Revlon and had failed. Just the year before, an investment group which included Martin Revson (Charles's younger brother) and Kaiser Steel Corporation's chairman Joseph A. Frates considered bidding $50 a share for Revlon. Bergerac, a tall, courtly Frenchman, dismissed the offer and refused to meet with the investment group.

Perelman's executives leaked news of the talks between Perelman and Bergerac to Wall Street. Speculation was rampant during the next few weeks of hush-hush negotiations in August 1985. Despite the takeover talk, however, Revlon stock continued to languish around the $45-a-share mark.

After their introductory meetings, Ronald Perelman met once again with Michael Bergerac on Friday, August 16, for what appeared to be a definitive session. Adding confusion to the scenario, foreign investors including Unilever, a British-Dutch consumer products company, as well as the West German chemical firm, Hoechst A.G., were said to be preparing counteroffers for Revlon.

A week of quiet passed as Wall Street waited and wondered.

Finally, on August 20, Perelman made a formal offer: $47.50 a share for any or all of Revlon's 38.2 million shares in a deal potentially worth $1.81 billion to Revlon's shareholders.

At this, Michael Bergerac broke his silence. "Revlon is not for sale," he said in an interview with the *New York Times*, dismissing Perelman as a "breakup artist." Bergerac acknowledged that they had several meetings. "He wanted to look at the possibility of acquiring Revlon at a low price and bust it up. Initially, he mentioned he was thinking about paying around the market value, about $40," Bergerac added. "He kept saying he was a friend, but was ready to be hostile."

Bergerac asserted that he had "absolutely no interest" in selling Revlon, even though Perelman had offered to keep him on as head of the company at a salary in the range of $1.3 million per year. "I'm not going to be bribed into shafting my shareholders," he added.

Bergerac also announced that he was planning to issue shareholders a "special dividend"—a so-called "poison pill" defensive step that would effectively add $750 million to the price tag of the company.

Perelman responded by saying Bergerac's actions were a "blatant attempt to deny shareholders the right to decide for themselves," adding that the poison pill proposal was all the more outrageous because it came at a moment when discussions between the two were "only minutes" away from resuming. "Our offer is real," Perelman said, "and Revlon's misleading and irrelevant rhetoric about junk bonds and bust-up offers can't alter that clear fact."

Bergerac was appalled at Perelman's persona and his pushy, tenacious method of doing business. There was no way he ever intended to see Revlon sold to such a person. "Never," he said, adding that he only agreed to see Perelman several times because "before going to war, one should try to make peace."

At the end of the day, when the dust had settled, one thing was clear. Revlon and Perelman were at war, and the bloody battle they intended to wage would allow for only one winner.

THREE

Fire and Ice

Ronald Perelman was surprised by the outrage in Michael Bergerac's message. He had honestly wanted this to be a friendly takeover. Moreover, he was hurt. As one wealthy entrepreneur to another, he had expected respect. What he received was arrogance and dismissal.

In his office on East 63rd Street, Perelman paced with pent-up anger. He puffed rapidly on his cigar, distressed not by the battle that he knew lay ahead, but rather by Bergerac's failure to acknowledge who he was, what he had accomplished. The Revlon head had toyed with him, led him into a false sense of progress, while privately mocking him for his impertinence at even suggesting that Revlon would consider becoming a division within the Perelman empire.

In fact, Bergerac had worked too long in his ivory tower full of yes-men and creative artists to entertain the concept of stepping down or giving in. After ten years at the top of the cosmetics giant, he felt that Revlon was his to develop or destroy as he saw fit. Had Charles Revson been alive, he might have thought differently.

Revson was the son of a cigar packer who had emigrated

49

from Russia, instilling in his family his own strong, unrelenting drive and uncompromising standards. More eager to discover life than to seek an education, Revson had left home at the age of seventeen and, in a small way, entered the world of fashion in New York. Through the help of a cousin, he found work selling dresses at $16.75 on Seventh Avenue for the Elke Co. Eventually he moved into the firm's piece-goods department, where he sold the nail polish of the day—thin and translucent, and available in only three colors: light, medium, and dark red.

While still in his early twenties, after being denied a position as national distributor, he struck off on his own. It was then that he and his older brother Joseph met a young chemist, Charles Lachman—the "L" in Revlon—who had been experimenting with a colorful nail polish, heating his concoction at home over a Bunsen burner. Pooling the sum total of their cash—some $300—the three went into business together in a dingy room on Manhattan's Upper West Side.

They produced a supply of revolutionary non-streak, creamy nail glaze (as it was then called) and, with prophetic vision, took advantage of the economic hardship caused by the Great Depression. Despite the bread lines, Revson recognized that, rich or poor, Americans continued to spend what money they had on two things—entertainment and grooming. In the case of women, that meant beauty salons, which, at the time, were booming because of the popularity of the permanent wave. Hitching his success to the salon, Revson concentrated sales of "Revlon" nail glaze to professional beauticians, who did much of the introduction of the novel product.

By the beginning of World War II, Revlon had a near monopoly in the nail polish industry, supplying over 100,000 salons across the country, and they expanded into department and drug stores as well. Charles Revson would often be seen at work, his nails dabbed with polish and hands streaked with lipstick. He soon embarked on his first national advertising campaign. It was truly inspired: "Matching lips and finger-tips." In 1951, Revson followed up with equally catchy commercial poetry: "Fire and Ice." The advertisements are now classics. They elevated Revlon into the first division of fashion society's big leagues.

The advent of television was a godsend for Revlon's ideas. The medium was made to order for Revlon's expansion into hair spray, shampoo, fragrances, and men's products. Following Revlon's imaginative advertisements on "The $64,000 Question" television series, sales skyrocketed 200 percent and Revlon's newly issued stock leaped from $12 to $30 a share in three months.

During the early sixties, brother Joseph and chemist Charles Lachman both retired from the company. A younger brother, Martin, who had entered the executive suite in the thirties, left his biggest impact on the firm with a bitter multi-million dollar lawsuit in 1958 in which Martin charged fraud, misrepresentation, and breach of agreement over a stock deal gone sour.

By 1973, Revlon's ad budget for its cosmetics division was $52 million, spread among such trade names as Princess Marcella Borghese, Ultima II, Moon Drops, Miss Balmain, Bill Blass, Braggi, and Ethera. By that point, the Revlon principality had diversified into pharmaceuticals, which soon accounted for nearly a quarter of the sales and 27 percent of the profit for the growing concern.

It was with that diversification in mind that Michael Bergerac was recruited from ITT Europe. He got a $1.4 million bonus just for signing on the dotted line. Revson believed that Bergerac, with his international background and skill at administration, could continue the expansion of Revlon long after his passing. Indeed, Bergerac had only been president of Revlon for several months when Revson revealed he had cancer, from which he died in 1975.

Pompous and autocratic, Bergerac ruled over Revlon's empire like a dictator, expanding into health industries at the expense of the core beauty business. But he refused to spend money on product development or new makeup lines and cosmetics, and turned his back on the department and drug stores which formed the basis for its distribution network. The result was a dearth of new products and a drop in Revlon's cosmetics market share to just over 20 percent.

Over the decade he ruled Revlon, Bergerac made eleven acquisitions, adding such brand names as Tums and the Oxy line of acne medication. While Revlon's cosmetics lines wallowed, an outdated reflection of its former glory, the corporation itself increased its profitability. As the takeover battle commenced, profits from the health care divisions were generating 66 percent of the company's profits of $298.3 million and 54 percent of its $2.4 billion in sales.

The booming health care industries were the real reason for Perelman's interest in Revlon. If he could buy Revlon and divest the company's health care operations, conservatively valued at a bargain basement $1.5 billion, it would mean he had acquired the Revlon beauty business for nearly nothing. The idea was far from theoretical. When Perelman announced his intention to buy Revlon, the phones at MacAndrews & Forbes–Pantry Pride began to ring as buyers sought to be first on the list to scoop up the conglomerate's health care and prescription drug operations. Insiders revealed that among them were Bristol-Myers, Procter & Gamble, American Home Products, Hoffmann-La Roche, SmithKline Beecham, and Boots, the British drug company. In fact, Pantry Pride had already signed a formal agreement with Morgan Stanley to handle the sales.

When he heard the news, Bergerac was offended. "This man is trying to offer pieces of Revlon without authorization," he claimed, labeling the actions "outrageous and irresponsible." Felix Rohatyn, the famous Wall Street advisor to Revlon, canceled his vacation in Austria and raced to Bergerac's side. "The Pantry Pride offer is financially inadequate," Rohatyn stated, privately amused at the small grocer's endeavor to absorb the giant corporation's assets. "Preposterous," was his haughty prediction for Perelman's undertaking.

After a four-hour emergency meeting with Revlon executives, the litigation attorneys Wachtell, Lipton, Rosen & Katz announced details of the proposed "poison pill" offer. It would kick in if anyone acquired 20 percent or more of the company and would allow stockholders to swap individual shares for $65 in one-year notes. There was a single notable exception: should the buyer of the 20 percent offer to purchase the remaining Revlon shares at $65, the poison pill offer would become void. While refusing to entertain Perelman's bid of $47.50, the executives essentially had set their sales price at a figure nearly 33 percent higher.

Bergerac struck back at Perelman in a second way as well. He lashed out privately at Chemical Bank for allegedly agreeing to help fund Perelman's $1.8 billion takeover bid. Revlon considered it a conflict of interest since some of its European customers were Chemical Bank clients. Placing a call to Chemical's chairman, Walter V. Shipley, Bergerac expressed his "surprise" at Chemical's involvement in the hostile takeover, saying it was a violation of Chemical's corporate policy, which generally refused financing in such cases.

While Chemical remained mute on the subject, Perelman did not. Through a spokesman, he said: "I don't think banks like Chemical lend half a billion dollars without knowing what they're doing." Apparently not. It was later confirmed that

Chemical had agreed to provide additional funding for the takeover should Perelman require their help.

Behind the public rhetoric, the precise combat lines were being sketched out in the boardrooms of the two firms. Pantry Pride's first move was to sue Revlon in Delaware Chancery Court to invalidate the poison pill provision, claiming that the move was at odds with the best interests of Revlon's stockholders.

Equally important from a stockholder consideration was Revlon's next move to cut off Perelman's takeover attempt. The company announced plans to buy five million of its own shares, having reached an agreement with Manufacturers Hanover Bank to fund the repurchase with a $1 billion loan. Within days, Bergerac increased his plan to add an additional five million shares to the buyback scheme. When pressed for his reasoning, Bergerac sniffed, "We wanted to respond to Pantry Pride's offer, of course."

The company's repurchase plan was more than a response; it was an expensive and deliberate move to plunge the company into enormous debt. Bergerac planned to repurchase the common stock for new notes and preferred stock valued at $57.50 a share. If Bergerac wanted to get Wall Street's attention, he did. The gambit also drew the attention of Judge Simon H. Rifkind, who happened to be on the board of both Revlon *and* MacAndrews & Forbes. When approached about this peculiar predicament, Rifkind smiled, "I'm keeping my ears plugged and my eyes shut." It was an interesting spot for the attorney whose name was part of Paul, Weiss, Rifkind, Wharton & Garrison, legal counsel for Revlon.

When the Revlon team stormed into action, the conventional wisdom was that they would swiftly prevail. Bergerac confidently shuttled between his private dining room with his own chef; his lavishly appointed office with his two secretaries and a butler; his limousine with a round-the-clock chauffeur; and the company's private 727 jet with kitchen, bedroom, living room, backgammon board, and a custom-made big-game gun rack—just in case the plane found itself on safari in Africa.

Perelman's battalions worked more clandestinely. They labeled the takeover attempt Operation Nicole (after Donald Drapkin's seventeen-month-old daughter), and attorneys at Drapkin's Skadden, Arps, Slate, Meagher & Flom law firm were in continuous touch with Dennis Levine of Drexel Burnham Lambert. Joseph Flom cleared his calendar in order to map out a strategy that would have the effectiveness and firepower of a modern military exercise. Stuart Shapiro and Michael Mitchell, two merger and acquisition specialists on Flom's staff, handled litigation filings and responses. Both knew their every move and countermove could be booby-trapped. And no one was more acutely aware of the dangers than Perelman himself.

His first significant reaction to Revlon's stock buyback plan was the revelation of his own plans for the cosmetic "supercorp." His filing with the Securities and Exchange Commission confirmed what had been widely speculated. If Pantry Pride succeeded in its takeover attempt, it would strip Revlon of all but its cosmetics divisions immediately, anticipating between $1.7 and $1.9 billion from the divestitures.

In addition to the $500 million in ready cash from its Chemical Bank loan and a little over $750 million in junk bond proceeds, Pantry Pride indicated it was prepared to get another $500 million from Drexel Burnham Lambert to cover the purchase. It would repay the investment banking house as well as its other takeover debt from the sale of Revlon's noncosmetic assets.

Speaking to the press after the filing, Perelman called

Revlon's debt-for-stock defense "outstandingly absurd and horrendous." He had taken his offer to the stockholders, Perelman said, hoping that they would see its wisdom. "We are not liquidators," he stressed. "I am a builder whose job it is to maximize the inherent value of the companies we purchase. Basically, what we've done in every transaction is to bring a company down to its basic core business and build that core business to new levels of performance. We've done it consistently in everything we've bought."

In spite of the fact that what he was saying was true, many in the press responded by referring to his opulent lifestyle and to his celebrity wife and by criticizing his reluctance to speak out in the past. "I'm a very private, media-shy person," he countered ingenuously.

Revlon's Michael Bergerac seemed to regard Perelman as almost comical. He felt the entrepreneur's pleadings were the fumblings of an amateur in a professional's league. As if to prove the point, Revlon countersued in Delaware Chancery Court, asking the court for a dismissal of the Pantry Pride suit and a ban on its takeover attempt.

In a separate filing with the Securities and Exchange Commission, Revlon confirmed that its offer to buy back its own stock would increase its debt to $956 million, while creating "significant new interest costs." In the sixty-five page filing, Revlon even cast doubt on its own ability to pay back the loan, suggesting that it would be totally contingent on earnings from sales, and adding that the company's capability to repay "could be severely impaired." The intent of its filing seemed to be to make it appear that the company was weakening its corporate position, thereby making the junk bonds that Pantry Pride was selling to finance the takeover too risky for even the most liberal investors. Predicated on the news and weak sales,

Revlon's shares continued to slide, reaching a low of $44.50 at the end of August.

As the stock dipped, Perelman reacted typically. While Wall Street had anticipated that Pantry Pride would raise its offer to further entice Revlon to accept a takeover, Perelman did just the opposite. He *reduced* his proffer, dropping it by $5.50 a share to $42. Moreover, the new Pantry Pride offer came with conditions. It demanded that 90 percent of the outstanding stock be tendered and not withdrawn. That was the stick; the carrot was a statement that "if Revlon should drop its 'poison pill' offer, Pantry Pride will consider increasing its price" and also would reconsider the 90 percent provision.

The Revlon stockholders' response was immediate and predictable. As they saw Pantry Pride's dollars flying away from their wallets, they began to put pressure on the board of directors of the cosmetic giant to take steps to increase the value of the stock. Instead, the price continued to drop—down to a low of $43.25.

Bergerac, however, still considered Perelman's maneuvers little more than scare tactics and boldly told his board that he did not even want to consider dignifying the offer with a response. Given its legal obligation to do so, however, Bergerac issued a terse and prompt rejection, calling Pantry Pride's latest bid "grossly inadequate and not in the interest of Revlon shareholders." With that news, Revlon's stock fell again, this time to $41.63.

After debating their strategy in light of the harsh and immediate Revlon response, the Skadden team decided their best approach would be to patiently wear down Bergerac and his allies. They called the strategy "Yertle the Turtle" after the Dr. Seuss character whose own slow and steady pace eventually won the race.

Said a wise insider at the table, "The object was just to keep the ball in play. Skadden realized that if they kept hitting it over the net, sooner or later Revlon would make a mistake."

But merely keeping the ball in play was not Perelman's way. He wanted to smash his serves, and did just that on September 27, 1985, when Pantry Pride reversed itself and upped the ante by 19 percent to $50 a share—a surge of $8. Ironically, the increase in share cost would not require more capital from Pantry Pride because Revlon had followed through on its announcement to buy back ten million of its outstanding shares at a cost of some $575 million in debt. With only 28 million shares still on the market, Pantry Pride's offer amounted to a bid of $1.4 billion—a decrease in real dollars of $405 million from its previous obligation.

"We extend this offer in friendship," Perelman told reporters. "We want this merger to work as a partnership, not a takeover."

Unfortunately, while Perelman was passing the peace pipe, the executives of Revlon weren't even at work. The threat of Hurricane Gloria had closed most of New York's financial district and businesses, Revlon and the New York Stock Exchange among them.

But while the Exchange was closed, the independent brokerage house of Jefferies & Co. was not. According to Jefferies & Co. records, Revlon stock rose four points to 46¼ on the strength of the Pantry Pride announcement.

Perelman wrote Michael Bergerac a more-in-sadness-than-in-anger letter saying, "As you know, we have always been interested in a negotiated transaction. Unfortunately, you have always been unwilling to negotiate with us." The charge was fair. Bergerac had not only rejected the past offers, but flatly refused to meet again with Pantry Pride attorneys even to discuss the matter.

At first, silence was the answer from Revlon to Perelman's

latest offer. Analysts were convinced that Bergerac believed Wall Street would operate in his favor as it had so often done in the past. When Revlon finally did respond a few days later, it revealed that it had been privately negotiating with a "major American corporation" that was interested in taking the company private. While Bergerac refused to say who it was or how much the mystery player was prepared to bid, financial insiders were speculating that the white knight was either the The Gillette Co. or American Home Products Corporation.

Not content to wait out the competition, Pantry Pride slammed back even before its $50-a-share bid was formally rejected. It offered $53 a share. On the strength of that announcement, Revlon stock shot up to $54.37½ a share as analysts shook their heads in wonder at the epic warfare.

"One thing is certain, this whole thing will be over soon," one brokerage house commented. "They can't keep going much longer. This bidding is crazy."

Revlon's board of directors met in a session so secret that even secretaries were told to leave the building early. And Ron Perelman, for his part, was frustrated, eager to end the nerve-frazzling weeks of standoff, determined to bring an agreement to some favorable conclusion.

"Those were rough days," said an assistant who once kept track of Perelman's appointments. "He would call in continuously to find out if we had heard even the smallest rumor. Like a man possessed."

On October 3, Revlon announced it had agreed to be purchased by the investment firm of Forstmann Little & Company. The buyout would require a total restructuring of Revlon into three separate organizations. While saying the entire deal was worth $3 billion, Revlon announced that Forstmann Little would pay stockholders $1.6 billion, or $56 a share. The difference in the two figures was due to amounts that Forstmann

Little would get for selling off portions of the cosmetics firm. Forstmann Little had agreed to fund the takeover with $445 million in cash, with the remainder coming from bank loans.

The speed with which the sell-off was negotiated left even the most astute Wall Street analysts astounded. So, too, did the proposal's complicated nature. Revlon's cosmetics division was to be sold separately to the New York investment house of Adler & Shaykin for $900 million. Forstmann Little would then take control of the remainder of the company, but had already agreed to sell Revlon's Norcliff Thayer unit, which manufactured Tums antacid and Oxy acne creams, as well as its Reheis specialty chemicals division to American Home Products Corporation for an estimated $350 million. Perhaps most astounding of all was that Forstmann Little was being joined in their buyout by Michael Bergerac and other members of the board of directors, who had cut themselves an ownership position.

To most analysts watching the developments, Bergerac's latest maneuver showed an amazing lack of perception. "He was treating his stockholders as if they were idiots," a broker with Merrill Lynch was quoted as saying, pointing to the fact that for all of Bergerac's negative comments about Pantry Pride, he was essentially *doing* what he had for months been accusing them of attempting to do. He was helping to break Revlon apart and was selling off the pieces. Another analyst pointed to Bergerac's insistence that the firm was worth in the neighborhood of $65 a share, even as he agreed to sell it for $56.

From the outside, it appeared that Michael Bergerac's sudden change of heart was motivated by immediate gain. Not only would he be able to liquidate his own 261,633 shares in Revlon (for a total of $14.7 million) as part of the sellout to Forstmann, but he would be able to continue to run the corporation's health care divisions much as he had in the past—with autonomy. By becoming part of the buyout, he would manage the company of which he was an owner—and a large company it would remain.

While beauty products still accounted for one-third of Revlon's operating income, and the Norcliff Thayer and Reheis divisions added another 11 percent, that would still leave the remaining 56 percent of the former Revlon under Bergerac's control. That included the Vision Products division (13%), the Diagnostic division (15%), and Ethical Pharmaceuticals (28%).

"It looks to most people as if Bergerac and his group have taken the cream," Allan Mottus, a consultant to the beauty industry, told the *New York Times*. "He never felt that comfortable with the cosmetics group. That wasn't his legacy. Bergerac's legacy was making the acquisitions that made Revlon a full-blown health care company."

A pragmatic, formula-type executive, Bergerac was said to have little ability to gauge the mood of the creative fashion industry. "He came from an enormous company that was highly structured and was a big believer in financial analysis, market research, and five-year plans. It is impossible to make a five-year plan for a lipstick collection," is the way former Revlon executive Stanley Kohlenberg put it.

For its part in the breakup/merger talks, the investment house of Adler & Shaykin wasted no time in moving to take control of Revlon cosmetics. Concurrent with the announcement of its plan to buy the division, Adler & Shaykin announced the appointment of Linda J. Wachner to head up the company. Wachner, the strong-willed and controversial ex-president of Max Factor & Company, had come to the investment house the previous year after failing in her own attempt at a leveraged buyout of Max Factor from its corporate owners, Beatrice Companies.

Hard-driving and impulsive, Wachner was looked upon by

analysts as a question mark in the Revlon acquisition. "She's provocative," said consultant Alan Mottus. "Those that are loyal are fiercely loyal, but she creates a lot of alienation among her staffers. This is not your basic polished manager."

In the days that followed Revlon's announcement, Ronald Perelman was silent, but certainly not inactive. He toiled sixteen-hour days right through the weekend with his team of lawyers and acquisition advisors, working and reworking Pantry Pride's response strategies. In addition to being furious at his treatment by Michael Bergerac, he was aggravated by the aspersions the company had cast on his corporation and its ability to meet its offer.

In sum, far from being out of the contest, Perelman was getting his second wind. He raised his offer for Revlon stock, this time to $56.25—not a significant cash amount over the Forstmann Little bid, to be sure, but with a very significant difference. The Pantry Pride offer was a tender offer—so called because stock must be tendered from shareholders by a specific date. In this case: October 21. The Forstmann Little deal was a leveraged buyout offer, an ownership bid which is subject to a protracted stockholder vote.

Perelman's tender offer was like a buyer telling a farmer he'll pay him twenty-five cents for an apple. The farmer gives the man the apple, and the buyer gives him the quarter. The deal is clean, simple, and immediately complete. In a leveraged buyout, the company's assets are used as collateral on the purchase loan. It's like taking out a mortgage to buy an apartment building and then using the rent on the apartments to pay off the mortgage. After the weeks of uncertain stock roller-coasting, for Revlon stockholders Ronald Perelman's straightforward tender offer looked very tempting.

This time there was no personal note from Perelman to Bergerac. All thought of diplomacy was abandoned. "Why should we?" questioned the Perelman team. "They never answered any of our other letters." Instead of a letter, Pantry Pride filed an amendment to its lawsuit in Delaware Chancery Court, adding a charge that the directors of Revlon's board breached their fiduciary duties in agreeing to the Forstmann Little deal. At the same time, Pantry Pride asked the court to disallow an agreement that Bergerac had signed with Forstmann Little offering to pay the brokerage house $25 million if the deal was not accepted.

While responding only through a spokesman, Bergerac left no doubt that the heat of the corporate war had heightened. Pantry Pride's offer, Bergerac said, was "another typical, highly conditional proposal that lacks financial backing," while adding that Pantry Pride was out to "filch" Revlon's assets.

It was a martial melody that everyone had heard before— particularly Revlon's stockholders, who began to let their own chorus be heard. Pressure was brought on Bergerac and his fellow directors by stockholders to respond directly to the Pantry Pride bid. Stockholders were also outraged when it was uncovered through Pantry Pride litigation that Bergerac had been afforded a "golden parachute." The wily executive was due to have a $21 million payday should his present job cease through a buyout, even one of his own making. In fact, Bergerac was using the $21 million to finance his own portion of the takeover.

This pressure from the stockholders, the scrutiny from the press, and litigation from Pantry Pride led Bergerac to make a momentous decision on October 13. Just as Forstmann Little raised its leverage buyout offer for Revlon by a dollar a share over the Pantry Pride bid, to $57.25, Bergerac removed himself from the agreement. Rather than being part of the buyout, Bergerac retreated to a neutral position. He "didn't want to be in a position where it would look that I would have some conflict of interest between doing what might be good for me and what might be good for the shareholders," he said piously.

In a further statement, Bergerac put his entire future with Revlon in doubt by refusing to confirm that he would stay with the company. He would only comment, "There are many options which will be looked at." For its part, Forstmann Little declined any comment on Bergerac's future. The investment house had little more to say about its offer either, other than the fact that it had been awarded a "lockout" option, allowing it to buy Revlon's vision care group and its National Health Laboratories for $525 million, if anyone else should succeed in gaining control of more than 40 percent of Revlon. Importantly, Revlon's poison pill was being dropped.

Revlon's stock rose, and Wall Street reacted wildly. All calls to Bergerac were diverted to a spokesman who would say only that Bergerac's move was aimed at putting "to an end criticism in the media" which had suggested the executive "was having his cake and eating it, too."

In a formal response to the outcry, Bergerac issued a statement saying, "I asked to be relieved of my equity participation in the new venture so that there would be no confusion as to the motivation behind this agreement—to get the best possible transaction for Revlon stockholders and note-holders and, therefore, gain for them the greatest value possible."

In a separate move, Judge Joseph T. Walsh in Delaware Chancery Court stopped Revlon from transferring any of its assets to Forstmann Little, including any assets from National Health Laboratories or its vision care group. The Perelman team had won a victory, limited but consequential.

"It set the tone for what was to follow," said a Skadden, Arps attorney. "We weren't sure we would win, but we knew we had an ear in the Delaware court at least."

Nerves at the Fifth Avenue headquarters of Revlon were

stretched taut. The chiefs there were still hoping for a victory, but rumors began to circulate about who would still have a job if Pantry Pride suddenly became the boss. There were jokes about the "Panty Raid," as it was labeled, but they were jokes whose punch lines were laced with fear and cynicism. Revlon spokesman Roger Shelley, for example, made up T-shirts which said, forebodingly, "It's not over 'til the fat lady sings." While Revlon may not have heard any joyous arias, there was plenty of reason for happy singing around MacAndrews & Forbes's East 63rd Street town house office suites nearby.

Buoyed by the court's ruling and not wanting to allow the momentum to stop, Pantry Pride renewed its "Yertle the Turtle" philosophy and stroked the ball back into Revlon's court. On October 19, it upped its ante to $58 a share and extended its offer until midnight on Halloween, October 31. Simultaneously and smugly, it announced that its bond offer from Drexel Burnham Lambert had been fully subscribed and that it had the necessary $1.9 billion in place to finance the takeover. Pantry Pride's offer came with a stern condition, however. Perelman insisted that any rights granted to Forstmann Little to buy Revlon's crown jewel health care divisions must be eliminated.

The luck that Pantry Pride seemed to be having in Delaware court not only held but also hit a jackpot shower of gold and prestige. On October 23, Revlon was ignominiously vanquished. This time, the court found that Revlon had breached its fiduciary duty by giving Forstmann Little the right to buy the two key operations. Additionally, the court, in its thirty-page ruling, came down in favor of Pantry Pride when it found illegal an arrangement in which Forstmann Little had gotten Revlon to promise that it wouldn't use the Forstmann Little offer to shop around for a higher bid.

While shocked Forstmann Little partner Theodore Forstmann called the court ruling "unbelievable" and the case "a
very troubling suit," legal observers said the all-important
court decision would bear on all leveraged takeover buyouts
in the future, including those to be handled by Pantry Pride.
Perhaps most telling, in making his ruling, Judge Joseph T.
Walsh also ruled that Pantry Pride was "entitled to market its
latest bid without the entanglement" of Revlon's poison pill
offer.

In his blistering attack on Revlon, Judge Walsh stated that
"the directors' role changed from that of a board fending off
a hostile acquirer bent on a breakup of the corporation to that
of an auctioneer attempting to secure the highest price for the
pieces." Additionally, Walsh said that Revlon's repeated claim
that Forstmann Little was better able than Pantry Pride to finance their deal "does not withstand hard analysis." Revlon
had been slugged, and slugged mortally.

"This is a great victory for the stockholders of Revlon," Perelman proclaimed after Walsh's ruling was announced. "This
decision now clears the way for Revlon's shareholders to partic-
ipate in Pantry Pride's generous offer."

Judge Walsh had also sent a message to all of corporate
America. No ordinary judge, Walsh was an honored adjudica-
tor who had only the month before been elected to the Supreme Court of Delaware. And, in fact, his ruling set a
precedent that is accepted today. For while roadblocks like
"poison pill" offers are still acceptable tactics for boards of
directors to use when fighting a hostile takeover, there can no
longer be so many obstacles erected by the board that it affects
bidding and thus hurts the stockholders the board is elected
to represent.

At MacAndrews & Forbes–Pantry Pride, they leapt to celebrate. Champagne was broken open by Perelman's executive

assistant Sue Strachan and passed around to all those who had labored so long and so hard for the past four months.

As is often done, the day after the Chancery Court ruling, the Delaware Supreme Court, with Justice Walsh among those on the bench, delayed the preliminary injunction granted the day before in order to allow Revlon time to appeal the crucial ruling. With a hearing scheduled for the following week, Revlon and Forstmann Little were given a green light to pursue whatever actions the board selected. It was a small liberty handed the corporation.

Three days later, on November 1, the Delaware Supreme Court upheld the Chancery Court's ruling against the cosmetics giant. Revlon, at last, hung out the white flag with the announcement that Revlon would "do nothing to impede the Pantry Pride takeover," adding that all directors on the board would immediately sell their stock to the Florida supermarket chain as an indication to their stockholders to follow suit. "We assume that, by the end of tomorrow, they will have control of the company," Roger Shelley announced, his "fat lady" T-shirt nowhere in sight. "That's the end of the battle."

At the law firm of Skadden, Arps, Slate, Meagher & Flom, there was a wild victory celebration as grown men hugged each other like children and law clerks jumped with joy. The round-the-clock work load of the past four months had forced lawyers and staff alike to sleep some nights in their offices. All that was finally over.

"I don't think any of us ever worked so hard on a deal," Skadden partner Stuart Shapiro said. Part of the problem had been keeping Ronald Perelman contained during the drawn-out process. "He's impatient every day of his life," said Shapiro. "If there's a Ferrari he can drive, he doesn't want to drive a Jeep."

For Forstmann Little, it was a double loss. Not only was it

no longer in contention to own Revlon and divide up the company's assets, it also had been denied by the court two things written into its deal—its right to collect the $20 million consolation prize and its right to retain $4.4 million for services rendered. While refusing to comment on the ruling, Forstmann Little indicated that it intended at least to ask for a hearing in order to collect the comparatively paltry fee.

Perelman had won. On the surface, his price for the Revlon takeover was $1.8 billion. Yet, when debt refinancing, income taxes, takeover expenses for lawyers and investment bankers, and severance pay were factored in, the price for Perelman to own his own lipstick company rose to $2.7 billion. It was quite a shopping day, even for someone of Ron Perelman's enthusiasm.

With Donald Drapkin at his side, Perelman happily announced to the press that, once Pantry Pride took control of the Revlon board, he expected to be elected chairman and chief executive officer. While officially making no comment on Michael Bergerac's future with the company, he silently made the motions of someone appearing to wave "bye-bye."

As parties continued over the weekend following the takeover announcement, lawyers on both sides worked to make the transition of power as smooth as could be hoped for given the hostile atmosphere. One loose end that had to be tied up, and quickly, was Revlon's previously announced plan to sell its cosmetics division to Adler & Shaykin. Leonard Shaykin had left little doubt that he expected Ronald Perelman to follow through on the terms of Revlon's deal. "I have no reason to believe the contract would not be honored," Shaykin said. "It's a breathtaking price. I can't imagine they wouldn't want to go through with it." Little did they know.

On Monday, November 4, Perelman walked into the executive offices of Revlon with the authority that only $1.8 billion—or more—can bring. According to those who watched from the wings, his reception was anything but warm. "We looked upon him as a something slightly vulgar," said one secretary in the executive suite. "The entire 49th floor smelled of cigar smoke," she said.

Perelman was ushered into Michael Bergerac's office—the same office that once belonged to Charles Revson—and, like a victorious general accepting the surrender of a defeated enemy, he received Bergerac's resignation. Apart from a short, civil conversation, there was no attempt at friendship or real social grace. Bergerac walked out of his office that night and never looked back. In his hand was paperwork worth $34 million in severance pay—$7 million in cash, $14 million in stock, and another $14 million in stock options.

"We have accomplished our goal," Bergerac said in a final self-serving statement. "Our diversification program over the last ten years of pursuing major acquisitions in the health care industry has been successful. We bought companies at the right prices and we built their values. Once the sale of Revlon became inevitable, we obtained maximum value for shareholders."

It remained for Judge Rifkind, still on the boards of both Revlon and MacAndrews & Forbes, to have the final word. "It is the demise of this enterprise as we know it," he said, a look of distinct sadness in his eyes.

It took only one day for Perelman to move into Bergerac's office. In his customary blue cardigan, a cigar in his hand, he was already ruling by decree. "There is something to be said for winning," he said, taking a long draw on his cigar and luxuriously releasing the smoke.

On his second day in the office, he was shocked to discover the dust-covered bronze bust of Revlon founder Charles Revson dismissively relegated to a corner closet. Michael Bergerac had made sure there was scant evidence of Revson around the company during his tenure as chief. As a symbol of the *new* Revlon, Perelman ordered the bust restored to a place of honor in the lobby of the company's executive suite.

His victory was hard-earned, and sweet. The glory days, however, were complicated, for on November 22, less than three weeks after he had won control of Revlon, he was hit with a lawsuit by Adler & Shaykin. The company had been in negotiations with Perelman over their attempted acquisition of the cosmetics division of the firm. When the last few meetings became heated and a breakdown in talks occurred over what Shaykin said were "unresolved questions involving a lot of money," the investment house went back to Delaware Chancery Court to try to force the new Revlon into completing the sale.

"We are requesting that Revlon allow us to complete our investigation of the cosmetics operations," Leonard Shaykin said, "and to close the deal. We have every intention to honor our contract, and we have intentions to have Revlon honor their side of the contract as well."

It was a busy day for the man in Charles Revson's office. While refusing to comment on the Adler Shaykin lawsuit, Perelman announced that England's Beecham Group had agreed to pay $395 million in cash for Revlon's Norcliff Thayer patent medicines (including Tums and Oxy acne cream) as well as its Reheis Chemical Company division. This was the same group of companies that Michael Bergerac had attempted to sell to American Home Products Corp. for $350 million only two months before.

A week later, Rhone-Poulnec Rorer Group announced its agreement to purchase Revlon's worldwide prescription drug operation for $690 million in cash. The prescription divisions included USV Development Corporation Pharmaceutical and

Armour Pharmaceutical, makers of Hygroton and Regroton blood pressure medication, as well as Lozol, a diuretic, and Calcimar, a drug used to treat osteoporosis and Paget's disease. With that buy, Rorer, whose Maalox antacid was its best-known product, more than doubled its business overnight. In the course of one week, Perelman had recouped over $1 billion of his $1.8 billion purchase price.

On the legal front, Perelman decided not to challenge Forstmann Little's $20 million claim, which the Delaware Supreme Court had ruled Pantry Pride did *not* have to pay. Instead of risking a trial and judgment on the issue, Perelman struck a deal with Forstmann Little that essentially gave them $20 million in cash and allowed them to keep the $4.5 million in fees which they had already been paid. In exchange, Perelman got the investment house to drop any claim to Revlon's vision care group and National Health Laboratory division.

In the meantime, Howard Gittis, who had left his Philadelphia law practice and moved to New York to become MacAndrews & Forbes's vice-chairman, began the work of pruning down Revlon's staff, which had grown by thousands under Bergerac's domain. He first looked at its legal staff, an area he understood very well. Within a month, the troop of over one hundred attorneys had been winnowed to twenty. He also arranged to auction off valuable real estate holdings near Revlon's Arizona manufacturing plants, and disposed of Revlon's customized Boeing 727 corporate jet (safari gun collection and all). The lucky purchaser: socialite Ann Getty.

Gittis also dropped a bombshell on Adler & Shaykin directly in the face of its lawsuit. He summarily canceled Revlon's commitment to sell the investment firm the cosmetics division and the Revlon name. According to Gittis, Adler & Shaykin had failed to meet its closing deadline scheduled for 2 P.M. the day after Christmas, 1985. Leonard Shaykin was astounded by the news. "There was no closing because Revlon has not performed in accordance with the terms and conditions of the agreement," he countered.

Gittis contended that they had been prepared to close the deal. The executives were at the law firm where the closing was to take place, he said, and had been waiting forty-five minutes when John Quigley of Adler & Shaykin arrived carrying a letter saying that the investment house needed more information before proceeding. Inside sources suggest that Revlon was refusing the Adler organization access to its financial records.

To those who cared to look, Perelman's desires were becoming clear: to keep the cosmetics division of Revlon intact and restore it to its former prestige position as the number one makeup line in America.

As 1986 began, Ronald Perelman was flushed with all kinds of success. He continued to be wildly in love with Claudia Cohen, even though much of his energy and time was expended away from the social whirl she preferred. She adapted to her husband's schedule, however, and played the role of royal homemaker and decorator. Throughout the town house on East 63rd Street, Cohen's touches began to appear, including new pink marble in the bathrooms of their private suites. Her impromptu appearances in the corporate offices of MacAndrews & Forbes were announced with her bellowing cry of "Ron! Oh, Ron!" Her husband, the corporate potentate, was always pleased to see his bride and was not shy about showing it, no matter who was around.

Regardless of his affection, Perelman turned his focus to Revlon. Chief among his projects was restoring the fading complexion of Revlon's beauty creams and makeups. "No one buys a company that's going to go down," Gittis was overheard to say. "Of course, we intend to bring it up." The question was, how? Everything in the beauty division had been allowed to slide under Bergerac's reign—from packaging, which desperately needed to be updated, to advertising campaigns, which were hopelessly out of step with the times. It also fell to Perelman to improve the relationship between Revlon and its retailers, who had long felt the company was the most arrogant of their suppliers.

Perelman's dramatic response was to walk into department stores unannounced and meet with store managers. His very presence in stores like Saks Fifth Avenue and Bloomingdale's caused crowds to gather and sales clerks to stare. He was treated like visiting royalty, and it paid off. Soon department managers began to heed his pleas of cooperation and to accommodate themselves to his suggestions.

To further his campaign, Perelman and his wife took frequent trips abroad. Internationally, Revlon was a loser. Its failures abroad had cost the parent firm a $28 million loss in 1985 alone. Part of the problem was Revlon's inadequate distribution network in Europe. In an effort to shore up this weak area immediately, Perelman mounted another takeover—this time a friendly one—for the Max Factor, Halston, and Almay beauty divisions of Playtex Products. All it took was $340 million, pocket change for the new guru of the gigantideal. For an additional $160 million, he also added the fashionable cosmetics lines of Germaine Monteil, Yves Saint Laurent, and Charles of the Ritz.

Perelman's lust for Max Factor can be traced both to its valuable brand name identification (second only to Revlon in the beauty business) as well as its sales leadership position. Seventy percent of Max Factor's business was outside of the United States. Almay was an ideal addition to the Revlon family for its hypo-allergenic skin products—then the single fastest-growing aspect of the makeup industry. The new high-fashion lines of Monteil, Saint Laurent, and Charles of the Ritz allowed

Perelman to claim more shelf space in department stores, and he convinced the stores to group all the Revlon products together for more impact.

Perelman installed Sol Levine as the company's president. Levine was senior vice-president of Revlon before the Perelman buyout and a longtime executive under Charles Revson. Perelman also hired a new advertising agency, Bozell, Jacobs, Kenyon & Eckhardt, and gave them $25 million to spend. Claudia Cohen had sat in on the meetings as various agencies pitched for the Revlon account. Cohen, as it so happened, was a friend of Barbara Walters, while Perelman was chummy with Walters's then-husband Merv Adelson. Adelson at the time owned Lorimar-Telepictures, which coincidentally owned Bozell, Jacobs, Kenyon & Eckhardt. To Carl Spielvogel, chief executive officer of Backer Spielvogel Bates, an advertising agency on the losing end of the draw, the entire selection process was rigged. "It was a charade, and we are outraged by it," he told a reporter for *Adweek*. Perelman himself was said to be amused.

The new ruler of Revlon also sought to improve its factories, which were the oldest in the industry. Perelman investigated state-of-the-art production lines in Europe and the United States and spent millions to equip his factories with automated lines called "Pick 'n Pack," which not only automatically filled lipstick orders but simultaneously kept track of inventory and shipments.

Perelman also increased Revlon's research and development budget, insisting that his company be on the cutting edge of innovation. Unfortunately, the old Revlon had carved its niche among middle-level customers when it was low-cost and high-end cosmetics that were beginning to make most of the sales. As a result, Revlon's sales had fallen from its first-place standing in 1975—at the time of Charles Revson's death—to a distant third behind market leaders Maybelline and Cover Girl. Third place was *no* place as far as Perelman was concerned. The financier was determined to change Revlon's course—whatever it took.

FOUR

Revolutionary

With the takeover of Revlon, Perelman gained what he wanted most from his fellow businessmen, investment bankers, and Wall Street analysts—respect. There was no denying that the "little engine that could," his nickname from the people at Revlon, had made it to the top of the mountain.

Yet, for Perelman, the thrill was not in the accomplishment but in the pursuit. Like a big game hunter, he constantly needed the excitement of the stalk and the bagging of the prey. Merely displaying his trophies was not enough. While devoting much of his time to reinventing Revlon, he soon was also tirelessly looking for his next acquisition. At the same time, the lawsuit filed years earlier by Michael Forman and Cinerama Corp. took an unexpected turn.

During the process of discovery by Forman's attorneys in California, some fascinating new elements were uncovered. Fascinating, and potentially illegal, according to Forman, who filed a second suit in 1986. This time he charged that the entire negotiation process had been tainted by gross negligence and conflicts of interest among the Technicolor board of directors.

Trial depositions in California and New York disclosed the extent to which Perelman had attempted to influence individual directors of Technicolor. While it was publicly announced to all Technicolor stockholders that Fred Sullivan, a director, was being paid $150,000 for introducing Perelman to then-chairman of the board Morton Kamerman, several other facts were only now coming to light.

Perelman admitted in his deposition that he had promised Kamerman a seat on MacAndrews & Forbes board of directors if Technicolor became a Perelman company. Additionally, Kamerman conceded in his deposition that the investment house of Goldman Sachs, analyzing the potential sale for Technicolor's board, had some doubts. Goldman Sachs said that while Perelman's offer was fair, Kamerman himself should consider doing a leveraged buyout with the other board members for an even higher return. According to the court documents, Kamerman considered the idea, then dismissed it—but without ever discussing it with the other directors.

Additionally, Kamerman admitted that as further inducement for the deal, Perelman had led him to believe that he would continue to run the company after the transfer of ownership and that Perelman had offered to add an extra $50,000 in consulting fees for Kamerman covering the last five years of his Technicolor contract.

Additionally, Perelman also made contact with Technicolor's president, Arthur Ryan. Perelman conveyed messages to Ryan through mutual friend Martin Davis (then chairman of Gulf + Western). Ryan and Kamerman were approached separately because the relationship between the two Technicolor executives was so strained that the pair weren't even speaking at the time, with Kamerman having removed most of Ryan's power at the company. According to Ryan's deposition, Davis led him to believe that Perelman intended to restore his decision-making authority at the company once the Technicolor sale was complete.

When the Technicolor board met on October 29, 1982, with more than a dozen investment counselors and attorneys in attendance, Kamerman not only recommended that the entire board unanimously support the Perelman takeover, he even distributed a press release announcing that the approval had been given. Each of the directors was given a chance to speak and all seemed eager to approve of the sale, until finally seventy-two-year-old Charles Simone had his turn.

According to Simon's deposition, not only didn't he approve of Perelman's offer, he was upset that outsiders were permitted in the room while the subject was being discussed. Furthermore, he didn't like the fact that he and some of the other directors had not been informed of the proposal before the meeting and suggested that other offers be considered. Additionally, Simone objected to Sullivan's $150,000 fee. As chairman of Technicolor's compensation committee, Simone was supposed to pass on the proposal first, but, in fact, he had not seen it.

At that point, according to Simone, he was abruptly cut off by Kamerman, who adjourned the meeting. Almost instantly, Simone swore, Perelman rushed into the room, arms flailing, fists clenched in the sign of victory. As a token of his appreciation, Simone testified, Perelman offered to take everyone out to a celebration lunch at the posh eatery, Le Perigord East. Simone was unable to say what happened at the lunch, since he refused to attend, or even to shake Perelman's hand. "I only had one thing in my mind . . . this whole thing was not right. . . . I feel that a crooked deal has been done," Simone testified.

According to *Forbes* magazine, Kamerman, who was fired in February within thirty days of Perelman's takeover of the corporation, was soon soaking up sun on an island in the Caribbean where he would collect $35,500 a month for the first six years of his retirement, before having the figure reduced to $12,500, to continue until 1993. At the time, Ryan became chairman of Technicolor, having been appointed by Perelman to run the company. And Sullivan joined the board of directors of MacAndrews & Forbes, having been paid his $150,000 fee by Technicolor.

Perelman's attorney, in fighting the Forman lawsuit that was filed in Delaware Chancery Court, stated in 1986 that "it would be grossly negligent to indicate . . . [the plaintiff's] claims have a basis in fact." The double hearing was set to be heard over three years later, in October 1989.

Yet, while Perelman's attorneys tackled the intricacies of the lawsuit, the financier himself was more interested in expanding his empire. In mid-September 1986, stock analysts reported that speculators were showing increased interest in Transworld Corporation (the owner of Hilton International Company), Spartan Food Systems, and Canteen Corporation. With Transworld rumored to be the next Perelman target, the stock price rose steadily from 22¼ in the latter part of September to 39⅜ a month later.

USA Today chronicled: "As the curtain rises again this week on the play 'Target Transworld Corp.,' the mysterious force behind the unexplained rise of Transworld stock has been unmasked. The spotlight closes in, the audience gasps. It's not Donald Trump. Not [former president] Charlie Bradshaw either. Behind the mask are the basset hound features of Ronald O. Perelman."

Perelman, at this point, had purchased 15 percent of Transworld. The company was not impressed by the new King of Makeup, and announced its plans to restructure to optimize stock value and thus thwart a Perelman takeover.

A week later, CPC International, the New Jersey–based food products company that made, among other brands, Hellman's mayonnaise, Skippy peanut butter, Thomas' English muffins, and Mazola corn oil, said it was going to do likewise. The reason: "to discourage an investment group, believed led by Ronald O. Perelman, from acquiring a majority share of the corporation." James R. Eiszner, president of CPC, authorized Salomon Brothers, the firm's financial advisor, to handle the repurchase of 10 million shares of the then 48.7 million outstanding. Speculators began boisterously buying stock in anticipation of a Perelman takeover attempt, rapidly driving its price from $75 to $84.50.

Even though Perelman owned only 7 percent of CPC, it appeared that the mere mention of the name Perelman was enough to strike terror in the hearts and souls of both Transworld and CPC. But a closer look uncovers another factor driving the corporate panic. His name was Donald Drapkin. The investment attorney and acquisition genius had turned in his resignation at Skadden, Arps, Slate, Meagher & Flom to join MacAndrews & Forbes Group. Perelman had picked Drapkin to be his merchant banker and acquisitions chief. "The Drapper" had been lured away with a multimillion-dollar contract and the promise of personal involvement in Perelman's buying sprees.

The frantic activity was all over as suddenly as it had begun. Coaxed by Salomon Brothers to sell back his shares, Perelman cashed in his chips on November 6. To reduce the boil to a simmer, Salomon Brothers bought the shares back at $88.50, giving Perelman a quick $80 million profit. He had held his stock for less than a month. Others were not so lucky. After news spread of Perelman's sale, the price of CPC stock dropped to $78. Wall Street professionals were trapped with as

80

many as five million shares of the stock, some bought as high as $80 a share.

The about-face by Perelman did more than sting Wall Street speculators; it generated a lot of negative feeling about him. "A few lucky deals and he thinks he's J. P. Morgan," one stock analyst huffed. "It's only a matter of time before his maneuvers will backfire."

Transworld did not wait for an overt Perelman move. Its board of directors assembled to deal with what it labeled "the Perelman agenda." Transworld chairman Edwin L. Smart had had several meetings with Perelman in which the investor's takeover plans were discussed. Perelman said he expected to conduct a "detailed review" of the company, but insisted that he had no "specific plans to dispose of any specific parts" of Transworld.

Insiders generally believed that it was the Hilton Hotels International division that had caught Perelman's attention. A hostile takeover of Transworld would be difficult, however, due to a variety of anti-takeover measures adopted by the board over the years. Among them: staggering the terms of its directors, a requirement for a "supermajority" for certain actions, and an "antigreenmail" provision that specified all stockholders must be compensated equally if a takeover loomed.

Greenmail is the practice in which a company buys back one stockholder's shares at a substantial premium in order to end that stockholder's threat of a takeover. Ronald Perelman not only understood the principle, he was the beneficiary of it with the CPC buyback. In that case, while Wall Street cried foul, Perelman claimed innocence, saying that he was paid the going market rate for his stock, no more. Perelman said that he could not be held accountable for speculators who drove up the stock price based on his takeover explorations.

Transworld, in an effort to stay independent, was prepared

to rip itself to shreds, selling off various divisions of the firm until it became too unattractive to be a Perelman target. Not surprisingly, at the top of its "sell" list was Hilton Hotels International. They even gave Perelman first option to buy the hotel chain.

Once again a company was armed, looking out from its bunker only to find suddenly that there was no enemy out there. Perelman had already moved on, not abandoning Transworld forever, but salivating at the prospect of bigger prey. This time, Perelman was about to open Revlon's wallet for $4.12 billion to purchase The Gillette Co., the Boston-based manufacturer of shaving equipment.

Perelman was cruising at top speed through corporate America looking for buys at the very time that the bottom had dropped out of investor confidence. Ivan Boesky, notorious Wall Street arbitrager, had been arrested and charged with insider trading. He agreed to pay a $100 million fine to the Securities and Exchange Commission as well as cooperate with the continuing investigation that promised to bring down other high rollers.

Perelman was polite but granite-like in a November 14 letter he sent to Gillette chairman Colman Mockler notifying him of a $65-a-share offer he was making for the shaving company. In it, Perelman outlined his plans for a friendly combination of Gillette and Revlon, while making clear he wouldn't walk away if things got heated. Perelman made his bid through a new company, Orange Acquisition Corporation, a combination of MacAndrews & Forbes Group and Revlon Group.

"It's mogulmania." That's how one cosmetics industry analyst viewed Perelman's behavior. "It's a case of power at the rawest. He makes Carl Icahn look like a polished stone." The analyst, as an example, pointed to a department store which reported that when a Revlon executive didn't like the way the store was displaying its product, he warned, "You'd better watch it or we'll buy you."

On November 18, Gillette unfolded its defense, not in a direct reply to Perelman, but through a suit. The shaving giant asked a federal court in Boston to block Revlon and its ownership or affiliated companies from buying any more Gillette stock while it considered Perelman's proposal.

When financial papers clamored for interviews, a coy Perelman would only comment to the *New York Times,* "You really don't gain a lot of advantage by talking a lot. It makes it more difficult to do business."

In reality, Perelman *was* talking. Not to the press, but to his financial advisors. He resolved that the Gillette foray would be a fight to the finish. "He calmly explains what his bottom line is, and he protects it," a competing attorney asserted. "He's very cordial and friendly [with the target]. But there's no room for doubt that there are teeth behind the smile."

If cordial and friendly were to be the ground rules, no one bothered to enforce them on Gillette. In a futile attempt to destroy his credibility, the lather giant publicly charged Perelman with insider trading, saying he gave inside information to Wall Street as part of his attempted $4.12 billion buyout.

"It's a desperate and untruthful attempt to taint this offer in light of totally unrelated events of the past week," was the official MacAndrews & Forbes line. The statement was referring to the widening Boesky investigation by the Securities and Exchange Commission which had then begun to focus on Michael Milken and Drexel Burnham Lambert, the investment house that had committed to raising the funds necessary for the Gillette takeover. "The charges are totally without merit and self-serving," the Perelman spokesman said. And, in fact, the charges went nowhere.

Four days later, on Sunday night, Eric Gleacher of Morgan Stanley met with Perelman at his East Side Manhattan town house and informed him that Gillette had succeeded in securing a commitment from another corporation for a 20 percent block of Gillette preferred stock. Gillette was going to go ahead with the deal, with Gleacher handling the sale. While Perelman didn't know the name of the competing corporation at that moment, indications were that it was Ralston Purina.

"We were faced on that Sunday with the prospect of fighting two corporate establishments and a different kind of capital structure," Perelman stated in an interview in *Cigar Aficionado* years later. With Ralston Purina having a vise-grip on 20 percent of the company, Revlon's chances to take over control would be dim. Gleacher recommended that Perelman give up his attempt to acquire Gillette. Given the circumstances, Perelman decided on the spot to sell his 13.8 percent stake in Gillette to Ralston, and asked Gleacher to convey his intentions. It wasn't until later that same night that Gillette executives telephoned to say that the Ralston deal had yet to be completed. Gillette asked if Perelman would sell *them* the stock, adding that Gillette would sell the shares to Ralston the following day. Perelman agreed and went back to sleep.

On November 24, Gillette paid Perelman about $550 million to buy back the stock that MacAndrews & Forbes Holdings had purchased in the company. All 9.22 million shares of it. The deal made the financier a profit of more than $35 million overnight, in addition to reimbursing Perelman $9 million for expenses incurred during the takeover attempt.

In truth, Ronald Perelman had been suckered. It took only twenty-four hours for Perelman to realize that he had erred, big time, labeling his call "probably the worst decision I have ever made." It was made all the more obvious when it was confirmed that Ralston had backed out of the deal as well.

"We were in a spot," Howard Gittis told *Institutional Investor.* "We didn't have Donnie Drapkin on our side [Drapkin, who had yet to make his move to New York, had a conflict of interest since his law firm, Skadden, Arps, represented Gillette], the financial world was in chaos over the Boesky business, and we had to worry about a potential loss for our public shareholders."

When asked to explain his sudden turnaround, Perelman released a statement that said "we were strongly persuaded that Gillette was pursuing alternate transactions that would effectively deprive Revlon and MacAndrews & Forbes of the opportunity to acquire control of Gillette and would cause Revlon and MacAndrews & Forbes substantial losses. We reluctantly dropped our offer to protect the interests of Revlon shareholders."

"Outrageous" was Gillette's formal response when they heard the Perelman version of his takeover scuttle. "We strenuously disagree with the characterization of the events leading up to the withdrawal of the Revlon Group's tender offer. However, we think it would be unproductive to engage in a debate over matters that are in the past."

For the moment, it appeared that Perelman was finished with Gillette. As part of his deal in selling back the stock at an inflated price of $59.50 a share, he promised not to buy Gillette stock again for the next ten years. Additionally, Drexel agreed not to finance the acquisition of Gillette stock for three years.

Wall Street continued to look down on Perelman's sellout with suspicion. Some, like Tom Larkin of the Trust Co. of the West, wondered aloud: "Why would you want to put your money on a company if the guy is going to pull the rug out from under you?" Claude Rosenberg of Rosenberg Capital

Management hung his response on talk of greenmail: "If Gillette was willing to pay $59.50 a share now, the company should have been buying up stock months ago. They better have something wonderful in mind for shareholders," he stated.

While Gillette's executives moved to reassure their stockholders, Perelman could not contain his own frustration at having allowed the shaving giant to slip through his grasp. "He was angry at himself," Howard Gittis later recalled, "and just couldn't let it go." In reality, the Gillette incident was an isolated failure in a plethora of successes. The Perelman companies were all showing enormous gains. MacAndrews & Forbes's licorice extract business was booming, its sales five times greater than when Perelman bought the firm. Profits had shot up 400 percent to $90 million. Its chocolate division had been sold off during the year for $41 million, recouping nearly all of Perelman's initial investment in the company. Consolidated Cigar was making more money than ever, and was acquiring additional brand names that even convinced Perelman to appear in its ads: "The man—Ronald Perelman. The cigar—Don Diego." Technicolor, too, was showing vivid growth. Its processing and videotape divisions had quadrupled their profits in the four years of Perelman's ownership, spurred on by the sale of five operating divisions. Revlon was poised for a turnaround with a new advertising campaign watched over by Claudia Cohen featuring photographs by Richard Avedon. The name Pantry Pride had ceased to exist, rolled into the newly formed Revlon Group, which included Charlie Co., named after its famous perfume for the masses. Revlon's name had taken on new luster in every way. In fact, Perelman felt so confident he had advanced Revlon into a profitable future that he prepared to pack up his files and evacuate Charles Revson's old office in favor of a hippity-hop back to East 63rd Street.

There was only one irritant for Perelman as 1987 commenced. It wasn't the troubles of Boesky or Milken. It wasn't that his wife was tugging him to celebrity parties with increasing frequency. He didn't even mind joining Cohen as co-chair of the Actors Studio fundraising premiere of *The Color of Money*, hobnobbing at the Palladium with the likes of stars Tom Cruise and Paul Newman. It was that Ron Perelman simply couldn't shake his anger over losing out on Gillette.

The defeat chewed at the financier's insides for several months. Nevertheless, there were other items on the calendar—like toying with taking Revlon private. He talked it over with Gittis and Drapkin, then ran the concept past Drexel Burnham Lambert. He threw out the figure of $18.50 a share at a time when Revlon stock was selling at $15. Revlon stock had bottomed out months before at $11 a share, after Perelman had disposed of some its highly profitable health care lines.

As usual, Perelman was impatient. He didn't like the fact that he had to explain his actions every quarter to stockholders who ultimately controlled his moves. He didn't want to report profits or losses for all to see, or respond to the investment community about his plans. Going private was the quintessential friendly takeover. With 65.4 percent of the Revlon shares outstanding, the deal would cost an estimated $715 million.

Drexel Burnham Lambert rallied once more to Perelman's cash call, selling some $880 million in newly issued MacAndrews & Forbes Holdings junk bonds to finance the purchase.

Given the chaos reigning on Wall Street, it seemed to analysts that Perelman had stretched his spending rope to the limit. While his companies were performing well, he would have to bring down his debt load, and quickly, in order to keep his interest payments from robbing his bottom line of profit and available cash. Everyone thought so. Everyone, that is, but Ron Perelman.

There was one more company he wanted—no, *needed*—to buy. Now it was as much ego as anything else. It didn't matter that he had promised not to utter those two syllables ever again with his checkbook in hand. "Gill-ette" was on his lips. On June 17, 1987, Donald Drapkin called up his old buddy Bruce Wasserstein of First Boston to get him to intercede on Perelman's behalf with Gillette. Perelman wanted to make another stab at buying the company. A $4.66 billion stab.

The answer was the same as it had been the previous November. "Thank you, but no thank you." It mattered little to Gillette that Perelman's offer of $40.50 a share was 24.6 percent higher than his previous offer. The company wasn't interested and planned on holding Perelman to his agreement not to attempt a takeover of the corporation.

There were many who thought that Perelman's obsession had another motive altogether, one based on a different part of the agreement. When Gillette paid Perelman the equivalent of $29.75 a share for his stock (adjusted to account for a stock split), it also promised that if Gillette should be sold for more than that share amount in the forthcoming year to anyone— including Perelman—it would give him the difference in cash. By stirring up interest in a new Gillette takeover bid, Perelman increased the chance that another purchaser would actually buy the company, thereby kicking in the condition of his stock bonus. Either way, Perelman would win.

The Gillette board's peremptory rejection of Perelman's offer offended many of the company's stockholders who were tired of the constant flux of the corporation's stock. These stockholders filed suit in Delaware court in an effort to force Gillette to seriously consider the bid. The court denied the request, ruling instead that the case be filed in federal court in Boston, the headquarter city for Gillette.

If the stockholders were concerned that Perelman might lose interest in Gillette and go away mad, they had little reason to fear. In a particularly sweet move, Perelman pointed to the "standstill" agreement he had signed against any further hostile takeover and held out a conciliatory hand. This time, it was to be a friendly takeover. He was even willing to forego his over-$29.50 provision which, at his offered price of $40.50, would have amounted to a little more than $200 million in cash. "Now *that's* friendly," said one stock analyst.

But not even that added incentive was enough for Gillette to enter into serious negotiations. They answered Perelman's latest query with veiled threats of a lawsuit for breach of contract, citing a 1985 Pennsylvania court ruling that upheld and enforced a standstill agreement.

If Gillette thought a threat was enough to make Perelman stop what had been labeled the Wall Street version of *Fatal Attraction*, Gillette was dangerously wrong. Perelman disappeared, all right, but only for six weeks. In August 1987, he was back again, with another letter to Gillette—this time extending his "friendly" hand—and this time it was holding $5.4 billion.

Perelman's third offer for Gillette amounted to $47 a share. In a three-page letter, he asked Gillette not to make up its mind before September 15. Gillette chairman Colman Mockler was irate. Perelman's third offer drew the same answer his other two bids had—a firm no. This time, however, Mockler added the testy comment that he would "not be subject to arbitrary conditions or deadlines or affected by strident statements made by Revlon in its own self-interest."

Meanwhile, Perelman placed the "sold" sign on Revlon's Vision Care division. Pilkington Brothers, a glass maker from England, agreed to pay $574 million for the business. The British firm was already well known for making glass lenses, and the Vision Care division allowed it to branch out into the contact lens field.

With $574 million in his pocket, Perelman waited. Labor Day came and went, and a new Revlon advertising campaign began: "Unforgettable," featuring Liza Minnelli in a series of photographs by Richard Avedon. Madison Avenue delighted in the slick, high-style ad. Revlon had reascended to the top— if not in sales, at least in image. Yet, even in victory, his thoughts were elsewhere.

Unable to conceive how Gillette could arbitrarily ignore his offer of $5.7 billion, Perelman tried still again to sweeten the deal. In yet another letter to Colman Mockler, Perelman unilaterally waived his right to a windfall payment by Gillette— waived it unconditionally—effectively removing any inference that his offer was precipitated by a desire to put Gillette in play as a takeover subject in order to activate his windfall payment. He sent the letter on September 14, the day before his offer was due to expire, and extended his proposal to pay $47 a share for Gillette.

For all his apparent restraint up to now, Ronald Perelman was tiring of the Gillette game. His letter made that clear. "We were chagrined at your hasty and ill-considered rejection," he wrote. "We believe that you still have not given our request a fair and thorough review and, accordingly, we extend our request until October 15, in the hopes that you will be more responsible in your evaluation.

"We have no interest in profiting on the sale of Gillette to any third party," Perelman added. "Our action today mandates your reconsideration."

Despite the fact that Gillette had paid generously for Ron Perelman to remain far from their corporate door, the financier had no intention of leaving the giant alone. This was not about money alone. Perelman had more money than he could spend in ten lifetimes. What he wanted was the same thing he had *always* wanted—from his father, his bankers, his friends, his foes. Respect. He wanted to be respected as an astute manager of businesses, respected for his skill at nurturing companies toward their maximum potential. Yet, despite his genuine accomplishments, most of Wall Street and certainly Gillette continued to sniff at him as, at best, a ballsy raider.

And, in a way, Perelman was his own worst enemy. He was perceived by many as pushy, arrogant, and single-minded. At MacAndrews & Forbes, he threw tantrums—and ashtrays—as a way of getting attention.

His marriage to Claudia Cohen only seemed to strengthen his bombastic personality. As the pair grew in mutual affection, so too did they in belligerence toward others. While not intended, perhaps, to be rude or cruel or both, their comments nevertheless were conspicuous for their lack of delicacy. Domestic help were commanded in the royal sense, for servants were meant to serve and know their place.

While Perelman refused to give up on Gillette, Cohen redecorated the East 63rd Street town house. Color schemes, inspired and integrated by famed New York architect Peter Marino, changed with her whim of the moment. It is said that Cohen rejected as many as twenty of Marino's designs for the breakfast nook, and more for the redo of the master suite.

And then there was the saga of the Perelmans' air conditioner, an appliance that became the subject of cocktail party conversation across Manhattan, thanks to the notoriety it received in *Spy* magazine. It seems the Perelmans—he and she— liked temperatures on the chilly side. As the story goes, the day the air conditioning was activated for the first time was particularly sweltering. Fifteen minutes after the start-up, Cohen arrived home. It little mattered that the room temperature in the giant dwelling had dropped from 90 to 78 degrees in a mere quarter hour.

"You call this cool?" Cohen was said to have asked. "This isn't cool. What I want from an air conditioner is that you turn it on—and it's cool." The size of the air conditioner was promptly doubled, causing many to recall Roy Cohn's words: "It knocks me out that God made a couple this compatible."

While impatience was permeating the roost at home, it found a favored perch in the office as well. With Ronald Perelman's pursuit of Gillette going nowhere, he became ever more eager to make his next acquisition. His palms itched to feel the rush that only an acquisition fix could give him. If he couldn't have Gillette, then he needed something bigger, something even more dramatic, a firm that would get Wall Street talking and keep it talking. In September 1987, he found a perfect and awesome target—the esteemed investment banking house of Salomon Inc.

At the time, Salomon was the parent company of Salomon Brothers, the country's leading underwriter of corporate securities. The firm had gotten millions in commissions by advising its clients how to evade hostile raiders. Suddenly, they found themselves in bad need of advice.

The concept of buying into Salomon hadn't come to Perelman as pure, midnight inspiration. Rather, it was instigated by a telephone call from First Boston's Bruce Wasserstein. A slab of Salomon Inc. stock, Wasserstein told Donald Drapkin, was coming on the market via South Africa. That country's Mineral & Resources Corporation (Minorco), Salomon's largest shareholder, needed to sell its Salomon stock to finance its rescue of Newmont Mining Corporation, which was involved in a hostile takeover by raider T. Boone Pickens.

Salomon said it wasn't interested in meeting Minorco's asking price of $65 a share—above the market at the time—so

Minorco contacted Felix Rohatyn, senior partner of Lazard Freres & Company (the same Felix Rohatyn who was on the losing side of the Revlon buyout), to handle the sale. Rohatyn called Wasserstein, Wasserstein called Drapkin, and Perelman couldn't wipe the grin off his face for days after hearing the news. The takeover of an investment banking firm! And with his old adversary Rohatyn as a middleman. The challenge and the irony alone made the deal inviting.

Perelman met with Salomon chairman John Gutfreund on September 23 at Gutfreund's home to inform him that he planned to buy the Minorco stock for $809 million. During the meeting, according to Gutfreund, Perelman informed him that he intended to ask for Minorco's two seats on the Salomon board. Perelman remembered it differently. "If they want to give us a seat, fine; if they don't, they don't," he said.

The staid Gutfreund not only didn't want Perelman to have a board seat, he didn't want Perelman at all. "I told him that I would not work for him, and that I thought our people wouldn't work for him," Gutfreund was later quoted as saying. Perelman left Gutfreund's Manhattan co-op only to be replaced by Felix Rohatyn, who arrived minutes later. Moving quickly to limit Perelman's involvement, Gutfreund told Rohatyn that Salomon would buy back the Minorco block for $38 a share. Rohatyn relayed the news to Minorco, and the company was quick to accept the offer.

Later that same day, Gutfreund contacted his longtime friend, Berkshire Hathaway chairman Warren Buffett, a man considered by most to be an investment genius. Buffett had previously expressed interest in owning some Salomon stock, and now Gutfreund was offering him a substantial slice of the pie.

The deal cut by Buffett was shrewd. Salomon would sell Buffett the stock, but in a different form. Buffett was, in effect, offered a 12 percent interest in Salomon for $700 million. The stock would be in the form of convertible preferred, paying a dividend of 9 percent per year. In addition, Buffet was given the right to convert it into ordinary shares at $38 a share after three years.

On Monday, September 28, Perelman sent a letter to Gutfreund. In it, Perelman expressed his "desire to consummate a transaction." Although he must have known the futility of his effort, his pitch was, as usual, both to the point and economically seductive. "We will purchase preferred shares in Salomon on exactly the same terms and conditions as you were prepared to accept from Berkshire Hathaway, except that the conversion price would be $42 a share rather than $38," Perelman's letter said.

While congenial, the letter contained a veiled threat. "We have filed under Hart-Scott-Rodino to seek clearance to buy shares in the open market in the event you are unable or unwilling to conclude a transaction," Perelman said. The Hart-Scott-Rodino Act requires buyers to inform the federal government of any purchase larger than 15 percent of a company. This gives the Justice Department time to study the antitrust implications.

An hour after delivering the letter, Perelman called John Gutfreund. He was told that the board of Salomon had rejected his offer, despite the fact that it bettered the Buffett deal. Gutfreund would later remark that he liked working with people he knew, and that Buffett was a longtime friend.

"I don't really know these folks at Revlon, but I do know they ran a bootstrap operation that was financed by Drexel to make some heady acquisition," Gutfreund later told *Business Week*. "I feel that our clients would be totally uncomfortable with them," he said.

The deal with Buffett was finalized while Perelman was preoccupied with observance of the Jewish New Year.

For Perelman, the strict observance of the Sabbath and other Jewish holy days was not negotiable, so strong is his Orthodox belief. And its practice extends far from the boardroom to all areas of his life.

·

FIVE

Orthodox, or Maybe Not

A faithful worshipper at the Fifth Avenue Synagogue, Perelman keeps a kosher household. He wears a custom-made yarmulke and is devoted to the teachings of the Jewish scripture.

As further evidence of his Orthodox beliefs, he has, for several years, been a fan of Rebbe Menachem Schneerson, the leader of the Lubavitcher sect of Hasidic Judaism. The Rebbe (Yiddish for Rabbi) was introduced into Perelman's life via cable TV where the keen-eyed, thick-bearded old man in a black coat and fedora speaking in Yiddish held forth on his own late-night talk show.

Those in his studio audience occasionally leaped up, singing and chanting with great joy. The Rebbe would wait patiently, even encouraging the outbursts, and then continue with his message of hope after all had quieted. While the spectacle almost appeared to originate in an ancient synagogue in medieval Russia, the program was actually broadcast from Crown Heights, Brooklyn—a mostly black neighborhood which Schneerson called home.

Schneerson's gabled brick house on Eastern Parkway had

a new roof installed thanks to Perelman's generosity. To the Rebbe, Perelman was no different from many of his other 200,000 followers from around the world—Budapest to Bogotá. However, Perelman *was* different, for he not only believed in the Rebbe's teachings but also donated millions to help spread the word.

To most traditional Jews, the Lubavitchers are an extreme group who trace their movement back to eighteenth-century Russia. Even then, the sect was looked upon as a splinter group born from reaction to rabbinical aridity and thwarted messianic prophecy. Lubavitchers called a rabbi named Shneour Zalman their father. It was Zalman's son who moved his followers to the Russian town of Lubavitch and gave the sect its name.

In the late 1980s, Schneerson, the seventh in the Rebbe line, updated the teachings with the help of Perelman's money and Madison Avenue savvy. Among his additions were full-page advertisements in the *New York Times*, subway posters featuring the Rebbe's countenance, bumper stickers, roadside billboards, and the cable show—all proclaiming the same message: "Prepare for the coming of the Moshiach." Moshiach is Yiddish for Messiah. Many Lubavitchers believed Schneerson himself was a divine holy one.

While Schneerson never came out and claimed that he actually was the Messiah, he also never denied it, even when followers called after him with the title. In fact, when dozens of books were published, many in Hebrew, asserting there was positive proof that Schneerson was the son of God, he did nothing to debunk them.

While Perelman was caught up in this theology that seemed to speak to his Russian Jewish heritage, Claudia Cohen Perelman was less convinced. She thought of the Hasidim as "Ronald's people" and respected them as that, but she didn't exactly clutch them to her bosom and invite them home for dinner.

Spy magazine chronicled that on one particular day, Cohen was shopping for something expensive to add to the $6 million-plus East 63rd Street town house renovation. She directed the chauffeur of her Jaguar XJ6 to Brooklyn's Crown Heights. Perhaps she wanted to add something pious to the predominantly Georgian Jewish decor she had selected for her Manhattan mansion. Her exact purpose is unknown. Her comments, however, were reported.

"Ronald, Ronald," she is said to have exclaimed into the car's telephone. "We're with your people! We're with the Hasidim!" Peering out from her vantage point in the rear seat of the car, she stared with amazement at the bearded men in their black coats, high-crown black hats, and long beards. Children ran along the streets, *payot* curled down from the sides of their ears.

The women, pushing their baby carriages, walked behind their husbands. Their dresses were long and plain, in stark contrast to Cohen's designer ensemble and studiously made-up face. Directing her driver to pull up to a Hasidic bakery, she bought an assortment of pastries for her husband. Temptation got the best of her before reaching home. Cohen nibbled enough to finish the entire bag. Ronald was never the wiser.

In September 1988, Perelman sold his controlling interest in Technicolor for $780 million to a British firm, Carlton Communications. The selling price was nearly eight times what Perelman had paid for it, but as Perelman proudly told anyone who would listen, Technicolor was "ten times the company" than when he had bought it six years earlier. But the Technicolor story in years to come was to turn into a grade B courtroom movie for Perelman. At this time, Perelman saved only one small piece of the former Technicolor for himself. The

Compact Video division had been quietly liquidated of its assets and was reduced to a shell corporation with a new name: Andrews Group. Andrews was a kind of proof that while Technicolor was gone, Perelman's interest in Hollywood remained.

Immediately following the Technicolor sale, Perelman agreed to turn over control of his long-treasured Consolidated Cigar Corp. to a leveraged buyout group for $128 million. The company wasn't really on the block at the time, but he would later say that the offer was a good one for the value of the company. Even with a cigar, business was business, and a $4 million profit was good business.

Less than a week later, Perelman was ringing his sales register again, dumping his 15 percent interest in TW Services (the restructured and slimmed-down former Transworld Corp.) for $137.3 million. Including the cash available from his earlier Revlon sales, which had not yet been used to significantly reduce his debt, Perelman's war chest stood at well over $2 billion.

Wall Street was awash in speculation about what Perelman was planning. Companies with such familiar names as Sears Roebuck, Kimberly-Clark Corporation, PepsiCo, May Department Stores, McGraw-Hill, McDonald's, Colgate-Palmolive, and Procter & Gamble were all rumored to be his takeover targets during the weeks following his selling spree. Perelman reveled in the attention, adding water to the waves by proclaiming his next acquisition was "going to blow people away."

The venerable Dan Dorfman, whose "Inside Talk" column in *USA Today* was widely quoted for its accuracy, jumped into the forecasting arena. "The guessing game—who's the mystery target of Revlon Corp. CEO Ronald Perelman—gets wackier by the minute. Or maybe not," he wrote. "The latest: Philip Morris. Estimated 1988 sales: just under $30 billion." Even Michael Milken, who at this point was breathing his last at Drexel

Burnham Lambert, was said to be quietly raising $15 billion for Ron Perelman in an effort to show he hadn't lost his ability to produce money.

But during October and November, the Perelman camp was atypically quiet. As if to make up for the paucity of corporate activity, Ronald and Claudia were soon around Manhattan at fund-raisers, film premieres, society parties, and birthday events. Perelman also made a major donation of $10 million to his alma mater, the University of Pennsylvania, to build a new student and faculty activities building with his name over the door.

Late in December, in typical year-end accounting style, Perelman made his move. He had promised something big. What he delivered was staggering and caught every analyst on Wall Street unprepared. The front-page banner headline of the *New York Times* on December 28, 1988 blared the news: $5 BILLION RESCUE OF 5 SAVINGS UNITS IS PLANNED BY U.S., with the subheading adding, "Cost Stuns Some Analysts."

What Perelman had pulled out of his hat was more crocodile than rabbit. The deal was expensive, dramatic, and, as with most other Perelman deals, likely to yield a sizable profit. While all of Wall Street had guessed about giant brand name corporations as acquisition targets, Perelman's team had been quietly talking with the Federal Home Loan Bank Board, and cut a remarkable deal.

In what was labeled the most costly bailout of a savings and loan to date, Perelman, through his MacAndrews & Forbes Holdings, agreed to invest $315 million ($160 million in cash, the rest borrowed from Shearson Lehman Hutton) for controlling rights to First Texas Savings Association, with its $3.2 billion in assets; the Gibraltar Savings Association of Houston, with $6.3 billion; the Home Savings and Loan Association of Houston, with $568 million; the Killeen Savings and Loan Association of Killeen, with $256 million; and the Montfort Federal Savings and Loan Association of Dallas, with $1.8 billion.

The deciding factor for Perelman, however, was the guarantee from the federal government of $5 billion in assistance over the next ten years. While many were stunned by the size of the government guarantees, even more were surprised that Perelman would get involved in the enormously controversial and potentially lethal Texas savings and loan game.

The history of First Texas and Gibraltar Savings was a labyrinth of questionable financial maneuvers, beginning in mid-1982 when former Democratic Party Chairman Robert Strauss received a call from his longtime friend J. Livingston Kosberg, the Houston millionaire whose money came from nursing homes and a few savings and loans. Kosberg was about to invest in the ailing Dallas-based First Texas Savings Association, and he wanted to cut his buddy Bob in on the action.

Strauss went along for the ride, pumping $400,000 into the thrift in exchange for a 10 percent equity position. His son, Richard, a land developer, was added to the board of First Texas and together with Kosberg began to invest in commercial real estate. Unfortunately, they were not alone. Nearly everyone in Texas in the early eighties seemed to have caught land fever, and despite rising prices for property, overbuilding threatened to bring the entire enterprise crashing to a halt.

Rather than backing off and cutting their losses, the Kosberg-Strauss duo increased their land buys and, in 1984, added another S&L to their embryonic realm—the state's largest, Gibraltar Savings of Houston. In a land where large means better, Kosberg and Strauss were avidly adding property to their assets, as evidenced by their outbidding H. Ross Perot in 1985 for a 6,230-acre ranch a casaba melon's throw north of Dallas. Perot had already offered $108 million for the spread called the Flying M Ranch, when Strauss and Kosberg waved

$135 million in front of the sellers and walked away with the property.

Perot cried foul, and had his lawyers demand compensation. Rather than risk a lawsuit, First Texas sent Perot a consolation prize in the amount of $8 million. Kosberg had grand plans to develop the Flying M into luxury homes, and signed a deal with Richard Strauss's land development company to manage the complex. Strauss's take: upwards of $2.9 million a year for twenty-five years, plus a quarter of the profits should the development be sold.

By 1987, as giant chunks of Texas were suffering foreclosure, First Texas Gibraltar was at the front of the line, padlocking buildings and gates with dazzling speed. Handling the legal work for the S&L was Robert Strauss. It's the Texas way.

By the time the government realized what was going on, much of Texas was in the hands of banks that themselves were insolvent. As for First Texas Gibraltar, its available cash was said to have slipped to just 1.8 percent of its assets. (Federal law requires a minimum of 3 percent.)

When it finally heeded the wake-up call, the federal government placed M. Danny Wall in charge of the Federal Home Loan Bank Board and hoped for a miracle. What Wall created fell somewhat short of that, but, nevertheless, he did offer a way out of the calamity. Bring in private investors to save the ailing S&Ls by offering them tax shelters and covering a percentage of their projected losses, he reasoned. Legislators, afraid that perhaps they had overcompensated their rescuers at a time of panic, eventually amended the Wall plan to cut its benefits on January 1, 1989.

With that deadline in place, all the elements combined to create a modern-day gold rush during the waning moments of 1988. The pressure was on everyone to conclude the complicated Perelman deal within days. It was to be the culmination of long bargaining sessions that had begun five weeks before under cover of deepest secrecy.

The day before Thanksgiving Howard Gittis received the initial call about the prospect of Perelman's involvement with the Texas S&Ls. On the other end of the line was longtime buddy and Perelman money machine Michael Tarnapol with Bear Stearns & Co. Tarnapol had heard about the availability of First Gibraltar and the four other failed savings and loans, and wanted to know if Perelman would like to perform a rescue.

Gittis committed thirty of MacAndrews & Forbes's analysts to crunch the numbers on the "misery banks" and, despite the holiday weekend, had an answer for Tarnapol the following Monday. The word was "go" and the deal making began.

Despite the fact that Perelman was assuming control of malfunctioning Texas S&Ls that had been hemorrhaging profits for years, he had several aces up his sleeve. First, he was only paying three cents for every dollar of assets he was receiving. Second, in spite of the drop in land values, the S&Ls were still holders of a great deal of valuable Texas real estate. Basically, with $5 billion in government guarantees, Perelman had been given a ten-year option on Texas real estate with very little personal risk.

Part of his protection came by way of a partner. Perelman went into the S&L deal linked with Gerald J. Ford (not to be confused with former President Gerald R. Ford), chairman of the Ford Bank Group. Ford was a wizard on the day-to-day operations of lending institutions, for he had begun purchasing them as far back as 1975. Given the Ford expertise, industry insiders estimated Perelman's risk as nonexistent.

In addition to the value built into the guaranteed Federal subsidies, Perelman stood to benefit in other ways. His deal with the Federal Home Loan Bank Board allowed him to use

the net operating losses of the ailing savings and loans to reduce the future tax burden of any of his businesses that were
making a profit.

Even as the final papers were being signed on December
29, Congress was already being pressured to do something
about the bonanzas possible under deals like Perelman's. Rep.
Charles E. Schumer (Democrat, New York) held a press conference to declare that "Congress has explicitly said that you
can use some of the tax losses to get a sick institution off the
ground, but if you are passing the tax breaks up to a holding
company, then you better watch out. Congress will come down
hard on that."

Yet other members of Congress pointed out that the government wasn't putting up any hard cash to save the savings
and loans or, at least, not at that point. What the fiscally broke
Federal Savings and Loan Insurance Corporation was doing
was promising to cover future losses caused by previous management, in addition to the tax breaks. An added bonus: the
government retained 20 percent ownership in the institutions.
Essentially, the government was banking on Perelman's and
Ford's abilities to run the savings banks at a profit, despite
years of failure.

When the financial trade papers caught up with the news
just before the end of the year, much of Wall Street was taken
off-guard, impressed by Perelman's speed and tenacity in land-
ing the banks and squeezing such large concessions from the
federal government. As the media scurried to cover their
bases, the Perelmans escaped to the south of France to spend
the remaining holiday at the luxurious Hotel Du Cap in Cap
Ferrat.

In early 1989, the Perelman home on East 63rd Street hosted another kind of event altogether. There was major

fumigation going on. A noxious odor had worked its way through the entire brownstone, courtesy of the super-efficient air-conditioning ducts in which some disgruntled employee had apparently placed a family of dead gerbils. Although Perelman would later deny it was true, some on the scene swear by their story, as did those who spread the report around Manhattan's best tables at Elaine's, 21 Club, and Le Cirque.

When Perelman returned to his office, his acquisition chiefs had finished work on what was to be his first important buy of 1989—Marvel Entertainment Group. It was said that because Perelman worked his way through grade school at his father's knee and boardroom, he never had time to discover The Amazing Spiderman or The Incredible Hulk. The comic book publisher that created and owned the licenses to those superheroes and others had been on the block for four months. Perelman scooped up the property for a reported $82.5 milllion as his first acquisition of his Andrews Group holding company in California. Manufacturers Hanover Trust Company provided the cash.

After he sold Compact Video's assets and renamed the company Andrews Group, Perelman hired William Bevins as its chief executive officer. Perelman had met Bevins when he first bought Technicolor and while Bevins was building Ted Turner's operation as his chief financial officer. It was Bevins who brought Marvel Entertainment to Perelman's attention, and who pushed for its acquisition.

Perelman bought the division from Los Angeles–based New World Entertainment, a film and television producer that had fallen on tough times after several box office failures including *Hell Comes to Frogtown* and *Nice Girls Don't Explode*. Not part of the deal was New World's Marvel Productions unit, which had ongoing commitments for two Saturday morning animated children's series—"Muppet Babies" on CBS and the syndicated "Marvel Action Universe."

While the deal made Wall Street wonder why the owner of a licorice extract manufacturer, a makeup giant, and the largest savings and loan institution in Texas would include comic books in the mix, Perelman immediately began a major Marvel licensing program that dispelled their doubts. Stealing a page from the highly successful Walt Disney Studios, Perelman sold the rights to Spiderman and Incredible Hulk lunch boxes, toy figures, T-shirts, costumes, and posters. It was, at that time, a virtually untapped market. When Perelman bought the company, its skimpy profit of $2.3 million came exclusively from its publishing sales.

Marvel made an amazing "Bang-Pow" turnaround that even its own superheroes would have found amazing, but its former owner, New World Entertainment, continued to struggle. No one was surprised when New World went hat-in-hand to Drexel Burnham Lambert in an effort to find a fresh source of funding "to position it for future growth and possibilities."

Overall, films and television were part of the creative world that Perelman had always considered too volatile to ever interest him. He knew the players, but he continued to watch in silence when, at the end of February, Pathé Entertainment chief executive Giancarlo Parretti said he would buy the struggling New World for $138 million in cash and notes, plus assume its $125 million debt.

In any case, Perelman had more pressing problems. Congress was feeling the backlash of the generous deal it had approved that allowed Perelman to buy the five Texas savings and loans. There was even talk of undoing the entire package, and the prospects sent most of the Texas banking industry even deeper into a tailspin.

But by March 1989, Perelman had consolidated Gibraltar

Savings Association, First Texas Savings Association, Montfort Savings Association, Home Savings and Loan Association, and Killeen Savings and Loan Association into one large institution called First Gibraltar Bank, a division of First Gibraltar Holdings. With Gerald Ford running the show, the mechanism seemed to dictate pooling the assorted land deals and bad loans and arranging write-offs.

Then, suddenly, Ford found himself being called to San Antonio to testify in front of the House Banking Committee, which wanted an explanation of the exact nature of the deal to which the Federal Home Loan Bank Board had committed itself. The entire process was going to be reviewed and a report prepared by the General Accounting Office, the congressional watchdog.

Perelman's reputation as a major player was being questioned by members of Congress who thought he had pulled a fast one in the last moments of 1988. Far more than Ford's million-dollar-a-year management contract was on the line. So were Ronald Perelman's tax incentives.

Lawyers and consultants were rallied to support Ford's testimony as he charged that Congress was creating a smoke screen instead of letting businessmen get on with their salvation of the ailing banking industry. "They're looking at the meat of the deal," Ford said in a statement. "But below the surface is a thick layer of gristle they haven't seen. These institutions are losing $2 million a day. That gets lost in the translation. We plan to live up to our end of the deal, and we expect government to uphold its end."

Ford could have mentioned that during the first two weeks of owning First Gibraltar, he and Perelman had sold $2 billion of the thrift's assets, generating what was said to be about $200 million in tax losses. This alone gave Perelman a $135 million tax write-off. Others from Gibraltar were also doing fine. Robert Strauss's law firm, Akin Gump, was now the official outside counsel for First Gibraltar Bank, earning an independent fee for his services. Richard Strauss was still managing the land development project, now called Stonebridge. (The government had excluded the land deal from the S&L sale.)

While Ford was being grilled under the bright lights in Texas, Perelman stepped back in the news in New York. He announced that MacAndrews & Forbes had acquired the family-owned Coleman Company, a maker of stoves, lanterns, and camping equipment. The sale price was $74 a share, for a total of $545 million.

Coleman had come on the market only one month before when company president Sheldon C. Coleman and other family members sought to take the company private for $500 million. But in a compulsory action dictated by the firm's board of directors, Perelman outbid the thirty-six-year-old grandson of the founder and assumed control, promising to keep Coleman on to run the company. Within a month after signing the deal, the young Coleman was out of a job.

Perelman said that Coleman was dumped because he didn't "respond quickly enough or enthusiastically enough to suggestions about his role in the company." According to Coleman, every time he met with Perelman's team of "extremely intelligent, fast-moving, hard-charging executives," they would change their minds about his role and he would then ask for time to consider it. Eventually, Perelman's patience wore thin.

Coleman took his $250,000 in severance pay from Perelman and gave him a good-bye kiss. "I think they tried to treat me well," he said. "I'm extremely sad to be leaving a company that has been part of our family for eighty-nine years."

Two weeks after adding Coleman stoves to his crazy-quilt of companies, Perelman picked up another surprise acquisition—New World Entertainment, the very same New World Entertainment that Giancarlo Parretti thought he had bought only six weeks before. After being assured of its profit potential by Bevins, it appears that Perelman thought New World was selling itself short at Parretti's bid of $8.20 a share in cash and notes. He made his own offer: $8.95 a share, all cash, for a payout of $120 million. Never mind that Parretti's offer on the surface would have eventually paid them more, if the notes were held to maturity. Placing New World under William Bevins's leadership as part of the Andrews Group, Ronald Perelman was in the movie business.

His entrance wasn't cheap. New World had been founded by cult-film creator Roger Corman (*Attack of the Crab Monsters*) who sold the studio in 1983 to entertainment lawyers Harry Evans Sloan and Lawrence L. Kuppin for $2 million. Six years later, it was not only charming moviegoers with its films (the best being *Heathers*, starring Winona Ryder and Christian Slater), but it had managed to produce a string of hit TV series including "The Wonder Years" and "Santa Barbara." It also had managed to run up enormous debt.

Parretti was given an opportunity to top Perelman's bid but declined, saying that he didn't want to enter into a bidding war which would "push the price of New World past its utility to us." For his trouble, Parretti received a $3 million termination fee.

While many thought Perelman grossly overbid for New World and its assets, the billionaire disagreed, pointing to Bevins's experience in handling entertainment units, particularly television. But it was widely theorized that Perelman would dismantle New World's theatrical movie wing as a far too speculative venture.

With reassurances from Bevins, Perelman was satisfied to add the company to his Andrews Group holdings. Claudia

Cohen Perelman, on the other hand, was ecstatic. The newest Perelman acquisition gave the entertainment journalist instant access to a whole fresh crop of stories for her on-air segment as well as furthering her contacts in Hollywood.

Claudia Cohen was ready for a lift. In the three years since she had been Mrs. Ronald Perelman, her life had become a hectic routine of shopping, parties, shopping, parties, shopping, parties. It was enough to wear *anyone* down to their terminal nerve, and Mrs. Perelman increasingly was telling those who would listen that she had her share of misery.

Who in Manhattan had not heard of her problems with the redecoration of the house on East 63rd, with its air conditioner cold enough to do double duty as a snow maker on Mount Shasta?

And, she complained, the air conditioner was just one of many disasters. There was, for example, the incident of the bathroom marble. Claudia had originally thought white Thásos marble for the walls would be lovely as a mate for the white marble tub with its custom-fitted corners, the white steps leading up to the tub, and the specially crafted seat in the shower on which Claudia could sit and have the eight, or was that ten, shower heads massage every single inch of her perfect size-three body.

Given the abundance of white dominating the room, Claudia had selected hot pink marble for the floor. Unfortunately, *after* the marble had been laid by the tile man, Claudia discovered that pale hot pink wasn't the exact shade she had in mind.

Spy magazine captured the moment in print in an article titled "Mr. and Mrs. Perelman Build Their Dream House(s)," quoting Cohen as saying, "Pink? Pink? With all this white? That's insane. I never approved that color. I never selected that color. Take it out! Now! Now! Now!"

While the workmen grudgingly obliged, they did so under the impression that they would be paid for their work. After having been on the job for a year, the contractor—Civale & Trovato—abruptly walked off the job, charging the Perelmans with failure to pay some $402,134. According to the contractor, the Perelmans and their architect, Peter Marino, had made ninety-five changes in the original plans.

Not to be outdone, MacAndrews & Forbes countersued Civale & Trovato, claiming their work was substandard, and not at all as intended. There was mention of the air conditioner, of course, and the bathroom marble. There were additional complaints about kitchen cabinets, a leaky skylight, and a fireplace that simply wasn't right.

However, it is hard to fathom why Claudia insisted that the bathroom toilet be moved—six times. An inch this way, a smidge that way. Her instructions were to make it exactly, precisely, "the height of a throne."

There were also repeated attempts to adjust the bedroom television set to exactly the optimum angle so that it could be viewed without neck—or any other—strain. Television being such an important element of Claudia's life, the changes were understandable—except, of course, to the workmen doing the job.

The bed from which the television was to be viewed was planned as a king-sized lacquered unit with a quilted silk bedcovering and headboard (six feet in height) edged in sharkskin. The bed was to be placed against an orange silk damask wall. Because the design was somewhat avant-garde, a model was designed and built, right down to its flamboyant headboard.

When the unique piece arrived and was carried in by the workmen, reality set in. The featured word of the moment from Mrs. Perelman was "Out," repeated often and loudly.

111

Lest it be presumed that perhaps the contractors were making up their half of the story, a similar scenario was playing itself out on Long Island where the firms of Two Bears Builders and Bates Electric had been hired by the Perelmans to do reconstruction work on their recently purchased $6 million home in East Hampton on Lily Pond Road. The Perelmans' country home was undergoing major reconstruction to prepare it for the casual all-millionaires barbeque on Memorial Day, 1988.

The house re-do also ended up in litigation, this time in the New York State Supreme Court in White Plains. It seems that while the workmen moved mountains and a few other non-incidentals to get the job completed on time, they alleged the Perelmans withheld payment—$26,632.51 in the case of Two Bears, and $4,218 from Bates Electric. This was not, however, before Perelman's oldest son Steven had blocked the driveway with his car one afternoon in an effort to keep the workmen from wrapping up work for the weekend. The case was eventually settled out of court. The party was said to have gone flawlessly.

With his house remodeling completed, with acquisitions finalized, with a secure family life, with debt reduced, and with cash horde growing, Ronald Perelman seemed a man who, by the middle of 1989, had accomplished much of what he intended in life. At forty-six, he was still young by mogul standards. He even received some of the respect he so coveted when in its May issue *Institutional Investor* magazine featured Perelman on the cover and crowned him "the richest man in America."

The article, written by William Meyers, said the corporate mover and shaker was a "latter-day Midas. In barely ten years' time, Perelman has built an industrial empire worth in excess of $7 billion. After his debt is deducted, he emerges with a personal fortune that is approaching $5 billion—which makes Ronald Perelman the richest man in America."

Meyers went on to attack *Forbes* magazine for seeming to ignore Perelman's wealth altogether. "For the past several years," the article reported, "*Forbes* magazine has bestowed this distinction [of richest American] on Wal-Mart Stores founder Sam Walton in its annual survey of the country's most affluent citizens. But *Forbes* has lumped the Wal-Mart shares that Walton has given away to his four children into the patriarch's portfolio, thus considerably enlarging his reported net worth."

Meyers continued: " 'The methodology used to arrive at Walton's No. 1 status,' notes *Forbes* senior editor Harold Senecker, 'is the subject of lively debate around here. It's valid to argue it both ways.' As for *Forbes*'s reckoning that Perelman 'may be worth over $1 billion,' the magazine is understood to use ultraconservative estimates in cases where precise information is very hard to come by—and no one plays it closer to the vest than Ron Perelman."

Because of the fact that Perelman's holding companies were, for the most part, privately owned, he was under no obligation to release profit figures—and he didn't. There can be little question that Perelman's wealth had skyrocketed, but just how far remained the stuff of speculation and debate— particularly among financial reporters. And nowhere did the confusion about Perelman's bottom line occupy more workday hours than at *Forbes* magazine, whose editors prided themselves on keeping abreast of such news.

The anointing of King Perelman by *Institutional Investor* had a whiplash effect that cracked from the top of *Forbes* magazine right down the ladder. It set off a series of inquiring interoffice memos, published in the October 23, 1989 *Forbes* 400 issue as "The Perelman Letters," which illustrated how insiders viewed Perelman and his assets.

"The Perelman Letters" began with *Forbes*'s then editor-in-chief Malcolm S. Forbes, Sr., quoting from the cover of the May issue of *Institutional Investor* that labeled Perelman "the richest man in America." Forbes then sent the editor of *Forbes 400* the following memo on May 15, 1989: "????!!!!" Forbes seemed to be a man of few words.

Eight days later, the editor replied in a long, pithy memorandum of his own. "Were we 'scooped'? Hardly. Their $5 billion for Perelman looks like somebody was straining to come up with a big number. Our $1 billion estimate was, I admit, too low, we tend to be conservative. If I had it to do over again, I'd put Perelman near $2 billion last fall. But $5 billion? No way. Here's why. . . ."

The editor suggested that while the other magazine placed Revlon's worth at $4 billion, *Forbes* felt Revlon should be valued at $3.6 billion. Of the $1.4 billion that *Institutional Investor* credited to National Health Laboratories (NHL), the *Forbes* editor pointed out that Perelman floated 5 percent of the shares to make a public market. Their bottom line for NHL: $810 million.

As to MacAndrews & Forbes, the prominent editor wrote his boss: "Say they, 'Wall Street puts a valuation of $350 million on Perelman's licorice-root operation.' With cash flow at only $22 million last year, someone must be smoking licorice root to get to $350 million." On Coleman Co. being worth $545 million as *Institutional Investor* claimed, the editor said, "maybe."

And on First Gibraltar Bank: "This deal hadn't happened when we valued Perelman last year, but I am not yet convinced the trade publication is realistic when they say he could sell this $160 million equity stake for $360 million today."

The *Forbes* memo pointed out that *Institutional Investor* credited Perelman with $500 million in "undescribed assets." "I have no idea where this alleged [amount] comes from," the editor said.

The real math began when Perelman's massive debt was subtracted from his assets, which "conservatively" the *Forbes* memo seemed to have placed at $5.6 billion. The editor suggested that by *Forbes* figures, Revlon was carrying $2.5 billion in debt. "Now, where did the $705 million come from to pay for Coleman and First Gibraltar? Either Ron took down more debt to pay them, or he drew down his cash hoard. This has to be deducted from worth. You can't have it both ways."

What *Institutional Investor* had given, *Forbes* wasted no time in taking away. Bottom line, according to this interoffice memo sent from the editor to MSF, Sr., on July 31, 1989: "Add it all up, and we were too low on Perelman last year, by being conservative. The trade mag was $2 billion too high, for other reasons. I'm a lot happier to be in our shoes than in theirs."

Perelman, during the brouhaha, had his own shoes off, his feet up, his cigar out, and his shirt sleeves rolled. When there were fits of temper—and there were many—Ronald's apologists attributed them to intense stress and his need to tap the release valve when he was with those he could trust.

Only a few around this complicated, driven man actually understood him. Certainly not those who saw him at movie premieres with Michael Douglas, or watched him lunch at "his cafeteria," Le Cirque. They might admire him for his money, fawn on him, struggle to get closer to him, hoping to share in his wealth by association or occasional gift. But comprehend his inner workings? No chance.

If New York society looked upon him with awe, jealousy, or revulsion, certain elements of the business community continued to treat him with suspicion. Not even the hiring of publicist Linda Robinson (wife of then-American Express chairman James Robinson III) seemed to be able to shake their view.

Perelman wanted to be referred to as a "builder" or "industrialist," rather than a "raider." Wanting it and getting it were two distinctly different things, however. While business trades and the *New York Times* continued to call him anything but what he wanted to hear, it was left to gossip empress Liz Smith to tag him with a label even Perelman found delightful: "Papa-to-be." In December 1989, she revealed what the Perelmans had heretofore kept to themselves. Claudia was pregnant with their first child, who was due to be born in early spring.

The pending addition of a baby to the household meant fewer perfunctory dinners and casual social events. Perelman was becoming ever more cautious. Trusting few, confiding in even fewer, he pulled his inner circle tight.

There were less frequent drives in the back of his Bentley limousine. Instead, Perelman began taking long, solitary walks around Manhattan, disappearing into the energetic human swarm of the city, losing himself inside a mind that wouldn't, or couldn't, stop calculating, analyzing.

Daily 8:30 A.M. breakfasts at Perelman's East 63rd Street town house found the boss, Gittis, Slovin, Drapkin, and Tepperman still joking through lox and bagels and cups of coffee, assessing their stranglehold on a financial empire that was growing at such speed that even they were genuinely at a loss to place a precise dollar figure on the package. Their friendship derived from a shared dependency and lives that existed mainly for business. For them, the rest was little more than decoration. They were never without purpose, always under control, their motives firmly in mind.

Yet, no amount of close-to-the-chest, privately held, secret planning sessions about an enterprise the size of MacAndrews & Forbes Holdings could exist totally free from outside intervention. The mood on Wall Street was changing. With the

Securities and Exchange Commission's prying eyes and ears poised for any hint of impropriety, there was a feel of paranoia in the air, and not even the biggest players were safe from its tentacles.

SIX

Behind Closed Doors

As 1990 opened, Wall Street was, indeed, a different place. Michael Milken had been indicted, with his brother Lowell Milken and former Drexel trader Bruce Newbert, on ninety-eight counts of racketeering and fraud, to which they pleaded innocent. Their former investment firm of Drexel Burnham Lambert was about to declare bankruptcy—its 5,300 employees put out of work.

While others saw the investment world in shambles, Perelman saw opportunity. He saw it in the Wall Street firm Shearson Lehman Hutton, whose largest shareholder was American Express. Having learned from his successful bid for Salomon, Perelman attempted a very friendly relationship with Shearson in the last days of 1989, offering to inject as much as $250 million in cash into the firm in exchange for a 20 percent ownership.

Once again, relationships played a part in the maneuver. Perelman was a close friend of James D. Robinson III, the chairman of American Express, and Robinson's publicist-wife Linda was on the board of Revlon Group.

For Perelman to approach a beleaguered institution such

as Shearson Lehman Hutton, itself an amalgamation of venerable firms, was business as usual. Shearson et al. was a "brand name" in the industry, but it was suffering a lack of cohesive direction. While his Shearson bid would eventually be dropped, Perelman was more successful when he focused on another troubled savings and loan.

The San Antonio Savings Association had been struggling under losses of $890 million when Ron Perelman bid $10 million to add the thrift to his growing banking empire. Once again, the federal government was underwriting much of the risk and advanced Perelman $1.3 million to cover current and future bad debt. In the year and three months that had passed since his first S&L rescue, Perelman had seen Congress revamp its entire effort to bring solvency to the savings and loan industry. Gone was the old Federal Home Loan Bank Board, a victim of its past generosity. Supplying the government funds this time out was an eight-month-old entity called the Resolution Trust Corporation.

In a typical Perelman acquisition, the previous management would be fired or retired. The difficulty, however, with San Antonio Savings was not really incompetent executives. Gerald Ford, Perelman's banking chief and chairman of his First Gibraltar division, took the unusual step of extending an employment agreement to the thrift's former chief executive, W. W. (Bo) McAlister III, the grandson of the founder of the bank. According to Ford, it was the economy in Texas, not Bo's bungling, that caused San Antonio to fail.

While Wall Street watched and wondered at Perelman's latest achievement, his sole focus was no longer work. Perelman devoted his attention to his wife and watched her pregnancy slowly progress. Her countenance mellowed, her appearance was radiant. Claudia Cohen even took on a lighter, happier tone with her on-air broadcasts than in the past.

119

The previous September, Cohen got what can only be considered a gift from her husband. She was chosen as a judge for the Miss America pageant. Soon after her selection, Revlon became a major sponsor for the event. Fate had once again interceded in the life of Claudia Cohen Perelman. Even the often snide *People* magazine found little to fault as they profiled her in May 1990, other than reporting that in the January 4, 1983 issue of *Village Voice* Cohen was quoted as "hunting for a kind, middle-aged tycoon as a 'very special friend.' "

While not known for his kindness, and barely middle-aged, Perelman was a tycoon and was definitely having a happy run. The pair had even purchased a third home—this time a $9 million ocean-front mansion in the society-teeming stretch of sand known as Palm Beach, Florida.

The home, which had a 2,000-gallon aquarium in the living room, was originally owned by pharmaceutical heir D. Mead Johnson. Perelman had seen the house, located in an area known as "Raider's Row," and made an unsolicited bid of $8 million for the property. A subsequent offer added an extra million if Mead Johnson would vacate immediately. Johnson was packed that very night, and the 2.3-acre property was Perelman's.

For all his apparent happiness at home(s), trouble continued to bubble just beneath the surface at work. There was, for example, disenchantment from the employees at Coleman Co., where many took exception to Perelman trying to use an excess in the company's pension plan for paying down the debt he assumed in purchasing the company.

Also, the government continued to investigate the deal they gave Perelman when he purchased First Gibraltar and the other four insolvent Texas savings and loans. According to a memo from Jeff Potter, an analyst with the Federal Home Loan Bank, it would have been cheaper for the government to close

First Gibraltar and pay off its depositors than to underwrite Perelman in the deal he structured. Even more troubling was the Resolution Trust Corp.'s announcement that it intended to "look at every available opportunity to renegotiate those hastily put-together deals, including retaining outside law firms if necessary."

Some stockholders of the Andrews Group were audibly unhappy when Perelman announced his plan to take the company private. The problem came with the dollar amount Perelman offered to buy out the money-losing corporation. For every outstanding share of stock, Perelman offered stockholders a junk bond which he valued at $7.25 (the same price at which Andrews was trading the day he announced the deal).

Unfortunately, Perelman's bonds weren't paying very high interest as junk bonds go—just 10 percent—and weren't set to mature for $9\frac{1}{2}$ years. Another gripe from the stockholders centered on the fact that the junk bonds were more junk than bond and weren't actually worth anywhere near $7.25. Financial markets suggest their worth was somewhere in the neighborhood of $3 and that Perelman was attempting to buy the company at a bargain basement price. Such moves by majority stockholders like Perelman (who controlled 57 percent of the company at the time) are called "cramdowns." Minority stockholders have very little choice but to accept the terms or sue—which in this case they did, but to no avail.

Respected financial columnist Allan Sloan, writing in the *Los Angeles Times*, said, "Depending on how you look at it, Perelman over the years has sold Andrews-selected properties from his other companies on favorable terms and has kept the company alive by lending it money and buying new shares from it ([*Howard*] *Gittis's version*). Or he's bought a majority of the company's stock cheap and used Andrews as a corporate toxic waste dump for unwanted and overpriced businesses (the

121

version embraced by Andrews shareholders who are suing to block the deal). The truth probably lies somewhere in between." It didn't make shareholders feel any better, however, when Perelman's plan was railroaded through the stockholders' meeting on June 4, 1990.

There was even trouble at Revlon, where Perelman was under mounting pressure to pay down some of his colossal debt load. In May 1990, four co-agent banks—Chase Manhattan Corporation, Chemical Banking Corporation, Citicorp, and Manufacturers Hanover Corporation—had restructured their $1.8 billion share of the Revlon loan, and began to sell off portions of the loan. For his part, instead of the original $150 million due to be repaid on the debt by 1992, Perelman promised to speed up the process and repay $650 million. In an effort to raise capital, two months later he sold 13 million shares of onetime Revlon division National Health Laboratories, a company which *Institutional Investor* called the "Fed Ex of medical labs," in a bid to raise $182 million. Even with the stock sale, Perelman retained 80 percent interest in NHL.

In October 1990, after arguments and continuances, the Delaware Chancery Court finally reached a verdict in the first of the Technicolor suits filed by Cinerama. In the appraisal proceeding, Judge William Allen ruled that the fair price for Technicolor at the time Perelman bought the company in January 1983 was $21.60 a share. Perelman bought the company for $107 million by paying $23 a share, obviously not underpaying as Cinerama had suggested. (In its suit Cinerama had estimated the stock to be worth $62.75.)

While not ruling on Cinerama's second suit, which alleged fraud and conflict of interest by Technicolor's board of directors, Allen did say that he found "unpersuasive" the conflict of interest claim involving former chairman of the board Morton

Kamerman. It was a comment that left the Perelman attorneys smiling.

In fact, Perelman was far from devoid of humor and, on occasion, compassion and magnanimity. For example, he contributed $2.4 million of Revlon's dollars to establish the Revlon-UCLA Women's Cancer Research Program at the start of 1990. Perelman became involved in the project at the urging of Lilly Tartikoff, a friend and the wife of then-president of NBC Entertainment, Brandon Tartikoff. Again with Lilly, he was instrumental in launching the "Fire and Ice Ball" later that same year to raise additional funds for the program. At the end of 1990, Perelman again joined with Lilly Tartikoff to underwrite and produce a 30-minute video titled "Once a Year . . . for a Lifetime." Narrated by Jane Pauley and Phylicia Rashad, the documentary urged women forty and older to have regular mammograms.

On the savings and loan front, Congress continued to scream about Perelman's profits. During his first year of ownership of the five ailing savings and loans which were collectively known as First Gibraltar, Perelman (and co-executive Gerald Ford) had managed to take a thrift that was losing hundreds of millions of dollars and had earned more than $250 million in profits and tax benefits (thanks mainly to the government subsidies) on an investment of $171 million.

But such large profits were hardly guaranteed. Caroline Hunt, daughter of eccentric oil man H. L. Hunt, invested only $25 million to acquire Southwest Savings at the same time, and lost all of her money despite government subsidies projected to total $2 billion over ten years. Unlike Perelman, in her first year of ownership she gave the bank back to the government. Her reasoning was that the worth of the bank's real estate and loans had been so poorly estimated that there wasn't any way for anyone to make a profit regardless of how much was poured into the vault. Different billionaire, different result.

Despite his success with First Gibraltar, the noises being made in Washington were of major concern to Perelman. Adding heat to the already raging debate, a Texas developer named Gary Bradley was making the rounds of the Capitol with complaints about First Gibraltar's handling of his Circle C Ranch, a large Austin residential development. With debt on the property at $130 million and an assessed market value of $30 million, the bank had to either write off the bad debt or wait out the vacillating Texas real estate market. It chose the latter.

Bradley wanted to buy the ranch back through a consortium of investors, but First Gibraltar refused. According to Bradley, under normal circumstances any bank would have leaped at his offer, but thanks to the subsidies being allotted by the federal government, First Gibraltar could afford to sit tight and do nothing. Among those listening to Bradley's theory were Representative Joseph Kennedy II and Senator Timothy Wirth, both vocal protectors of the underdog.

According to MacAndrews & Forbes, Bradley's actual complaint was not that the bank wouldn't sell the property, but that it wouldn't sell the property back to him. "Ridiculous" was Perelman's public opinion of the complaint. Privately, however, he was worried that any change in the government's position on the savings and loan rescue could dramatically affect his pocketbook. (One Texas property that *did* sell was the one-time Flying M Ranch turned Stonebridge development. Originally purchased for $133 million by First Gibraltar in pre-Perelman days, with another $170 million spent to develop it, the ranch sold to Japanese industrialist Yuko Kitano for a mere $61 million.)

In an effort to reinforce his own position in Washington,

Perelman hired former Philadelphia mayor Bill Green. Green now worked for Howard Gittis's former law firm, Wolf, Block, Schorr & Solis-Cohen, and was brought on board by Perelman to lobby members of Congress into keeping his S&L agreement in place. Green was a former congressman who had been a member of the House Ways and Means Committee. While his lobbying successes with Congress were debatable, his fortunes with Perelman were not. Soon after, Green was appointed MacAndrews & Forbes vice-president for government relations.

Using his own form of government relations, Perelman also stepped up his political contributions. Despite his Republican leanings, he hedged his bets and laid out in excess of $100,000 both to Republicans and Democrats. Contributions or not, the government continued to look over Perelman's corporate shoulder. He plunged into ever longer workdays that slowly began to eat into his already limited social life. Now, there were fewer parties with Claudia, but she, at least, managed to continue her own social calendar. She met often with Kathie Lee Gifford and the girls for lunch, and kept up a round of film premieres which were, as she pointed out, "essential" to her job.

Perelman did manage to squeeze in an appearance at the eightieth birthday party of comedian Joey Adams, husband of reigning gossip reporter Cindy Adams. In a way, the party was *not* the place to be, what with Leona Helmsley, Imelda Marcos, and Bess Myerson in attendance—each with her share of major legal woes. As comic Jackie Mason was overheard to comment: "There's too many people here under indictment. I should go out and steal something to feel at home." Perelman was said to have left early.

Weighing heavily on his mind was the failure of Revlon to pull out of its third-place spot, despite dramatic pitches made by Perelman's team. Its most innovative move came in department stores, where Revlon had been the sales leader as late as the seventies. Because cosmetics firms pay for their own counter space and sales help within department stores, Perelman approved space-saving restructuring of the high-end Revlon lines such as Princess Marcella Borghese, Germaine Monteil, and Charles of the Ritz, and gathered them together under the umbrella "Nines" (as in "dressed to the nines").

While the program saved money on store space, it was expensive to retrain sales staff, produce elaborate displays, and launch advertising to inform customers about the shift. In the end, Perelman discovered that a Borghese customer didn't like being lumped in with the color-trendy Charles of the Ritz or the snobbish Monteil. And few department store customers grasped the "Nines" theme. The theme approach was abandoned, and with it much of Revlon's hopes of regaining its predominance in department stores.

Combing through Revlon for cash, Perelman decided to sell its Paris office building for $80 million. Then, the following month, he jettisoned the Germaine Monteil skin-care line for $60 million. In this critical time, Perelman turned to his chief financial officer, Fred Tepperman, for help. But he now found Tepperman distracted and unmotivated. The financial satrap had begun to miss meetings, had become less driven, less sure of details. When Tepperman finally revealed to Perelman that his wife of three decades had been diagnosed with Alzheimer's disease and admitted that his full attention by necessity was not on MacAndrews & Forbes's bottom line, Perelman reduced the pressure by calling more than ever on Howard Gittis. Regardless of accommodations made, by the end of the year, ill wife or not, Tepperman would be history.

In March 1991, Perelman opened discussions with Unilever, Procter & Gamble, and L'Oreal, all potential buyers of his prized Revlon empire. Although Wall Street speculated feverishly, MacAndrews & Forbes headquarters said nothing. After five weeks of negotiating, Procter & Gamble found itself in the winner's circle, acquiring the Max Factor line as well as the international Betrix label for $1.14 billion in cash. It was a win-win situation for both P&G and Perelman.

Perelman had purchased both lines after his Revlon takeover. Now he was selling them for a substantial profit. This injection of new cash not only permitted him to reduce a sizable chunk of his bank debt but also freed him up for new acquisitions, all the while allowing him to keep the bulk of Revlon intact.

For its part, Procter & Gamble, which already owned the market-leading makeup Cover Girl, got the plum Max Factor name and distribution network. And the German-based Betrix label was highly regarded for its distribution and manufacturing capability in Europe.

Ultimately, the sale did more than recharge Revlon's bank balance; it changed the cosmetics giant's direction. As part of his new concept, Perelman replaced president Sol Levine, the Revson veteran who represented old glamour, with Jerry W. Levin, the onetime head of Pillsbury's Burger King division.

Changes were on the way in the savings and loan business as well. While Perelman was negotiating with Procter & Gamble in New York, his lobbyists were trying to protect his interests in Washington. They were far less successful than he was. In early March, the Treasury Department elected to rescind some $2.5 billion in tax breaks given to investors during 1988 and 1989. Among them: the deal the government had struck with Ronald Perelman and Gerald Ford.

At this, there was also the genesis of tensions at home. According to friends, Claudia Cohen had begun to spend an increasing amount of time in the couple's East Hampton home on Lily Pond with her newborn daughter, Samantha. There had been a growing emotional distance between husband and wife, exacerbated, it seemed, by the stress of business combined with caring for a young baby. Even nature was conspiring. The rough seas of the Atlantic had begun to encroach on the house. Contractors were called and a stone revetment wall was ordered. The water was so near the house at times that the crew was delayed for up to eight days—waiting for a tide low enough for them to move in their equipment.

It wasn't their only housing emergency. *Spy* magazine had turned the Perelmans' dwelling calamities into a cause célèbre, centering on their fussiness and the resulting lawsuits. The renovation of the Perelmans' $9 million home in Palm Beach had now caught their attention. In a story of Dickensian proportions, this time it was *Perelman* who sued the contractor, Charles R. Wilson Construction.

When the Wilson company had signed the deal to renovate the sprawling single-story home for $989,433, they agreed to complete the work within two months. Perelman was impatient to have his home finished, but the company, which had been the area's leading contractor for more than five decades, found that the Perelmans, both Mr. and Mrs., had problems visualizing their wants and needs. According to the subsequent lawsuit, changes were ordered and reordered, repeating a scenario now all too familiar to Perelman's construction crews in New York.

Months passed and the bills began to pile up . . . and up. After ten months, the total had reached $1.86 million, and Perelman sued the Wilson firm for "unauthorized requests for additional payments" when it tried to collect an unpaid $511,170. The construction firm contended that the delays and charges were due to incessant demands by the Perelmans. The billionaire owner resisted payment for months.

Stories from subcontractors about doors which would have to be moved a quarter of an inch, causing entire sections of tile floors to be ripped out and replaced, made the rounds. There were changes in the ultra-precious Crema Marfil stonework, the never satisfactory air-conditioning system, a custom-installed stereo, and a high-tech security system that monitored the home for motion, heat, flood, and burglary.

After taking the matter to court, Perelman placed $491,868 in an escrow account to show good faith. The move only served to shorten the fuse of the Wilson Co.'s attorney, Michael Monchick. "I told [Perelman's lawyers], 'Look, you've withheld $500,000 from my client,' " Monchick said. " 'You acknowledge that $450,000 or so is owed, so why not just pay us that, and we can discuss the rest of it later?' " he asked, according to *Spy* magazine.

Logic aside, Perelman contended that he would let the court decide what payments were justified and refused Monchick's demand for a deposition—right up until the time that the judge of West Palm Beach Court ordered Perelman to appear. Only then did the loggerhead break. Perelman ordered his attorneys to settle out of court—but the details of the drama remained on the record.

The last word from the Charles R. Wilson Construction Co.: "Things like this just don't happen *here*." Apparently there's a first time for everything, even in staid Palm Beach.

Now turning his attention to Hollywood, Perelman opened a public door to Marvel Comics. In an effort to reduce his Andrews Group debt from the Marvel takeover, Perelman authorized 4.8 million common shares to be sold, or 39.2 percent of the company, for $16.50 a share.

As usual in Perelman's financial maneuvers, his timing was superb. Sales of old comic books were booming, and new comic book issues were being hoarded as potential collector's items. With characters like the Amazing Spiderman, The X-Men, the Incredible Hulk, the Silver Surfer, and Captain America, even the stock prospectus from Marvel looked, well, marvelous.

The public raced to join the Marvel team. Within weeks of the totally-sold-out initial offering, the market price increased to $25. Comics sales were up 31.2 percent during the period. So, too, were prices for Marvel comic books. A book that had sold for just seventy-five cents several years before now had a cover price of $1.25.

Perelman generated $80 million with his latest stock issue. Considering that he had purchased the company with only $11 million in cash (with the rest in bank loans), Perelman made back his investment seven times over, and retained ownership of about $150 million in Marvel stock. Ironically for Marvel stockholders, none of the cash influx was destined to help the company grow. Perelman had earmarked the cash for Marvel's corporate parent, Andrews Group, which was still wallowing in the mire known as New World Entertainment.

The investment community applauded his financial prowess, but Perelman was far from celebrating. He had just separated from Claudia Cohen after six and a half years of marriage, a fact he had managed to keep quiet for several months from all but his closest friends.

It was a Perelman-instigated break. Cohen was devastated. She watched the father of their daughter and her key to power in the city walk out the door of their East 63rd Street town house and take up residence at their eleven-acre East Hampton estate. While not admitting the exact cause of the separation, Cohen said through a spokesperson, "They are personal problems and problems a lot of couples face." In the evenings while Cohen and baby Samantha waited alone, Perelman was reported out on the town at various restaurants, including his new choice of the moment, Sapore di Mare. Yet, even after the split, the couple were friendly and talked daily, and Cohen continued to speak of reconciliation. The pair were even spotted at a concert in Central Park given by Paul Simon, a Cohen favorite.

As the temperature in New York rose to near record levels, so did Cohen's problems. With her husband roaming and her heart aching, the entertainment reporter also had to undergo surgery for an undisclosed ailment at Manhattan's Memorial Sloan-Kettering Hospital, known for its outstanding cancer treatment. Her surgeon was the hospital's chief of gynecological services.

For Perelman, bachelorhood meant freedom. Young, attractive, successful females were only too ready to help the executive forget his marital problems and celebrate his business successes. After his regular Tuesday night dinner with the "boys from the office," Perelman would speed into the night for clandestine meetings with a selection of women.

On the business side, Perelman had every reason to be happy. Despite continued trouble with congressional critics over savings and loan tax breaks and bail-out subsidies, Perelman's empire was growing apace. Revlon, under Levin, was refocusing its energy on the mass market, targeting drugstores and discount chains. National Health Laboratories' sales showed a 28 percent revenue growth since April, while MacAndrews & Forbes licorice, which had started it all, continued to improve, up 18 percent in the same period.

Perhaps the most unexpected turnaround, however, had occurred with Coleman Co. Before taking over the helm of Revlon, Jerry Levin had run the Coleman division for Perelman and had instituted dramatic changes at the venerable Midwest corporation.

Its plant operation was streamlined and parts inventories

cut using a model developed in Japan known as just-in-time systems. The success of the process is derived from the weakest link theory, which brings entire assembly lines to a halt if any one piece of equipment on the line should falter. Though at first look it would seem inefficient, the just-in-time process makes every element of the production line absolutely essential to the total success of the product. Therefore, all elements are maintained at their peak capacity.

Production at Coleman's Wichita plant improved 200 percent, with employees rewarded accordingly. Workers at all levels were given an opportunity to contribute to product development, and computers were installed linking store inventories in Wal-Mart and Kmart to plant production. The end result was an operating profit of $32 million on revenues of $435 million, exceeding even the most aggressive projections.

Of all the Perelman companies, however, Marvel Comics was the clear-cut winner. The stock offering of July 1991, at $16.50 a share, had risen vertically ever since. By November, the stock had tripled in value and was peaking at $42 a share. Even Wall Street analysts were hard-pressed to explain the phenomenal growth of the shares, pointing to the fact that Perelman had lost over $120 million by pricing the shares too low. Others within the industry, however, were crediting the industrialist with deliberately undervaluing his offering to make future Perelman offerings irresistible.

Socially, Perelman attended ABC's fifteenth anniversary party for Barbara Walters, accompanied by his wife Claudia, in an increasingly rare public appearance together. Still separated, the couple were working at a marriage fix. He also generously spread some of his wealth around by donating $10 million to the New York University Medical Center. Perelman had long been a trustee of the hospital and had previously given $1 million to the medical center's cardiac catheterization unit in 1983. With the addition of $10 million more, which Perelman earmarked for research in biomolecular medicine, the center was renamed the Ronald O. Perelman Department of Dermatology in his honor—a first for the medical school. The gift was certainly magnanimous, but there was a contretemps behind the smiles and handshakes. When Perelman originally offered his gift to the medical center, it was designated for the construction of a building. But the building costs ran over, and Perelman refused to ante up more cash. The building was named for someone else, and Ronald O. Perelman got the Department of Dermatology.

"I felt an obligation to do something," Perelman said modestly. "We in the cosmetics industry have benefited by the research in the field of dermatology." But apparently not enough for Perelman to pay for extra brick and mortar.

The following month, it was Perelman's turn to generate funds by placing the Princess Marcella Borghese and Halston cosmetics and fragrance business on the market. The unlikely purchaser for the pair of luxury lines was a Saudi prince and his family, who formed Halston Borghese International.

Howard Gittis traveled to London to consummate the arrangements, meeting with the prince in his Mayfair town house, which was luxurious even by Perelman standards. The Saudis were fascinated by the cosmetics business and saw in Halston-Borghese an opportunity to expand within the high-end, designer arena—an area that Revlon was only too happy to abdicate to them. Going with the brand names and products was Revlon senior vice-president Michael Marten, who became president and chief executive officer of the new company.

With the public biting at his heels for more stock issues, and hot on the success of his National Health Laboratories and Marvel Entertainment direct hits, Perelman raised even more ready cash by issuing 4.3 million more shares of common stock in Coleman Co. Initially released at $19.50 a share, the stock closed at the end of day number one up 29 percent at $25.12. In the course of a few hours, Ronald Perelman had made more than $100 million—at least on paper—on the substantial portion of Coleman stock he retained.

With three solid successes in his pocket, rumors began to circulate throughout Wall Street and beyond that a Revlon public offering was imminent. If it were true, Perelman gave little indication as he flirted with, laughed about, and generally sidestepped the issue. Why shouldn't he? He was enjoying his new notoriety and took a newfound pleasure in being seen at celebrity events and star-studded watering holes.

His repeated lunches with Barry Diller in New York and Beverly Hills set crystal balls flashing with predictions that the pair were laying the groundwork for a joint venture. In truth, they were just old friends sharing good conversation and tossing concepts around as they had for years. If Perelman's appearances with Diller had tongues wagging, it was nothing compared to the mileage he got at the Academy Awards with Revlon model Claudia Schiffer on his arm. Despite the talk, in this case it was more business than pleasure. Revlon was a large Oscar Award sponsor, and Schiffer was the cosmetics firm's model of the moment. Wife Claudia Cohen, who covered the event for "Live with Regis and Kathie Lee," was *not* too busy to notice.

By the middle of April 1992, word had begun to leak out that Revlon had arranged for a $500 million line of credit through its favored trio of banks—Chemical Banking Corp., Chase Manhattan Corp., and Citicorp. MacAndrews & Forbes Holdings' senior vice-president for corporate affairs dismissed speculation about the purpose of the credit line, indicating it merely replaced a 1990 credit agreement held with the banks.

Yet one particular stipulation of the loan started tongues wagging. Specifically, the loan contained a clause that would lower the interest rate if Revlon went public. "That wording is more important than the new bank loans," said Phelps Hoyt, an analyst with Duff & Phelps in Montpelier, Vermont. "Revlon would have to renegotiate the credit line anyway," he said, indicating that it expired in two months in any case.

A month later, Perelman ended the suspense by announcing his intention to release 23 million shares of Revlon to the public at $19 a share. Given the successes of his past three offerings, analysts with a few notable exceptions were predicting a rush to jump on the Revlon bandwagon.

The exceptions were brokerage houses that cited Revlon's uneven sales and profit picture. Also, unlike the Revlon which Perelman had hostilely taken over in 1985, this one didn't have many of its dependable money-makers left to, well, make money. Gone were the prescription pharmaceuticals, contact lenses, and medical diagnostic equipment divisions. No more Max Factor or Betrix. In fact, the offering didn't even include all of Revlon.

In a fascinating game of divide-and-split, Perelman announced that the stock offering was for a new company—New Revlon Inc. That entity differed from old Revlon, if you will, by the subtraction from New Revlon of such lines as Charles of the Ritz, Norell, Tatiana, Alexandra de Markoff, and Bill Blass. Those department store lines had been losing money, in any case. Perelman also excluded the highly profitable National Health Laboratories, as well as other "non-operating assets," including $37 million in cash.

The New Revlon, Perelman led potential investors to believe, was the cream of the company—Revlon, Almay, Ultima II in cosmetics; Eterna and Moon Drops in skin care;

Charlie, Jean Naté, and Jontue in fragrances; and Flex, Aqua-marine, and Mitchum in personal care products.

With the New Revlon offering, Perelman projected sales increases for that company of 20 percent, an amazing prediction since sales of the overall company had only been increasing 1 percent a year since 1988. But the focus of New Revlon had changed. The theme was "mass, not class." Perelman was targeting stores like Wal-Mart and Kmart, plus supermarkets and drug stores. Clearly, Revlon had all but given up on recapturing its department store preeminence.

In the company's S-1 registration statement with the Securities and Exchange Commission, Perelman did more than prophesy a New Revlon sales boom. He also went so far as to predict economic growth for countries—the United States and Canada, 3–3½ percent; Japan, 1 percent; Europe 1–3 percent. All this emphasis on the future, of course, avoided much mention of the past. In Revlon's case this was a good thing, since it had been struggling to earn even enough cash to pay the interest on its debt.

According to the registration statement, the company was said to have posted net earnings of $2.6 million in the first three months of 1991. It wasn't enough, however, to convince many institutional investors of the company's future earning potential. Many refused to buy into the Perelman issue unless the per-share price was dropped, and dropped considerably. Two months after announcing his intention to sell the stock and three weeks after lowering the price from $19 a share to $14 to $15 a share, Perelman withdrew the offering altogether.

"Selling our stock at the undervalued prices sought by domestic institutional investors would have been wrong," Perelman later stated. "Since the company was under no obligation to complete the offering, there was no reason to proceed under unfavorable circumstances." None, perhaps, but pride. And, at this point, Perelman was not about to eat humble pie.

Even with the fizzle of the Revlon stock offering, Perelman's finances continued to grow. He added another element to his growing Andrews Group empire by purchasing Fleer Corporation, the sports card–bubble gum house, as a division of his Marvel Entertainment Group holdings.

Additionally, the government announced its intentions to prepay $3.2 billion on the high-yielding notes that financed his takeover of First Gibraltar, thereby saving taxpayers millions in interest. But at the same time, the Feds gave up their future stake in 20 percent of the bank in exchange for a modest $35 million, opening the door for Perelman to sell the thrifts and pocket husky profits.

So well run were his savings and loans by 1992 that there were several bidders waiting when the FOR SALE sign was put on the front lawn. Copping the winning bid: Bank of America, which parted with $110 million in cash and stock to acquire 130 branches and some $7.5 billion in deposits from First Gibraltar. The sale price did not include most of First Gibraltar's assets—including $500 million in capital, its mortgage company, and a division that handled the sale of problem assets for the federal government.

By keeping that division, as well as First Gibraltar's federal savings bank charter, Perelman managed to preserve his tax advantages as well as other government benefits. Haggling over every word in the sales agreement, Perelman even managed to keep the purchase price out of the official announcement.

Financial columnist Allan Sloan, writing in *Newsday* and the *Los Angeles Times,* predicted that Perelman would pocket a cool $1.2 billion on the sale, in cash and tax benefits. The MacAndrews & Forbes folk, of course, reminded any who would listen that tax breaks are only valuable if they're used, and Perelman had yet to use any and might never use them. To that rationale, Sloan remarked: "I think the chances of Perelman, who plays some of the most clever tax games on the planet, leaving a billion dollars of tax benefits unused are roughly equivalent to the chances of the sun rising in the West tomorrow." There were few who would argue with Sloan's reasoning.

Given his business prosperity, Ronald Perelman made an effort to bring his happiness full circle by heightening his efforts to reconcile with his wife Claudia. Friends indicated that it seemed to be working.

Public appearances again became openly affectionate, stumping even the most seasoned star gazers. It was warmly evident at an early November book party the couple tossed for Kathie Lee Gifford. The celebrity-packed sit-down dinner at Le Cirque's L'Orangerie launched Gifford's autobiography, "I Can't Believe I Said That," written with Jim Jerome.

Amid the gold and orange foliage decorating the palatial room sat Rush Limbaugh, Alan Alda and wife Arlene, Ethel Kennedy and Eunice Shriver, Joy and Regis Philbin, the Neal Sedakas, Shirley MacLaine, designer Carolina Herrera, model Elle MacPherson, Barbara Walters, columnist Liz Smith, New York Mayor David Dinkins, and, of course, Gifford's husband Frank. As Perelman and wife cooed at each other, they were watched by Donald Trump, who attended the event with then-girlfriend Diana Roberts. Late in the evening, The Donald's on-again, off-again love Marla Maples also made an appearance and drew a frail wave from her sometime beau across the room.

When the holiday season rolled around, the Perelmans gave another bash for their very best friends—this time at their East 63rd Street town house. It was a Hanukkah party that became "the" invitation to receive by those who knew, or thought they did, in Manhattan.

Yet, for Perelman, no conglomeration of parties could make up for the business restlessness that forever drove him. In mid-December, he announced that he had once again acquired Consolidated Cigar, this time for $180 million, and folded it into his new investment company, Mafco (MacAndrews & Forbes Company) Holdings, now the corporate parent of MacAndrews & Forbes Holdings.

More than a company, Perelman was getting back his favorite handmade H. Upmann cigar. The production of the custom, rolled-for-Perelman cigar had been discontinued by Vestar, the buyout firm formed to purchase Consolidated Cigar in 1988 by former First Boston investment bankers and Consolidated Cigar's former managers, including Theo Folz.

With Consolidated Cigar back in the fold, Perelman's house would have seemed in order. Few looking from the outside could have imagined the changes that lay just ahead.

CLASS POLL

Class Pole—Banani
Done Most For Haverford—Bunting, Burnham
Most Likely To Succeed—Sabol, W. Howson, Vacca
Most Mature—Hughes, Barclay, Cromwell
Most Susceptible To Feminine Charm—Odiorne, A. Jacobs, Vacca
Best Athlete—Shoch, Bunting
Most Popular—W. Howson
Best Informed—Moxey, Carlisle
Best Build—Clarke, Scott
Most Playful—Rea, Bentz, Laplace
Best Dressed—Moxey, Richards, Scott
Most Handsome—Lyons, Cook, Perelman
Social Lion—Odiorne, Rea
Teacher's Bane—Dodge
Most Serious—Smith, F. Jacobs, MacFadyen
Most Original—Blum, Sabol, Winn
Most Poise—Walton, Auchincloss
Most Co-operative—Walters, Harkins, Craig
Funniest—Sabol, Winn, Gawthrop
Peacemaker—Mr. Baker, Burnham
Quietest—Richardson, Schwennesen
Optimist—Mr. Black
Sleepiest—Stafford, Dutton, Rutenberg
Wolf—Frazier, J. Francis, Whitesell
First Married—Hughes
Women Hater—Smith, J. Howson, Simmons
Scourge of the Roads—Dutton, Forstall, Dodge, Kendall
Pseudo—Skerrett
Most Incoherent—Crane
Class Rock—Rutenberg, Layton, Greifzu
Philosopher—Mr. Agade, Skerrett, Elliott
Best Dancer—Monsieur Agade
Favorite College—West Chester State
Best Man For a Dirty Job—Scott
Thinks He Is—Dodge, Guerrini
Bluffer—Simmons, Hunt, Sabol
Class Politician—Winn
Most Businesslike—Osgood, Johnson, Buell
Best Line—Gawthrop, Matthew
Most Curious—Theis, Sloane, Watt
Most Unique Build—Burnham, Drake, Anderson
Comes Up Smiling—Aldrich, Laplace, Bentz
Most Dignified—Guerrini, Roberts
Best Feature Around School—'60
Worst Feature Around School—'60
Biggest Brain—Kimball
Most Intellectual—Rutenberg
Most Musical—Howson, Skerrett, Sloane
Loudest—Hunt
Has Most Nerve—Mr. Johnson, Kimball
Most Conscientious—Smith, Anderson
Most Sarcastic—Mr. Dethier, Winn
Kidder—Hunt, Gawthrop
Most Unpredictable—Onthank, Trouant, Mr. Ness
Favorite Actor—Bret Maverick's Brother
Out To Lunch—Carpenter, Biddle
Big Man Around Campus—Mr. Severinghaus
Favorite Comic Strip—Peanuts
Favorite Theatre—Main Line Drive In
Favorite TV Program—All Nite Movies
Favorite Beverage—Milk

High School Memories:
Haverford School's Class Poll listing Perelman as "Most Handsome."

Ronald Perelman Haverford
School yearbook photo.

College Days:
Ronald Perelman in the
University of Pennsylvania
yearbook.

Facade of 21 East 63rd Street office building

Facade of the 35 East 62nd Street office building.

Front view of the Perelmans' Elkins Park home.

Claudia Cohen and
Ronald Perelman at the
Central Park Paul Simon
concert.

Claudia Cohen at the
Winter Antiques Show
Gala Preview Party.

Ronald Perelman with Patricia Duff at the Bill Blass Fashion Show (Fall 94).

Perelman with Daisy Fuentes, Donna Shalala, Lauren Hutton, Claudia Schiffer, and others at the National Breast Cancer Coalition Awards Gala

Perelman and wife Patricia Duff at the Metropolitan Museum of Art's 1995 Costume Institute Gala.

Ronald Perelman and fashion empress Diane Von Furstenburg in 1991.

Ronald Perelman with Cindy Crawford and others at Revlon's 1993 "Unforgettable" launch.

Ron Perelman and Veronica
Webb in the Hamptons

Ronald Perelman and Claudia Cohen
at Malcolm Forbes' 70th birthday
celebration in Morocco.

SEVEN

The Small Screen

Television. It was more than America's favorite pastime. It was a way of life for those who provided and those who consumed news, sports, and entertainment. It was also an arena that Ronald Perelman had once said he would never enter. He changed his mind in the first months of 1993.

In a complicated deal structured as part of a bankruptcy reorganization, Perelman offered to pay $100 million in cash for a 51 percent stake in SCI Television. SCI owned stations in Boston, Detroit, Atlanta, Cleveland, San Diego, and Milwaukee, and had plans to purchase a seventh station in Tampa, Florida. Perelman also agreed to assume the company's staggering $1.3 billion debt, some $570 million of which could be eliminated through bankruptcy restructuring.

Perelman's one-hand-washes-the-other plan called for the stations to be placed under Bill Bevins's control in the Andrews Group, with SCI using the $100 million payment plus $63 million in new debt to acquire the Tampa outlet. Perelman purchased the SCI station from an investment group called Apollo Partners, which had taken control of the broadcast holdings of George Gillett, a onetime media mogul. Gillett had bought the stations just six years before for a pricey $365 million. Of the six stations, four were CBS affiliates. When the network reduced its affiliate compensation soon after Gillett purchased the group, the broadcasters began to bleed red ink, plunging Gillett into a financial crisis.

While providing a way out of financial disarray for the sellers, the buy promised Perelman a way to tie this new TV enterprise into his other media companies—Marvel Entertainment Group and New World Entertainment. The Hollywood rumor mill began to speculate that Perelman might use the TV outlets as a testing group for New World programming, or even that the stations would become the cornerstone of a fledgling network.

Such speculation was not welcome news in the corporate offices of Laurence Tisch. The chairman and chief executive officer of CBS, Tisch was already at odds with the general managers of SCI stations. The group regularly preempted CBS network shows including "This Morning" (in the Detroit and Atlanta outlets) plus all the network's late-night programming in favor of locally produced fare. Additionally, Tisch controlled CNA Insurance, a company which held bonds in the bankrupt SCI. With the Perelman purchase, those bonds suddenly became write-offs in the bankruptcy reorganization.

The two billionaires were known to be social friends, but they practiced different methods of doing business. Tisch was, more or less, a conventionally conservative industrialist, while Perelman, though also a master of numbers, allowed instinct to play into his equation. In the present case, CBS's standing with its own SCI-owned affiliates was in jeopardy, given Perelman's unpredictable nature. And no one knew that better than Larry Tisch.

Resting uneasy on Tisch's mind was Perelman's attitude toward broadcasting itself. While investors in television stations are typically executives who are either experienced or enamored with running broadcasting facilities, Perelman saw the outlets no differently from the way he viewed National Health Laboratories' analysis of urine samples or MacAndrews & Forbes's licorice root extract. TV outlets were commodities on which he expected to make money. Why, therefore, would Perelman remain loyal to CBS as a provider of programming if he could find a better bottom line elsewhere? Larry Tisch was worried, big time; and Ron Perelman could not have cared less.

Perelman was preoccupied with the orderly transition of power at the varied stations and related matters. For instance, he announced that he was buying 11 million shares of Marvel Entertainment Group at $25 a share, a full 30 percent *above* the price at which the stock was currently trading. While Marvel shareholders cheered the sudden rise in value of their shares, Wall Street scratched its analytical head in wonder.

After all, Perelman had only the year before offered the stock to the public for $5 a share (after adjustment for a split), and now he seemed to be paying far more than he had to in order to get some of it back.

The official word from MacAndrews & Forbes was that Perelman simply wanted to increase his ownership of the company to 80 percent (from his current 60 percent), in an effort to consolidate Marvel's earnings with those of MacAndrews & Forbes and thus offset other losses. Those who doubted Perelman's logic only needed to examine the MacAndrews & Forbes statement a little more closely to discover the truth.

Only by owning 80 percent or more of Marvel could Perelman legally claim the comic book company on his MacAndrews & Forbes tax return in a tax-sharing arrangement that held benefits far beyond the cost of the shares. Yet, even at what seemed like an inflated price, some stockholders weren't biting. Based on Perelman's own projections, Marvel was in for dramatic profit increases of 67 percent in 1994 and an additional 34 percent in 1995. "It seems that some of Perelman's shareholders have learned very well from the master," one Wall Street analyst with Salomon Brothers explained. "They're giving Ron a little of his own medicine."

To lure in these recalcitrants, Perelman upped the ante to $30 a share. Success. Perelman now owned 80 percent. At the same time, he invested $7 million in working capital for a 46 percent stake in Toy Biz, apparently interested in the company's product licenses. Avi Arad, the owner of the company, announced that with the Perelman contribution the name of the firm would now be New Toy Biz, lest anyone get confused.

This deal completed, Perelman began to growl at some of his own advisors for a slight mistake in calculations that put his name in the headlines unfavorably. He was given a public slap on the wrist by Washington, D.C., when the Federal Election Commission used a rarely imposed rule to fine him (along with nine others) for violating limits on political contributions by any one individual. In Perelman's case, he had exceeded the $25,000 limit by $7,500, and was fined $1,800. The billionaire was incensed—not so much that he was fined, but that his staff hadn't been on top of the matter long before the election commission intervened.

During the past several years, Ronald Perelman had contributed over $250,000 to various political campaigns and parties, spreading his money to cover every possible base without regard for his own personal beliefs. It was business, pure and simple. By structuring the contributions to be given by each of his various business entities, he could extend his reach well beyond the individual contribution limit of $25,000 in any one election year.

While maneuvering his way through tax loopholes and

political contribution constraints, Perelman made still another detour, this one out of his town house on East 63rd Street and into an eighth-floor co-op on Park Avenue near 73rd. The efforts at reconciliation had failed. He dropped a cool $10 million for the swanky address in an attempt to separate himself completely from his and Cohen's on-again, off-again marriage. Perelman's only remaining marital challenge was to keep his fortune intact. As for the quidnunc Claudia, she seemed finally to accept the permanency of the split and consoled herself with her look-alike daughter Samantha, who remained with mom.

The premature death at age 43 of one of Perelman's favorite art dealers, Thomas Ammann, gave Perelman cause to reflect on his own age and accomplishments. Ammann's gallery had supplied the now fifty-year-old industrialist with many of the works in his growing collection, which included such artists as Warhol, Miró, Nevelson, Dubuffet, Henry Moore, Twombley, and Giacometti.

As he hit his first half-century, Perelman was riding the crest of skill, intuition, and luck. It had boosted his combined personal fortune to an estimated $4 billion. If he had been twice unlucky in love, they were minor missteps for an entrepreneur whose life revolved far more around business than love and family.

Perelman had few outside distractions. One notable exception was an unusual Memorial Day weekend jam session on the drums. Dressed in all black, including a black silk shirt buttoned at the neck, Perelman joined Paul Anka on stage at the Concord Resort Hotel's Imperial Room. He had played with Anka once before, when the singer performed at two Revlon parties in Palm Beach. The singer and tycoon connected both socially and musically, leading someone in attendance to quip:

"Ron just might have a second career." Not that he needed the work.

As it turned out, the Memorial Day weekend was a busy one for the billionaire. The day before his drum recital, he went house shopping to the tune of $12 million. He had been in the market for another home in East Hampton for four months, ever since his wife-on-the-outs, Claudia, had taken a shine to the digs they had on Lily Pond.

The home he viewed on that Saturday was known as The Creeks. It had a reputation even more vivid than Perelman's. The ninety-four-year-old stucco mansion was owned by the late artist Alfonso Ossorio, who had given innumerable scandalous parties in the 12,000-square-foot building and its fifty-seven extensively shrubbed acres—parties where the champagne flowed as easily as sex.

Real estate broker Tina Fredericks, a Long Island legend herself, convinced Perelman to take a look-see. He arrived at 12:30 P.M. According to *New York* magazine, Perelman, clad in Sabbath attire of smart blue linen shorts and crisp blue broadcloth shirt, took a quick spin through the property—or at least some of the property—scanned the waterfront view, and left, telling Fredericks that his lawyer would take care of arranging the deal.

Like previous Perelman properties, this one would need extensive renovation. The exterior of the house was painted black—an Ossorio attempt to set off the groves filled with over a million dollars' worth of rare blue and yellow evergreens, as well as Japanese cedars and thirty types of pines. Yet that was the least of its problems.

The following day, Perelman was back on site with his favorite architect, Peter Marino, to talk about the need to rip out walls, install an air-conditioning system (!), redo the bathrooms, rewire the circuits, redo the plumbing, and on and on.

Perelman wanted the work completed by the Fourth of July, less than five weeks away.

Less than twenty-four hours later, despite the fact that it was Memorial Day, no fewer than thirty-six workers descended on The Creeks and began to perform major surgery. The outside walls were restuccoed to their original sandstone shade, while the formerly red, white, and blue trim was painted a sophisticated white. Original stairways and windows that had been closed off or boarded over by Ossorio were reworked back to their original condition, and the theater, which Ossorio had turned into a studio, was totally restored. By the time July 4 came around, the job had been completed with a week and a half to spare. Amazing? Not for Perelman. He was overheard to wonder why, at the price he was paying, it had taken so long.

It wasn't until August that Perelman opened up the house for a small dinner party and private showcase, to which he invited some close friends. He invited his architect Peter Marino (and his wife Jane) to view the fruits of his labor, as well as record-film mogul David Geffen, artist Roy Lichtenstein (with his wife Dorothy), Larry Gagosian, Ross Bleckner, and Perelman's oldest son Steven (who brought his girlfriend Abby Rose). Not on the guest list: Claudia Cohen, whom he was now officially divorcing. The group marinated in the luxury of the place, supped on a rich menu that included three separate dessert courses, and then retired to the screening room the size of a miniplex to watch *The Man Without a Face*, starring Mel Gibson—perhaps not the best film to watch on a full stomach.

But watching films, playing drums, and supporting the Long Island real estate market would never be Perelman's real métier. He never strayed far from corporate acquisitions, and sometimes in unpredictable industries. There are few who could explain Perelman's sudden interest in boats, particularly in light of the fact that he personally became sea-sick just looking at a launch. Yet, in mid-1993, Perelman entered the boating industry in a minor way, creating another new holding company as a by-product. Called Meridian Sports Holdings, the corporation was formed to cater to the fishing, water-skiing, and scuba diving set, and to handle the acquisition of boat maker Boston Whaler, which Perelman purchased outright from Reebok International for $20 million.

Reebok, which had only owned the company for five years (and had paid $45 million for the manufacturer), was eager to dump what it saw as a declining business. In addition to Boston Whaler, Perelman added boating brands MasterCraft and Skeeter as well as O'Brian water skis (offshoot divisions that came with the Coleman Co. purchase) under the corporate umbrella of Meridian.

Regardless of his other businesses, however, Perelman's overwhelming priority during mid-1993 was his growing media empire. In addition to his seven television stations, Marvel comic books, Fleer sports cards, and New World Entertainment, Perelman added a 50 percent ownership in Genesis Entertainment, a television syndicator whose distribution network both nationally and internationally was well known and respected. At the time Perelman bought Genesis, it had just canceled its single new production, "The Whoopi Goldberg Show." While folding this company into New World Entertainment, which itself was under the Andrews Group, Perelman persuaded Genesis to handle the distribution of Marvel Entertainment's syndicated "Biker Mice from Mars" cartoon. Such is the power of a 50 percent voting block.

Insight into Perelman's plans for his media division could be gleaned from an SCI stockholder's agreement in which he pledged to seek "vertical integration of television programming and distribution activities." While SCI stock was traded

147

over the counter (in this case it was sold only through several large stock brokerage houses), Perelman pushed to get it listed on the Nasdaq Exchange. Speculation remained ripe as to Perelman's plan for the business. Few analysts were convinced the entrepreneur would limit himself to his current seven TV stations. Since the FCC allowed individual owners to assemble as many as twelve stations under one corporate umbrella, Perelman had some major shopping to do. Word on the street was that he was doing just that.

Shortly he announced a $25 million investment in Guthy-Renker Corporation, the leading infomercial producer in the country. That bought him a minority interest. The entertainment community began to generate rumors of a secret Perelman strategy that would eventually lead to a new television network. In truth, his plans for Guthy-Renker were more basic.

Headed by the creatively agile thirty-six-year-old Greg Renker, Guthy-Renker was considered the Tiffany of infomercial houses. With such hits as Tony Robbins's "Personal Power" (more than $100 million worth of tapes sold), Vanna White's "Perfect Smile" teeth whitener, and Victoria Principal's "Principal Secret" beauty products, Guthy-Renker had the ideal marketplace experience to leapfrog Revlon productions into home shopping. In fact, Guthy-Renker's infomercial introducing a new Dolly Parton line of Revlon products had already convinced Perelman how good the company was.

The Guthy-Renker buy was Perelman's first step toward the vertical integration he had promised SCI stockholders. Step two was the hiring of Farrell Reynolds, a onetime senior sales executive with Whittle Communications and a former colleague of Bill Bevins at Turner Broadcasting System. Reynolds's addition to the Andrews Group signaled the building of a sales rep company within the Perelman media holdings to peddle its own advertising time. Ironically, SCI originally had

148

its own internal rep company, but it was disbanded by George Gillett when he took over control of the stations.

With the new companies came new wealth. By the end of 1993, Perelman's total net worth was estimated by financial magazines to be $5 billion. While few others in the world could make that claim, it was not the only point of pride for Perelman. It was his ability to *run* companies that he continued to insist was his legacy, in spite of the media denigration of this genuine skill.

Concerned by the possible danger his spectacular wealth had thrust upon him, Perelman restructured his security force. To top his team of bodyguards, Perelman hired the best—Floyd I. Clarke. It was Clarke, as the number two man at the Federal Bureau of Investigation, who ran the FBI when Director William S. Sessions was called on the carpet by President Clinton for the botched and fatal assault on the Branch Davidian compound.

Clarke, a onetime street agent, had risen through the ranks of the FBI to ultimately head the agency's worldwide criminal investigative, budget, and administrative operations. In no small way, Perelman's appointment of Clarke as his Vice-president of Corporate Integrity pointed to his intensified concern over not only his personal security but also over numerous opportunities for leaks in corporate strategy.

One personal matter that Perelman managed to deal with effectively was his divorce from Claudia Cohen. Although the gossip journalist remained enamored of Perelman, she accepted a settlement which insiders tallied at $80 million, a house and an office in the East 63rd Street corporate headquarters, as well as child support for young Samantha.

As 1993 came to a close, however, there was no lack of romance in Perelman's life. Actress Melanie Griffith, who was having marital problems of her own, played Cupid and introduced Perelman to her friend, liberal political activist Patricia Duff. Duff was beautiful and intelligent. She was newly separated at the time from TriStar Pictures executive Mike Medavoy.

During that holiday season, Perelman began to be seen at late-night restaurants, parties, and private clubs. He attended the wedding of "The Donald" and his newest Mrs. Trump, Marla Maples (she wore white), at the Marble Collegiate Church. He even took another turn at the drums, this time at the Revlon Group Christmas party with 1,000 in attendance. The billionaire maestro sat in with the entertainment—the rock group Jukebox Heroes—at Club U.S.A.

Perelman bought himself yet another house, this one on the West Coast, close to Duff and his media conglomerate. He parted with over $4 million in cash for a sixty-seven-year-old, Spanish-style Bel Air estate on one acre. The four-bedroom mansion formerly belonged to Keith Barish, the film producer who delivered such hits as *The Fugitive* and *Sophie's Choice.* Barish had paid $2.1 million for the house fourteen years earlier.

In an effort to restructure his media businesses and establish more credit leverage, Perelman consolidated all his television holdings under a new company name. According to his SEC filing, the deal worked this way: Perelman sold his production entity, New World Entertainment, plus Four Star International, a film library, to SCI Television in exchange for 25.4 million shares of SCI stock valued at $230 million. The merged companies were then renamed New World Communications Group, which looked much better on a letterhead than the initials SCI. In addition to merging those companies together, he also was buying the remainder of both Genesis Entertainment and Guthy-Renker Corp. that he didn't already own.

In typical Perelman style, New World Communications Group was owned by Andrews Group which was owned by MacAndrews & Forbes Holdings which was owned by Mafco Holdings which was owned by Ronald Owen Perelman. It was an old trick he had learned very well at his father's knee.

In essence, by "selling" New World Entertainment to SCI, Perelman was making $130 million in profit—$230 million in stock minus the $100 million in New World debt he promised to retire. With New World and SCI TV merged, his producing wing now had access to the cash generated by his TV stations. As stated in his SEC filing, he planned to develop "relatively low-cost programs, such as game shows, reality programming, and talk shows, that meet the needs of the stations and are suitable for syndication."

His programmers already had begun to develop a game show titled "Family Circle"; a talk show geared to the daytime audience; a reality series; plus a weekly series based on the Jacqueline Susann novel *Valley of the Dolls*. In addition, there was to be "animated programming, especially in conjunction with Marvel Entertainment," a separately held division of Andrews Group. And all the shows would be distributed by Perelman's in-house Genesis Entertainment.

The arrangement did more than keep everything under Perelman's control. It allowed him to use his own companies to sell services to other companies he owned, thereby making money from each internal transaction. It was the ultimate profit machine, a business without any middlemen.

While this media complex was certainly looking like a future moneymaker, Perelman's cosmetics giant Revlon was wallowing in disarray. Unable to get on its feet despite the changes instituted by Jerry Levin, Revlon wasn't even generating enough cash to pay the interest on its debt. On top of that, its share of the marketplace was dwindling, making future profits look even less likely.

When he was attempting to go public with Revlon's stock,

151

Perelman had predicted a 1992 sales increase of 20 percent. In fact, sales rose only 11 percent, and Revlon showed an operating loss of $82.6 million, more than three times what his 1992 stock prospectus had predicted. In the first nine months of 1993, sales fell 6 percent, with operating income down 54 percent. Yet, if Perelman was worried, he wasn't showing it. He gave Levin a total vote of confidence. At least for the moment.

Once again, Revlon continued to lend its name and sponsorship to Hollywood's Fire and Ice Ball, the annual event to raise funds for cancer research. Perelman co-chaired the event with Lilly Tartikoff and Jane Semel, the wife of Warner Bros. president Terry Semel.

He donated $10 million to New York's Guggenheim Museum. Part of the gift was earmarked for a new sculpture by Perelman's friend, artist Roy Lichtenstein, to be placed on the outside of the museum's new tower building on Fifth Avenue.

Using Perelman's grant to kick off a $100 million campaign to raise capital, the museum's director, Thomas Krens, said that the museum wasn't naming any of its facilities after the financier. "He doesn't want his name on things," Krens said, apparently never having visited New York University Medical Center and its School of Dermatology.

In making the contribution, Perelman gave a rare public interview and said, "The Guggenheim is a fabulous institution, poised for great growth over the next decade, and I saw an opportunity to help accelerate that growth." He didn't mention that, several months earlier, the Guggenheim had nominated him to their board of directors or that his Marvel Entertainment Group sponsored the Guggenheim's recent Lichtenstein retrospective.

He also didn't announce that he wasn't actually giving the Guggenheim $10 million in cold cash. Nothing that simple. Perelman had instead given the Guggenheim title to a brownstone he owned in Manhattan's East 50s, said to be worth $5 million (although Perelman had been unable to sell it for that price). In addition, he gave the museum $5 million in securities which were to be delivered over a five-year period.

No matter; it was a generous move. Ten million was ten million, even though in New York it was becoming an increasingly common amount for individual donations. Perelman's gift to the Guggenheim was preceded a month earlier by a $10 million donation to the museum by developer Samuel J. LeFrak and his wife Ethel. The LeFraks got the landmark Frank Lloyd Wright building named after them.

Even *that* gift, which was cash, didn't exactly go as planned. The New York City Landmarks Commission said no to having anyone's name on the world-famous exterior rotunda. LeFrak began to get itchy feet, and the Guggenheim, sweaty palms. In a flash they scoured the floors, and on number five found a suitable gallery to name after the LeFraks.

Designer Bill Blass had no such problem. When he earlier had given $10 million to the New York City Library, they leaped at the opportunity and quickly named the public catalog room at its main branch on Fifth Avenue in his honor.

In the meantime, Perelman's buddy and Hollywood mogul, Barry Diller, who didn't donate $10 million to either the Guggenheim or the New York City Library, was nevertheless in a gift-giving mood. During a telephone conversation with Diller, Perelman just happened to mention that while out on his new Georgia Lake property in East Hampton, he spotted a Barnstable catboat that he thought would be a perfect complement to his empty dock at The Creeks.

Diller pitied his friend's empty-dock syndrome, and had his secretary ring the Barnstable Seacraft Company in Massachusetts to order one of the catboats for Perelman. Unfortunately, the small, busy manufacturer told Diller that all its boats were custom-made and that they weren't making any more this season. Not about to take "no" from a New England boat maker, Diller did what Diller does best—he bargained. The upshot was that Barnstable found a *used* catboat that could be refurbished to look like new. Perelman would never know. Barry immediately ordered the craft.

What he did not know was that Perelman, doing what *he* does best, also had asked his secretary to call the Barnstable Seacraft Company. For Ronald money-is-no-object Perelman, the company *would* make a new boat. Suddenly, the King of Cosmetics had two boats. When Diller found out what had happened, he had his gift delivered with a note: "Mine's faster."

The vessels, named Killer Diller and Creek's Cat, were docked side by side. There they floated, looking extremely picturesque on the edge of the fifty-seven acre estate, hardly ever used. Perelman had little time these—or any—days for fishing, sailing, skiing, or lounging on a catboat. He had just sniffed out another opportunity, this time with the help of his banking sidekick Gerald Ford.

Flushed with success from the First Gibraltar sellout to Bank of America, Ford was eager to pursue the purchase of a new savings institution. He turned once again to Ronald Perelman to provide the bucks to make it happen. In this case, Ford's target was First Nationwide Bank, a San Francisco–based savings and loan then owned by Ford Motor Company. With assets of $15.5 billion and 180 branches in eight states, First Nationwide ranked as the nation's fifth-largest S&L.

Although a thriving enterprise when Ford Motor Co. bought it in 1985, First Nationwide had been hit hard by the downturn in the California economy and by poor loan management. The automaker wanted out and placed the S&L on the block. Four different bidders made a pass at it, but the

Perelman-Ford proposal was structured most simply and didn't demand concessions such as credit guarantees.

The $1.1 billion deal contained none of the government guarantees that had accompanied Perelman's purchase of First Gibraltar six years earlier, so this time Perelman was flying without a safety net, putting his faith in the intrepid Gerald Ford. Ford's plan was to drop Ford Motors' emphasis on commercial real estate and to place all First Nationwide's efforts into residential home loans. Given a huge upswing in home construction as a result of the January 17, 1994, Los Angeles earthquake, analysts predicted the Perelman-Ford plan would produce a bounty. "With some well-placed deals, the returns could be astronomical," predicted E. Gareth Plank, an analyst with Mabon Securities, who followed First Nationwide.

In addition to being able to apply tax benefits retained from the sale of First Gibraltar, Perelman also managed to buy a relatively clean balance sheet by getting Ford Motor Co. to keep $1.2 billion of the bank's bad assets. As he had in the past, Perelman negotiated hard but wisely. Everyone involved seemed pleased with the outcome.

Particularly happy was forty-nine-year-old Gerald Ford. Divorced, with four children ages fifteen to twenty-one, the veteran banker was entering a new phase in his life, moving from his Texas home base to San Francisco. Having just recuperated from a mild heart attack, he was eager for the challenge. As one analyst said, Ford, having sold First Gibraltar, was "a passion in search of an object."

Despite the size of the S&L purchase and projections for its success, most of Wall Street still considered Ronald Perelman's major thrusts to be not in the banking world, but in his ever-growing media companies. The reason for the Street's preoccupation with New World Communications Group was obvious: Perelman was spending an increasing amount of time on the West Coast. And his continuing very public, very frequent lunches with Barry Diller at the power-padded Grill in Beverly Hills were the subject of speculation. A lot of speculation.

Diller, onetime chairman of Fox, had left the studio several years earlier to go into business for himself, and ended up with a major interest in and the chairmanship of QVC home shopping network. In mid-1994, QVC was putting its shoulders into an effort to take over Paramount. Diller had headed that film factory before going to Fox, and it was being loudly rumored that Perelman was acting as an informal advisor to his old comrade.

Diller, in turn, was said to be counseling Perelman on the television industry, an arena that Diller knew from the inside out. He had originally made his mark in Hollywood as a heavy-hitting honcho at the ABC network. Perelman needed all the skinny Diller could provide. The Revlon chief had already announced that he wanted to add five more television stations to the seven he owned through SCI. Just *which* stations remained a mystery. But not for long.

Perelman had been quietly looking at four stations owned by Great American Communications Company, which had just pulled itself out of bankruptcy. The stations, located in Phoenix, Birmingham, Kansas City, and High Point, North Carolina, were all then strong network affiliates that mixed nicely with Perelman's other station locations across the country. In May, he announced he had indeed struck a deal with the quartet of broadcasters for a bargain basement price of $350 million, plus a warrant for $10 million in common stock.

With the Great American purchase in place, Perelman's New World was only one station shy of the maximum allowed by the Federal Communications Commission. And in typical Perelman fashion, it was only a matter of weeks before he had added the last pearl to his string. But wait: Perelman didn't just add one, he bought *four* additional stations from Argyle Television Holdings for $716 million. The new stations were located in Dallas, Austin, St. Louis, and Birmingham, Alabama, and once again all were network affiliates. The planned purchase brought Perelman's total station ownership to 15— three above the legal limit.

A wave of his hand—the one with the wand in it—and Perelman dispensed with three stations in those markets which served him least. (It would take months, but eventually New World dropped the former Great American stations in Birmingham and High Point, plus the former SCI station in Boston.) Yet even as media watchers were trying to figure out who owned what, Perelman waved his wand again. This time, the resulting redistribution of broadcasting power would do more than just place him among the very top of television potentates. It would change the face of network broadcasting from one coast to another in the single most dramatic shift of affiliations that TV had ever known.

EIGHT

A Brave New World

R onald Perelman didn't mean to start a revolution in television. He was only doing what he had always done: gotten the best deal for his money. It made no difference whether the money was to be made in cigars, lipstick, or TV stations. He bought, he merged, and he maximized the potential for each of his businesses. And so it was with the New World Entertainment Group.

Yet, when the news began to circulate on Monday, May 23, 1994, that Ron Perelman signed a deal with Fox Broadcasting's owner, Rupert Murdoch, to switch the affiliation of all or nearly all of the twelve New World Entertainment television stations to Fox, it was earth-shattering. To the broadcast community, such mass defection was treason.

What Perelman and Murdoch had done was brilliant. The story began in a small way when Perelman bought his first seven stations from SCI. At the time, he knew next to nothing about TV. He didn't have time to watch it much; and when he did, it was typically to play a home video. His first lesson came from CBS, the network affiliated with five of the seven SCI stations. Those stations and CBS had not been on friendly terms for years, even in the pre-George Gillett days, when they belonged to Storer Communications Inc. (as in SCI). Storer did things that the network didn't like, such as preempting CBS programming for local shows on which they made considerably more money.

After Perelman became boss, relations did not improve. The strong-minded new owner didn't like having to get CBS's permission to take over the affiliations of three of the stations. He also didn't like it when the network refused to sign longer-term affiliation agreements he had requested. CBS, for its part, hated the fact that several of the stations delayed "Late Night with David Letterman," while another of the outlets refused to carry it altogether. When Fox Broadcasting outbid CBS for the franchise to broadcast NFL football games, the sound Perelman heard was nails pounding into a coffin, and the headstone on the grave said CBS.

"They would have actually been content to stay with CBS had it not been for the arrogant attitude of CBS affiliates head Tony Malara," said a high-level source close to the discussions. "They went in to CBS to discuss extending their affiliate arrangement with them, and New World was treated like they should be begging to do business with the network. CBS failed to realize that not only did affiliates have choices, it was now dealing with a company which had as much money as it did and wasn't about to be pushed around. And New World told them that—before they walked out of the meeting."

Perelman, a dozen television stations in hand, went trading. And he happened to run into Rupert Murdoch. Murdoch owned News Corporation, an Australian–U.S. corporation that controlled not only 20th Century Fox Studios and the fledgling Fox network, but also TV stations, a newspaper, some magazines, and a few other assorted companies. Murdoch had worked hard to launch the Fox network over the cackles of the entrenched TV Pooh-Bahs. They didn't realize at the time that Murdoch and his then-chief commandant Barry Diller were creating a new wave of "fragment TV." They didn't have a lot of viewers, but with shows like "The Simpsons," "Melrose Place," and "Married . . . with Children," the ones they had were loyal, young, and controlled the dial.

Then came the deluge that left the networks awash: Murdoch pulled a Perelman and outbid CBS for the rights to broadcast the games of the National Football League on Fox. The cost to Murdoch was tremendous: $1.6 billion for four years, but it guaranteed Fox an enormously expanded audience base. It also attracted the attention of Ronald Perelman.

Perelman referred to his alliance with Murdoch as "an interesting business opportunity." To say the least. It was as spectacular in its own way as anything that a Hollywood special effects department could have mustered.

To entice Perelman to bring over his twelve stations (seven of which he didn't even officially own yet), Murdoch promised to invest $500 million in New World Communications Group in exchange for 20 percent ownership. Perelman would then use Murdoch's $500 million and the $250 million he would get from selling his stations in Boston, San Diego, High Point, Greensboro, North Carolina and two in Birmingham, Alabama to buy the stations he didn't own.

For his part, Murdoch was raising some of the $500 million to pay for his New World investment from his sale of stations in Dallas and Atlanta, two cities already covered by more powerful outlets owned by Perelman. The rest of the money Murdoch could take out in loans, which were now easier to get, of course, because of the added Fox affiliates. It was a case of scratching each other's back to the point of shoulder dislocation.

When all the dust settled, CBS had lost eight affiliates—in

such cities as Dallas, Detroit, Atlanta, Cleveland, Tampa, Phoenix, Milwaukee, and Austin. CBS's president of affiliate relations, Tony Malara, had only learned of the switch in station alliances the morning it occurred. The stunner came in a telephone call from Bill Bevins. "It's a big blow," Malara commented. "But it's not Armageddon."

Perhaps not, but it was the next worst thing. It was the largest single affiliate loss to any one network—ever, and it sent CBS's stock to plummeting eighteen points in a single day. A day later, the value of CBS on Wall Street was 11 percent lower than it had been before the Perelman detonation.

In addition to the snatch it put on the CBS outlets, Fox also picked up a former ABC affiliate in St. Louis, plus one NBC affiliate in Kansas City, Missouri. Making the deal all the more remunerative for Fox and Murdoch, five of the stations were in cities with NFL teams.

In its own effort to run damage control, NBC began an all-out push to convince Perelman not to sell its affiliates in San Diego and Birmingham, Alabama, or convert those outlets to Fox affiliation. Eventually, the network's efforts proved successful. Perelman decided to hold on to KNSP (San Diego) and WVTM (Birmingham) in exchange for a guarantee that NBC would run up to an hour a week of New World Programming on NBC's seven owned stations: It was a small-screen version of having your cake and eating it too, and Perelman was licking the icing off his lips.

Having succeeded in scoring ten of Perelman's twelve stations, Murdoch and his Fox associates were smiling ear to ear. "They can't call us a 'weblet' anymore," Fox chairman Lucie Sulhany chortled at a media luncheon in Manhattan. Sulhany was referring to the frequent use of the slang term in the entertainment paper, *Variety*. Its competition, *The Hollywood Reporter*, took the opportunity to headline: A WEE-WEB NO MORE. Murdoch and Perelman were in their glory.

The ten-station affiliate swap began a swoop into the marketplace by CBS, ABC, and NBC to find replacement stations for those they had lost. In many cases, the three competing networks were forced to look at stations above channel 13 in the less powerful UHF band as alternative outlets, where viewership significantly decreased.

For Perelman, the alignment not only meant the welcome of football, it meant potentially lucrative open spaces in daytime programming on his stations, since the Fox network had yet to program those hours. The freeing up of those time slots was another incentive for Perelman, since inventive programming created by his New World division could now easily be test-marketed there. In addition, some prime-time slots opened, since Fox was programming only fifteen prime-time hours a week compared with twenty-two hours by each of the other networks.

It also served as a satisfying boost to New World's program development division. As part of the overall deal, Murdoch agreed to order a minimum of two prime-time series pilots per year from New World Entertainment as candidates for the Fox fall lineup, plus several miniseries and TV movies. Additionally, Fox and New World agreed to form a joint syndication arm that would produce programs for their stations. Included in the commitment by Murdoch were a two-hour block of daytime shows and two new late-night shows. Murdoch agreed to run any new New World shows on the stations he owned which, when combined with the Perelman-owned outlets, reached 45 percent of all TV households.

Perhaps the most lasting effect of the Perelman-Murdoch alliance, however, was the massive damage it did to the traditionally sacrosanct relationship between network and affiliate.

162

So strong was this relationship that some stations had been affiliated with the same network for over forty years. The statuary that once was thought to have stood on bedrock was suddenly discovered to have feet of clay.

Erik Sorenson, then-executive producer of "The CBS Evening News," put it succinctly: "There will never be trust again. Networks and affiliates could always count on each other to be there. Now, it's open season for the highest bidder."

For Perelman, this was a business deal, nothing more or less. It was aimed at boosting the bottom line, which in the case of New World needed a great deal of improvement.

Perelman negotiated the presto-chango in less than two weeks. While the excitable were referring to the move as the single most significant development in the medium after the invention of the picture tube, for Perelman it was just another day at the office. In fact, it wasn't even the only deal he managed to conclude during the time period. He was also choreographing plans for more home renovation, always a favorite Perelman pastime. Somehow, the master businessman had found time in between building a media empire and buying S&Ls to purchase another home. One is never enough when the town is Palm Beach. And Perelman found a treasure: Casa Apava. Located on eighteen acres of prime oceanfront, the house set him back a mere $11.6 million. Would-be rubberneckers at 1300 Ocean Avenue could gawk but see nothing, so far was the house from the road. It was ready to occupy, so Perelman had only to unpack and open his humidor—although finishing touches were necessary here and there.

He had two new pools constructed—one cool, one hot—to augment the just-tepid pool that came with the place. Then, in anticipation of entertaining on a grand scale, he expanded both the north and south wings of the mansion to accommodate more guests, along with such amenities as added cabanas and more extensive formal landscaping. His "other" beach house, at 641 North County Road, was almost a shack by comparison, although Perelman did place it on the market for $15 million including fish tank.

Meanwhile, his town house on East 63rd Street was also being overhauled. As his romance with Patricia Duff intensified, he asked her to help put a few new grace notes on the symphony left behind by Claudia Cohen. Friends were confirming that this time it really was "true love" for Perelman. More than a few were astonished when Duff's fortieth birthday came and went without an engagement announcement. Perelman did, however, toss a party for his favorite blonde on April 12 at his Park Avenue pad, with local and long-distance billionaire friends joining in the gaiety. And, engaged or not, soon after the party Duff discovered she was pregnant with Perelman's child. The expected one was due in January.

Yet Duff proved an elusive quarry for the investor who was used to being pampered by women. She was not dependent on Perelman for either her life or her power, and made no attempt to hide the fact. She would disappear for days at a time, involved as she was in various money-raising events for the Democratic National Party and for several big-ticket politicians including President Bill Clinton.

Over Memorial Day weekend, however, it wasn't Duff who was keeping Ron Perelman concerned. Rather, it was actress-turned-director Penny Marshall. The fifty-year-old former star of "LaVerne & Shirley" was spending the holiday weekend at Perelman's vast new East Hampton digs when she got chest pains during an early morning tennis game.

An ambulance was called to the posh estate, stirring the curiosity of the generally staid Georgica Pond set. Marshall was rushed to Southampton Hospital and admitted for observation, although a Perelman employee later confirmed that "it was nothing serious. The hospital checked her out and she was discharged."

Soon after the Marshall episode at East Hampton, word began to circulate that there had been a major rift in the Duff-Perelman romance. The office she had been given at Perelman's New World Communications and the secretary who went with it were reassigned, only to be mysteriously reinstated three weeks later. His Gulfstream jet was rumored to have been fueled and sitting on an L.A. runway for seven days waiting to depart, while Perelman pined away alone in Manhattan.

If the breakup was afoot, it was also brief, for in early June Duff was back as Perelman's date in Hollywood at a fund-raising event for Vice-President Al Gore, and looking particularly happy that night.

He also had Duff by his side when he held two highly successful fund-raisers at The Creeks in East Hampton—one for New York Governor Mario Cuomo, a Democrat to whose campaign Perelman would later write nineteen checks totaling $91,000, and the other for California Governor Pete Wilson, a Republican. Such high-profile, bipartisan events did not keep him from returning to the negotiating table to produce another communications surprise.

On June 14, 1994, in Manhattan, Perelman held a press conference to announce he had hired onetime NBC Entertainment president Brandon Tartikoff as chairman of New World Entertainment. By picking Tartikoff to run the programming wing of New World Communications, Perelman did more than secure a man known throughout Hollywood for pulling formerly third-place NBC into the first-place prime-time position thanks to his development instincts. If New World had been easy to dismiss as an also-ran in the past, that was no longer the case. With Tartikoff on board for programming and Bevins in charge of future acquisitions, New World

Communications was looking more and more like a glittering star in a town where appearance was everything.

Tartikoff's background held its own fascination. After leaving NBC, he subsequently became chairman of Paramount Pictures, releasing a variety of films including the highly profitable *Wayne's World*. For the fifteen months prior to the Perelman announcement, Tartikoff had been heading his own company, Moving Target Productions. On May 23, 1994, the droopy-eyed Tartikoff was busy attending the Cable Television Association annual conference on the floor of the New Orleans Convention Center, drumming up interest in Moving Target programming. The independent producer had been learning the realities of selling shows after years of buying them, first at NBC, then later at Paramount. It was a role that Tartikoff clearly did not like. *New York* magazine quoted him as saying that he was suddenly looked upon as a "content provider. . . . I felt like a Jersey cow."

On the convention floor, he was surprised to receive word that Perelman was trying to reach him, and immediately called the financier in New York. When Perelman asked for a meeting as soon as possible, Tartikoff agreed to see him the following day in New York. It was only after he hung up the phone that he heard the news that had stunned the broadcasting world—the massive reaffiliation of twelve television stations. Even then, Tartikoff had no idea that Perelman had hoped to get him involved in the deal. It took less than twenty-four hours for him to find out. After his meeting with Perelman, the lawyers did what lawyers do best, and two and a half weeks later the deal was done.

As part of the terms of his signing with New World, Moving Target was purchased by Perelman and folded under the New World banner. Moving Target had over twenty programs in development, including a syndicated late-night series titled "Last

Call," a two-hour pilot for CBS called "XXX's and OOO's," a Fox pilot titled "TV Guys," another pilot for NBC titled "The Book," plus "Weekly World News," based on the supermarket tabloid, as well as several miniseries—one for ABC to star Ann-Margret, titled "The Gospel According to St. Clair," and another by bestselling author Tom Clancy called "OP Center," for NBC.

In addition, Moving Target had options to do two specials based on *Passages 2000*, Gail Sheehy's newest bestseller, plus a "Dynasty"-esque serial centered on a rich black family and their hidden secrets.

Recruiting Tartikoff had taken Perelman all of three weeks. It was helped along, of course, by the fact that Perelman and Tartikoff were longtime friends. The financier was still actively involved in Tartikoff's wife's fund-raising campaign for cancer research. Mainly, Perelman was attracted by Tartikoff's reputation as the ultimate television programmer. Perelman himself knew *nothing* about programming, but he did know enough to hire the very best.

Perelman paid $9 million for Tartikoff's production company, spread over a six-year period, in addition to giving him an interest-free loan for one million shares of New World stock. According to Perelman, his goal in hiring Tartikoff was "to develop New World as one of the leading programmers in the industry." And he was well on the way.

In addition to paying top dollar for Tartikoff's Moving Target, Perelman agreed to allow the executive to remain based in New Orleans, despite the fact that New World Entertainment's headquarters were in Los Angeles. Tartikoff had moved to New Orleans from Beverly Hills in 1991 after his young daughter Calla was seriously injured in an automobile accident. Calla's rehabilitation specialist was located in the Louisiana port.

Additionally, Perelman offered Tartikoff an ownership stake in shows he developed for New World.

Even with the Fox alliance and Murdoch's promise to buy two pilots a year from New World, Tartikoff was not limiting his options to the fourth network. "The intention here is to make New World a powerful force in global TV production. In order to accomplish that, we will be selling our wares to all the major buyers, as well as cable where appropriate," Tartikoff stated.

For his part, Bevins, to whom Tartikoff would report, had every intention of letting him have his way. Admitting that he never read scripts and had no intention of starting, Bevins, forty-eight, remained detached from the creative aspects of the business, while proposing further expansion opportunities.

Bevins was cast in the Perelman mold. A workaholic whose life revolved around the office, Bevins loved nothing better than crunching numbers and making deals. He was equally well known for his chain-smoking, which took its toll on his heart. Bevins suffered two heart attacks while still in his thirties. Although those cardiac episodes put a crimp in his smoking habit, they didn't slow down his pace. The executive suffered a third attack after joining the Perelman organization and underwent quintuple bypass surgery. He was back at his desk within days of leaving the hospital.

With Tartikoff to mold his programming wing and Bevins to keep tabs on the $100 million he had dedicated to developing TV shows, Perelman returned once again to the buffet table of potential businesses that might enlarge his domain still further. There were more meetings with Barry Diller—including an oh-so-Hollywood exchange of hugs and kisses over the deli and fresh fruit platters in the green room the day NBC unveiled its new $15 million "Window on the World" digs for its "Today" show. He also attended a "smoker," a civilized get-together of 100 cigar smokers at Manhattan's world-famous "21." While there, he met, mingled, puffed, and palavered among such powerhouses as conservative broadcaster Rush Limbaugh, Interpublic's chairman Phil Geier, Condé Nast's president Steve Fiorio, and EMI Records' chief executive officer, Charles Keppelman. They had each parted with $1,000 for the honor.

While he had yet to convince Patricia Duff to become the third Mrs. Ronald Perelman, he did regularly point with pride to her two conspicuous photos in his office, routinely referring to her as "my boss." There was no doubt in anyone's mind, however, that Perelman was in love. In August 1994, he proved it—and in a very big way.

Esquire magazine writer Jennet Conant wrote a thirty-five-hundred-word profile of Duff under the title "Working Girl." The portrait she painted was one of a motivated, highly successful woman who had worked her way into a position of political influence and power in Hollywood and Washington, D.C. There were catty comments, to be sure. From her education at the International School of Brussels and Georgetown University to her entry into political circles as a researcher with the House Select Committee on Assassinations, the magazine portrayed a woman who had used her intelligence and good looks to maximize her dreams.

Of particular interest to the Hollywood crowd was how Duff arrived in town as part of the Gary Hart campaign in 1983. Connecting with stars like Jack Nicholson and Warren Beatty got her introduced in politically active show biz circles. When Hart imploded on his own lusty male ego, Duff used her new connections to help launch the Show Coalition—or Show Co for short. The organization provided a means for celebrities to donate their talents to fund-raisers. It also served as a way to connect candidates and celebrities at the hip, and Duff was instrumental in keeping them that way.

Obviously enjoying her life, she didn't hesitate to speak to *Esquire* about it, never realizing that the highly protective and oh-so-sensitive papa bear, Ron Perelman, might take offense at the reporting of some of the more critical comments directed Duff's way.

He made an attempt to get *Esquire* to drop the piece before it ran. As with any good publication, the ploy did more damage there than good, and the article ran, big time. Not to be outdone, Perelman picked up the telephone and made a call to *Esquire*'s parent company, the Hearst Corporation. He pulled all of Revlon's ads from their collection of magazines and TV stations. Among them: the widely read, very important *Cosmopolitan, Harper's Bazaar,* and *Redbook.* Estimates suggest that the loss to Hearst stood initially at $5 million. Some say the losses to Revlon were even bigger.

According to Perelman, withdrawal of ads from Hearst was unrelated to the publication of the "Working Girl" piece. Ronald O. contended that the tiff was over his lack of pull when it came to controlling Revlon's position in the Hearst publications. They would no longer guarantee him prime ad positions, he said.

Adding some credence to his side of the story was the fact that Perelman didn't show a ripple of reaction when *Harper's Bazaar* profiled then-wife Claudia Cohen in November 1989. And according to James Conroy, MacAndrews's senior vice-president and special counsel, "Position is the single most important issue in print advertising and it is taken seriously by all advertisers. We were at odds with Hearst long before this article came along." According to Conroy, Hearst, in an effort to encourage newer advertisers' spending, was giving the newcomers space that had formerly been reserved for Revlon.

Hearst pointed out that Perelman had pulled ads from magazines outside the United States, including those in Great Britain, as well as from broadcast advertising over Hearst's six television stations. Hearst also confirmed that a very angry Perelman called a high-ranking Hearst executive to ask that the *Esquire* story not run.

Regardless of which side was right and which spokesperson you believed, Perelman wasn't about to change his mind. Duff rode out the controversy by staying above the fray. As top Washington political consultant Bob Squier said in the Conant piece, "She is a major player. She is responsible for most of the political connections between the Democratic party in Washington and California. If you are a serious candidate, you have to talk to Patricia." But, Perelman felt, just don't talk *about* her in print.

Fuming or not, Perelman was pleased to see that Marvel Comics, which in recent months had plunged 52 percent below its previous peak, was finally beginning its recovery. Part of the rebirth came from Perelman's own purchase of a million or so shares of the stock to keep his percentage of the Marvel Entertainment Group at just above the 80 percent requirement for maximum tax benefits. His buyup of the stock translated into investor interest, and the price began a slow but steady rise.

There was a flurry of other Marvel activity, focusing investors' attention on the corporation. In a matter of weeks, Perelman concluded a licensing deal with MCA to develop theme parks using Marvel characters such as The Incredible Hulk, Spiderman, Daredevil, and The X-Men. Each park was expected to cost in the neighborhood of $100 million and offer a half-dozen rides and related attractions.

There were more Marvel-ous meetings. One was with the Italian sticker manufacturer Panini Group, which agreed to distribute a group of Marvel-themed products in Europe. Perelman's decision to put Bruce L. Stein, onetime chief of Hasbro Toys' Kenner Products, in as president of Marvel Entertainment suggested that the future of Marvel was going to be shifted to areas other than comic books.

And there were more Marvel-ous lawsuits: The Delaware Chancery Court finally dismissed the eleven-year-old suit brought by Cinerama and its owner, Michael Forman, challenging Ronald Perelman's acquisition of Technicolor. While agreeing with a previous opinion of the Delaware Supreme Court that Technicolor's board had been negligent in carrying out its duties to stockholders by failing to consider any other offers for the film-processing firm, it nevertheless found that Perelman's offer was "full and fair." According to Judge Chancellor William Allen, since the board had relied upon the opinion of lawyers and investment banks familiar with Technicolor's history, the price that Perelman eventually paid for the company gave stockholders as good a return on their investment as could be reasonably hoped.

Forman's attorneys immediately promised to appeal the decision.

"This ain't church. It's all about money," is the way Gerald Ford characterized opening day at the Perelman-controlled First Nationwide Bank. When the deal became official on September 30, 1994, more than a few investment houses wanted the credit and glory. Among those claiming to have dealt the winning hand as Perelman's advisor on the purchase: Salomon Brothers, Lazard Freres, Smith Barney, Goldman Sachs, J.P. Morgan, and Hovde Financial of Washington, D.C.

While Ford tended the banking fires, Perelman structured yet another holding company, this one named Mafco Consolidated Group. Mafco was formed to acquire in friendly fashion the assets and liabilities of Abex, a manufacturer of aerospace and industrial products. The sale was valued at approximately $200 million. At the same time Perelman was buying Abex, Abex (with Perelman's approval) was selling its brake friction division to Cooper Industries for $207.4 million. The money from the sale would go directly into Mafco, thereby making Perelman a profit of several million dollars and giving him the remaining assets of Abex for nothing.

Abex joined Consolidated Cigar and Mafco Worldwide "Flavors" (previously known as MacAndrews & Forbes Co.), the makers of licorice extract, as divisions of Mafco Consolidated Group. This group in turn was held by C & F (as in cigar and flavorings) Holdings, which was owned by MacAndrews & Forbes Holdings, which was owned by Mafco Holdings, which was owned by Perelman. As intricate as the breakdown of companies was, it was simple compared with the full Perelman flow-chart when one added Meridian Sports Holdings, Coleman Holdings, Andrews Group, First Nationwide Holdings, NHL (National Health Laboratories) Holdings, and Revlon Worldwide. Perelman, no doubt, was one of the few able to keep the many companies and divisions completely straight in his mind.

The 1994 holiday season meant celebrations. First, a black-tie dinner at the Rainbow Room to honor Perelman's continuing contribution to the Burden Center for the Aging, a pet charity for New York's wealthy. A week and a half later, Perelman had more to celebrate closer to home. Patricia Duff married him, agreeing to convert to Judaism and keep a kosher home. And then Duff gave birth to a baby girl, Caleigh Sophia, at New York University Medical Center.

To mark this event, there were baby showers aplenty. Barbara Walters gave one—the same Barbara Walters who had been such a good friend of Perelman's ex-wife Claudia Cohen. *Vogue* editor Shirley Lord threw Duff another shower, this one an afternoon tea at the home of socialite Gayfryd Steinberg. Joan Canz Cooney was in attendance, as was Diane Sawyer.

While Duff opened presents, Perelman reached into his wallet and lifted out $7.5 million for Lilly Tartikoff and her cause, the Revlon–UCLA Breast Cancer Center. Some of the money was also earmarked to permanently endow the Revlon Chair in Women's Health at UCLA.

With nary a company to acquire in the last week of 1994, Perelman accomplished the next best thing. He sought a casino license in Atlantic City. The red tape involved in such a filing is akin to being "put under the heat lamp," according to New Jersey political sources. The process not only takes up to six months, but by the time it's finished, "they know everything about you including the make of your underwear."

For Perelman to risk revealing everything about his business and private life meant he was eager to capitalize on the license when, and if, it was approved. An additional indication that this was no lark: a $100,000 check accompanied the application—only one-third of the eventual total he'd need to produce.

It was a small enough amount considering Perelman's now-estimated worth, which *Esquire* magazine figured to be $5.9 billion—over twice the amount generated by the entire Atlantic City casino industry. How Perelman intended to make use of the gaming license remained unknown, even to MacAndrews & Forbes Holdings' special counsel and senior vice-president, James Conroy. "After we've complied with the regulatory process, we'll see what our options are," he said. He also indicated that Atlantic City might not be the only gambling mecca in which Perelman was interested. "We are doing this just to get clearance in case an opportunity presents itself," he told reporters. Whatever the case, Atlantic City was *the* place to be at the moment.

174

The same week Perelman made his approach to Atlantic City, Bally Manufacturing Corporation bought one of the seven empty lots on the Boardwalk. It was the former site of the Shelbourne Hotel, in between Caesars Atlantic City and Bally's own Park Place, the city's most profitable casino. Just the month before, ITT had agreed to pay $1.7 billion for Caesars World, including Caesars Atlantic City.

Perelman, of course, knew nothing about running a casino, any more than he did eight months earlier about managing television stations. But he did know where to look for a bargain. In this case, Wall Street analysts were guessing he would turn in the direction of Circus Circus Enterprises, with eight casinos in Las Vegas and 13,660 hotel rooms. According to brokers, Circus Circus was undervalued and had a strong cash flow—two of Perelman's favorite things.

As for Atlantic City, Perelman knew it well. His parents owned a mansion in the Lower Chelsea section of the city at Plaza Place and the Boardwalk, its high hedge blocking the pool from prying eyes.

While Perelman was filing casino applications, his former wife Claudia Cohen decamped with their daughter Samantha and headed to Florida's Palm Beach to spend some time with her parents. Still upset over her split from her powerhouse husband, Cohen was fighting continual bouts of depression. "She was sad about the breakup," a friend confided on the guarantee of anonymity. "Real sad. She really loved the guy."

At that moment, fate—or, more precisely, publicist Peggy Siegal—stepped in on Claudia's behalf. Siegal had traveled to Palm Beach to be the houseguest of real estate developer Earl Mack and his wife Carol. As a way of welcoming Siegal, the couple tossed a little sit-down dinner party for sixty friends. Since Peggy and Claudia were longtime buddies, Siegal insisted that Cohen join them. At first, Cohen begged to be excused. She was in no mood to sparkle, let alone dress for a fancy do. Siegal, never one to accept a turndown, persevered until Cohen finally agreed to make an appearance. Also at the Macks' that evening was Alfonse D'Amato, the Republican senator from New York and chairman of the Senate Banking Committee heading the Whitewater investigation. The two were introduced, and Alfonse saw stars. While no one is certain exactly *what* Claudia saw, the word from those at the party was "love," despite D'Amato's mud puppy–like visage and frame.

The following evening, Cohen, dining with her parents at the posh Palm Beach eatery Amici, again crossed paths with D'Amato. This time the senator seemed unwilling to let her out of his sight. Sweeping her away from *la famiglia,* the senator and the lady went dancing at the nearby Chesterfield Hotel. It was only a matter of time before Perelman was only a memory.

LOVE CONQUERS AL, screamed the headline of the *New York Post* soon thereafter. They were referring, of course, to Cohen, *not* to D'Amato's wife, Penny. According to a Perelman spokesman, the billionaire was "not unhappy" about the budding affair. It was just as well, because it seemed to be out of his control in any case, and Claudia was spinning away on a life of her own. Suddenly, it seemed Cohen and D'Amato were everywhere together—film premieres, restaurants, the Super Bowl in Miami.

D'Amato believed the love match warranted a press conference. In February, he announced to reporters at the Water Club on New York's East River that he was indeed in love with the ex-Mrs. Ronald Perelman and planned to marry her. There was no mention of the fact that despite his thirteen-year separation from his wife, they still occupied the same Long Island home.

There was no talk of a divorce at that point, although there was some talk of his asking the Catholic church to annul his marriage. Cohen, it was pointed out, despite the fact that she was Jewish, would also have to ask the Catholic church to annul her marriage to Perelman. No matter the complications, D'Amato remained adamant. "I feel like the frog that has kissed a princess," D'Amato said at the press conference. There were those who whispered that in the fairy tale, the frog turned into a prince. D'Amato, from firsthand reports, did not.

He did, however, take the opportunity to sing. The last time D'Amato serenaded the public, it was on the floor of the Senate, where he bellowed to the tune of "Old McDonald Had a Farm":

"President Clinton had a bill,
E-I-E-I-O,
And in that bill was lots of pork,
E-I-E-I-O,
New pork here, old pork there,
Here a pork, there a pork,
Everywhere a pork, pork. . . ."

This time, the tune was "It's a Sin to Tell a Lie." God, for whatever reason, spared D'Amato from a bolt of lightning for that gush of hypocrisy.

As the relationship became the stuff of daily headlines, Perelman's patience began to run thin. He was said to be suddenly not very happy about the possibility that his daughter's future stepfather might take her to confession. He even hired attorney Stanley Arkin to represent him in the matter. This was the very same Stanley Arkin who had so brilliantly represented the *first* Mrs. Ronald Perelman in her divorce suit *against* him, and still later would take another case for him with the potential of scandal.

When he wasn't busy dealing with his ex-wife's public

displays of affection, Perelman was out business-shopping again. On the advice of the Andrews Group's Bill Bevins in Hollywood, he decided to acquire the independent television producer, Cannell Studios. Its owner, Stephen J. Cannell, previously hit paydirt with the Brandon Tartikoff–inspired series "The A-Team" plus "Hunter," both hour-long megahits on NBC.

More recently, Cannell had pioneered filming in Canada to cut costs, and left his mark on cable with the USA Network's "Silk Stalkings." Bringing this creative producer into the New World Entertainment fold might help Tartikoff jump-start the growing media conglomerate.

Meanwhile, on the East Coast, Perelman was named a trustee of the John F. Kennedy Center in Washington, D.C., by President Bill Clinton. The two men, fellow cigar smokers, were introduced by Patricia Duff. Around the same time, Perelman was given the added cultural honor of being named president of the Guggenheim Museum.

Eager to escape the love-headlines his ex-wife and the mouthy D'Amato continued to generate, Perelman took his current wife and new baby to Italy—more precisely, Milan, during fashion week and the swirl of the haute couture shows. It was Caleigh Sophia's first trip abroad, and she was all of three months old. Despite the spectacle on the runways, little Caleigh stole the show when she spit up what resembled risotto, but was surely formula, on Duff's shoulder while proud papa Perelman looked on at their table at Bice, the very fashionable Italian restaurant.

Back in the United States one week later, Duff took herself and her baby down to Palm Beach, while papa headed back to the salt mines of Manhattan. Perelman got a too-warm welcome when he lunched at the Four Seasons restaurant. He had just sat down with his "group" when smoke started pouring from the kitchen and all the all-too-powerful were asked to make a hasty exit through the front door. The smoke was caused by a two-alarm fire that had broken out in the kitchen duct of the Brasserie, the companion restaurant to the Four Seasons in the landmark Seagram Building. Perelman remained unfazed, completing his meal at nearby San Pietro.

In Florida, the current Mrs. Perelman was preparing to greet President Clinton and wife Hillary for a fund-raising dinner at Casa Apava, which had been redecorated in smart, warm Florida shades. Perelman arrived in time for the event that was the talk of the financially lacquered Palm Beach set. One guest commented that Donald Trump's Mar a Lago "is bigger, but this house is so much more 'livable.' " No small achievement for a paltry $11.6 million and a minuscule 14,000 square feet.

Just when Perelman thought it was safe to return to New York—there hadn't been a restaurant fire or word of the D'Amato-Cohen romance for weeks—he received news that the senator from New York had been granted a divorce from his wife. D'Amato made the news public himself from the steps of the state Supreme Court in Nassau County which had granted the divorce. This cleared the way for the Catholic church to begin work on an annulment.

After being briefly hospitalized soon thereafter, D'Amato used the excuse of recuperation to steal away to Florida with Cohen and visit his in-laws-to-be. The trip was more than a casual one. The Cohen family was said to be anything but pleased with Claudia's heartthrob, who by his own admission was poor. The Cohens, of course, *weren't*, and intended to stay that way.

Perelman was in Las Vegas as a guest of the National Association of Broadcasters which had chosen him as keynote speaker because of his chairmanship of New World Communications Group. Given the chaos he had created within the broadcast community, Perelman was a guaranteed standing-room-only sellout.

"We were simply trying to be as creative as possible in solving certain problems affecting our business," he asserted in his speech. He admitted that there was never a conscious effort to "rearrange the industry." At the moment he was giving his speech, Perelman's "creative" solution had caused sixty-six stations in thirty-three markets to realign their network affiliation. The networks themselves had anted up some $250 million in additional affiliate compensation to hold on to the ones who didn't jump out of the fold.

"We believed that our assets were underperforming," he went on, "and as a result would be undervalued in the marketplace. . . . In order to unlock the value of our stations, we felt compelled to go beyond the conventional."

Apparently the strategy was working. The New World station group had revenues the previous year of $445 million and turned a $193 million profit. In addition, the stations had increased their appeal to adults ages 18 to 34, vital targets for advertisers. Nearly 70 percent of the increases were in prime time.

Perelman acknowledged that the real appeal of the merger with Fox was the ability to launch syndicated shows on both Fox and New World–owned TV stations. He concluded his keynote speech by saying, "Change is inevitable. The world of broadcasting and cable in April 1995 is very different from that of a year ago. There is no reason to assume the coming years will be any less challenging or exciting. In fact, the pace of change is likely to accelerate."

At about this time, in his old home town of Philadelphia, the University of Pennsylvania was making plans to welcome their now-famous alumnus back to the downtown campus—or at least his name. In late April, the university announced a $20 million donation from Perelman.

"This gift expresses my deep regard for the formative role Penn has played in my life and the life of my family for three generations," he said. His father had gone to Penn, as had his three adopted children.

It had been nearly a decade since Perelman's first $10 million donation to the school. That money had been earmarked for a student activities building to be built at 36th and Walnut. The site, however, proved to be too far removed from the center of campus, and construction of the project was never begun.

Instead, university president Judith Rodin took personal interest in the project. Helped by consultants and advisors, Rodin came to the conclusion that the century-old Hudson Hall—the oldest student union in the country—just needed a refurbishing. With the new Perelman contribution added to his previous $10 million, Hudson Hall was about to get that and more. Other nearby buildings—College Hall, Williams Hall, Logan Hall, and Irvine Auditorium—were also to be given massive restorations to provide modern classrooms, performing arts facilities, and study lounges as well as eating areas.

The revitalized area was redesignated the Perelman Quadrangle in Ronald Perelman's honor. The project, designed by architects Venturi, Scott Brown & Associates, would take three years to complete. According to President Rodin, the Perelman Quadrangle was expected to achieve "a seamless integration of students' academic pursuits, their extracurricular activities, and their day-to-day lives."

While Perelman was giving away millions, he was cutting expenses at home. According to *Money* magazine, Perelman decided to stop splurging on French wine. While not quoting Perelman's Manhattan wine supplier, D. Sokolin Company,

Money did confirm that Perelman was no longer interested in paying $1,500 to $2,000 for a twelve-bottle case of 1970 French Haut Brions. In its place, he had substituted $500 to $800 a case for bottles of Italian Sassicaia, Ornellaia, Tignanello, and Gaja.

Whatever the state of Perelman's wine cellar, his checking account was rapidly multiplying. With Wall Street enjoying a bullish roll, on paper Perelman's assets were burgeoning at an astounding rate—so much so that financial magazines hedged their bets in guesstimating his worth, for fear their calculations would be out of date by the time their publications saw print.

Wall Street was also responding to an unconfirmed report that MacAndrews & Forbes's Andrews Group was about to make another media swoop. Not an insignificant one, either. This time out, the team of Ron, Bill, and Brandon were said to be stalking big prey—an endangered species called Time Warner.

The possibility of a Time Warner grab came on the heels of the purchase of a controlling interest in MCA, the parent of MCA Universal Studios, by Canada's Seagram Co. for $5.7 billion. In order to help finance its MCA takeover and to avoid any talk of antitrust violations, Seagram was rumored to be dumping its 15 percent ownership of Time Warner on the market. And Perelman seemed poised to scoop it up and then some.

In spite of the Wall Street speculation, Perelman was silent. But Time Warner was not. In an effort to boost its stock price, Time Warner divested itself of scattered assets in an effort to raise $2 billion to reduce its debt (then estimated in the range of $15 billion). While many on Wall Street saw the pairing of two conglomerates as a natural, Perelman did not see the advantages. Insiders say he never had any interest in a Time-Warner purchase.

182

Tiptoeing into an entirely new industry, Perelman was forming a partnership with Hachette Filipacchi Magazines to buy the barely profitable *Premiere* magazine from K-III Communications. The eight-year-old publication was once rumored to be a Time Warner target. *Premiere,* which reports on and reviews film projects, had a circulation of just over 600,000. The Hachette Filipacchi–Perelman deal was worth some $20 million.

Perelman was actually interested in the magazine for reasons other than publishing. By investing in *Premiere* and letting the editorial staff of Hachette Filipacchi run the publication, Perelman gained the right to use the magazine as a source of future programming ideas.

For *Premiere,* the Hachette-Perelman alliance was a sort of homecoming. When *Premiere* premiered, it was co-owned by Hachette and Rupert Murdoch's News Corp. Murdoch later bought out Hachette's interest but eventually sold the magazine to K-III Communications. Murdoch then, of course, joined forces with Perelman in New World, and with the Hachette-Perelman-*Premiere* connection, everything came almost full circle.

As interested as Perelman was in the new partnership possibilities with Hachette Filipacchi Magazines, he was far more preoccupied with the interminable lawsuit still ongoing between Cinerama and Technicolor. The suit was once again up for judgment, this time in front of the Delaware Supreme Court. To be sure, Perelman had won the crucial first and second rounds, but Michael Forman and his Cinerama-hired attorneys appealed for a third time to the top court of Delaware. All corporatedom was gripped by the case, for the outcome would determine the extent to which boards of directors of companies incorporated in Delaware could legally interface with potential buyers. Perelman was watching for another reason: his $780 million profit from his sale of Technicolor was in jeopardy.

As vital as the Cinerama-Technicolor suit was to the Perelman empire, even *that* paled in comparison to another suit about to enter the trial phase after three years of paperwork, depositions, and discovery. Records of the Supreme Court of the State of New York listed it only as *Fred L. Tepperman v. Mac-Andrews & Forbes Group, Incorporated,* Index No. 2481/92.

This suit, however, had the potential to rip open the swaddle of secrecy that had long kept Perelman's business behavior and deal-making methods largely hidden from the competition and the public.

NINE

Sex, Lox, Bagels, & Biz

On Thursday, June 15, 1995, the following fax was sent to the city rooms of newspapers throughout the New York City area. It was authored by public relations representative Mortimer Matz upon the instructions of Barry I. Slotnick, the attorney for Fred Tepperman.

Office of Barry I. Slotnick
225 Broadway, NYC 212-964-3200
Press Contact: Mortimer Matz 212-385-3800

NEWS ASSIGNMENT EDITORS

On Monday, June 19, 1995, in NY State Supreme Court, White Plains, the public and the media will have a chance to look into the secretive business empire of mega-billionaire Ronald O. Perelman, who is being sued for more than $25 million by his former executive vice-president and CFO, Fred L. Tepperman. Tepperman was a major player in all deals for Perelman, who is the sole owner of McAndrews [sic] & Forbes, the holding company that controls Revlon, National Health Labs, Marvel, Coleman, New Line Cinema [sic] and other companies.

Tepperman started with Perelman in 1984, coming over from Steve Ross's Warner Corp. As one of the four key players who met each morning in the town house with the Chairman, he was vital to many deals including the purchase from the government of First Gibraltar S&L, which was sold for a profit of nearly $1 billion and had a tax loss carry forward of nearly $3 billion.

In 1991, Tepperman's wife started to suffer from the early stages of Alzheimer's disease. From Dec. 20, 1991 through the holiday week, Tepperman promised to take his wife to their home in Florida, which was equipped with every technology that could keep him in constant touch with his office. In taking that trip so that he could have time with his wife before the incurable disease seriously progressed to the inevitable, McAndrews [sic] said 'he willfully failed to devote to his employer his entire time, energy and skill.'

On December 30, 1991, McAndrews [sic] notified Tepperman 'that his employment was being terminated immediately because of the foregoing material breaches and gross misconduct.' The company deprived him of his contractual agreements, and even cut off his medical coverage. His wife is presently in a nursing home in Florida, where he currently lives nearby.

Having been deposed, it is certain that Perelman will be called to testify during the expected three week trial and undergo a blistering cross-examination by Slotnick.

DATE: MONDAY, JUNE 19, 1995   TIME: 10 A.M.
LOCATION: NY STATE SUPREME CT., WHITE PLAINS
111 GROVE STREET

Despite the fact that Matz didn't seem to be aware of the correct spelling of MacAndrews & Forbes or that the holding company owned New World Communications, not New Line Cinema, the basics of the fax were accurate. Tepperman had been dumped after months of pining over his wife's condition. According to him, the termination was cold and calculated. Perelman, however, insisted it was carried out only after the financier had endured month after month of Tepperman's inept conduct and inattention.

Tepperman filed suit on February 13, 1992, against MacAndrews & Forbes when he failed to get a severance package he deemed adequate from his former employer. It was less than six weeks after his firing that the legal firms Slotnick & Baker and Davidoff & Malito sued in the Supreme Court of the State of New York.

In the complaint filed with Andrew J. Spano, County Clerk of Westchester, the attorneys laid out their case. They told of Tepperman's hiring on June 11, 1984, as executive vice-president and chief financial officer of MacAndrews & Forbes Group. His salary at the time of his firing was an astronomical $1,331,000 a year (not including bonus).

The discharge by MacAndrews was executed quickly, efficiently. The letter sent by registered mail to Tepperman in Florida began, "This shall serve as written notice of termination as a result of the material breach of the Agreement between you and MacAndrews & Forbes Group, Inc., dated June 11, 1984. . . ." With that letter, the fight began.

Tepperman's complaint alleged that he did not receive "salary, benefits and other perquisites to which he would otherwise be entitled pursuant to the agreement," as well as "certain retirement and pension benefits to which he is entitled." In addition, Tepperman contended that his wife's illness had caused him emotional trauma so severe as to render him disabled and incapable of performing his job.

Quoting from Tepperman's employment agreement, specifically section 4, paragraph a, the complaint left little doubt that his attorney would rely on medical testimony to support their claim.

> 4. (a) If, during the term of this Agreement, the Employee becomes disabled or incapacitated for a period of twelve (12) consecutive months to the extent he is unable to perform his duties hereunder ("Permanently Disabled"), the Corporation shall have the right at any time thereafter, so long as Employee is then still Permanently Disabled, to terminate this Agreement. If the Corporation elects to terminate this agreement by reason of the Employee becoming Permanently Disabled, the Corporation for the Unexpired term of this Agreement shall continue to pay:
>
> > (1) to the Employee 60% of his Base Salary at the rate in effect on the date of such termination . . .

According to his filing, Tepperman had "suffered a psychological injury which has rendered him, among other things, clinically depressed and unable to concentrate for extended periods of time, all of which has rendered him unable to perform the regular duties of his employment pursuant to the Agreement."

Tepperman was asking for nearly $30 million in damages in the suit and, despite his wife's deteriorating condition and his own psychological state, was prepared to testify in court about why he thought he should get it. He made no mention of those portions of his employment contract that had provided him with his enormous annual salary and such perks as "initiation fees and dues for one business club selected by Employee," a personal tax advisor, and a car—in this case, "a top-of-the-line Jaguar, Mercedes-Benz or like vehicle selected by the Employee."

Little more than a month later, on March 26, 1992, MacAndrews & Forbes fired back. This time it was Perelman's attorneys from the law firm of Chadbourne & Parke who had the court's attention, and they were quick to countersue, citing Perelman's side of the conflict.

Their counterclaim pointed to other terms of Tepperman's contract, including a paragraph that said the chief financial officer agreed "to serve [MacAndrews] faithfully and to the best of his ability; to devote his entire time, energy and skill during regular business hours to such employment; to use his best efforts, skill and ability to promote its interest . . . ; and to perform such duties as from time to time may be assigned to him by the Board of Directors or any of his superior officers . . ."

According to Perelman, Tepperman had increasingly neglected his responsibilities despite repeated warnings. Perelman's lawyers also addressed the subject of Tepperman's Supplemental Retirement Plan (the SERP), administered by Tepperman as part of his chief financial officer duties. It was added to Tepperman's contract as an amendment on July 1, 1989, to provide Tepperman millions of dollars. It would also form the basis for much of Perelman's countersuit that alleged Tepperman had engaged in fraudulent behavior.

According to Perelman and his attorneys, when Tepperman presented the SERP to vice-chairman Howard Gittis for his signature, he did it with assurances that it only represented "technical changes" as required by the IRS and was not increasing the company's liability to Tepperman. Not until later, after Tepperman's termination, did Gittis learn that the amendment put MacAndrews & Forbes on the hook for more than $5 million, the countersuit claimed.

From the corporate perspective, Tepperman "willfully failed to serve MacAndrews faithfully and to the best of his ability. He willfully failed to devote to his employment his entire time, energy and skill during regular business hours. He

willfully failed to use his best efforts, skill and ability to promote MacAndrews's interest. And he willfully failed to perform
other duties assigned to him by his superior officers."

Exactly what Tepperman *was* doing in place of his work was
also spelled out by the suit. Despite the fact that he acknowledged "to his superiors that he was not performing the duties
required of him under the Contract," he was said to have done
nothing to change his behavior. Instead of working harder and
concentrating more, Tepperman took time off.

"Tepperman announced that he would be absent from his
job the entire week prior to Thanksgiving. Tepperman was advised by his superiors that because this was an unusually active
and important time with respect to matters Tepperman was
working on, he should defer this vacation plans until Thanksgiving week," the MacAndrews countersuit formally stated.
"Tepperman," it said, "nonetheless willfully failed and refused
to follow this instruction, and instead responded that if
MacAndrews didn't like his decision, 'you should fire me.' "

The complaint continued: "In December, 1991, Tepperman announced that he would be absent from his job for seventeen consecutive days—from December 20, 1991, through
January 6, 1992. On or about December 19, 1991, Tepperman
was advised by his superiors that because of 'very significant
and substantive matters at year end,' being absent at this 'critical time' was 'not acceptable.' Tepperman was specifically instructed not to be away from his office for this seventeen-day
period."

In Tepperman's mind, he had planned this time as an opportunity to spend some quality time with his wife while she
was still able. Ignoring the orders from MacAndrews & Forbes,
he headed out on vacation, leaving for Florida, the sun, and
holiday weeks presumably filled with golf games and early-bird
dinners. Midway through the vacation, Tepperman received

his letter of termination—the single point upon which both defendant and plaintiff agreed. Not only was Tepperman fired, he was told to return "a top-of-the-line Mercedes-Benz automobile that was owned by MacAndrews and had been provided to Tepperman for his use in the performance of his employment duties." The MacAndrews folk also wanted back "a cellular telephone, a portable telephone, two facsimile machines, American Express cards, an AT&T telephone credit card, and V.I.P. cards for various private car services."

Three years later, when the court date finally appeared on the calendar of Judge Samuel G. Fredman, the items still hadn't been returned. For despite extensive depositions, later sealed by the court, there was little movement from either side. But the secret depositions and other court documents do tell quite a story.

In an affidavit to the court by Perelman's vice-chairman Howard Gittis, filed on April 27, 1992, the executive ripped into Tepperman for creating his own supplemental retirement benefit plan (SERP): "Tepperman never explained to the Board or me the vast sums of money that he would assert entitlement to under the Supplemental Benefit provision even if terminated for gross misconduct." Yet, Gittis himself was an attorney of considerable fame and experience in dealing with contracts, and he had signed the document authorizing its addition to the employment agreement.

"The role of Chief Financial Officer is crucial to the MacAndrews organization," Gittis went on. "MacAndrews is a multi-billion dollar company. It is controlled by a single shareholder, its Chairman. Tepperman was one of four executives of the company (including me) who met virtually every morning with the Chairman and with other senior executives having offices nearby. Clearly, as Chief Financial Officer, Tepperman's services were required in all aspects of MacAndrews's most important business dealings."

So vital was Tepperman to the success of the company, it appeared that his presence might be necessary at any hour. On October 1, 1987, Howard Gittis sent Tepperman a letter in which he offered to have the company pay for an apartment in the neighborhood of the East 63rd Street offices of the corporation to facilitate his availability.

"As you know all too well," the letter began, "experience over the last several years has demonstrated that your availability here in Manhattan into the late evening hours and on weekends is crucial to effectively deal with the crises which inevitably arise in the many transactions the company undertakes, as well as to permit you maximum input into strategic planning sessions with the company's other senior managers and its outside advisors. It is clear that, with your usual 8 A.M. arrival, departing for home very late in the evening is frequently not advisable nor convenient from the company's standpoint.

"Since suitable hotel accommodations are most often unavailable late in the evening, and to provide the company with the convenience of maximum availability of your time and attention, you have agreed to obtain an apartment within walking distance of East 63rd Street," the letter confirmed. "Such an apartment will also provide you with a suitable setting in which to conduct meetings dealing with highly sensitive subjects and to work more privately than is typically possible in your busy office. The company agrees to bear the monthly cost of that apartment, together with cleaning, catering and other sundry services reasonably incurred in connection with company business, of $30,000 a year." Tepperman later put his signature of agreement to the document.

It remained for Ronald Perelman himself to open the window wide on life inside the privileged walls of MacAndrews &

Forbes, and on much more. His deposition was also sealed by the court in an effort to keep its penetrating contents hidden. Small wonder. The deposition offered an unbridled look at raw Perelman—arrogant, often hostile, controlling.

To get Perelman to sit still for a deposition was not simple. Tepperman's legal team had waited nearly a year and a half to gain access to Perelman, who was finally deposed on April 1, 1993. Perelman appeared with his attorney Stanley Arkin in the offices of Tepperman's attorneys, Davidoff & Malito, 605 Third Avenue in New York, at 10:30 A.M. Barry Slotnick was asking the questions.

Q: Mr. Perelman, would you tell us where you reside in New York State?

A: New York City.

Q: Do you have an address?

A: Yes.

Q: What is that address?

A: I am not going to tell you."

The tone was set. So, too, the style. Perelman was not about to gently pass control of the situation to Barry Slotnick or any other attorney in the room. Unintimidated, Slotnick asked Stanley Arkin to direct his client to answer the question. Arkin, not about to be controlled either, refused, adding that he would give Slotnick Mr. Perelman's business address.

"I am not interested in his business address. I would like to know the residence," Slotnick said.

Q: How many residences do you have in New York?

A: One.

Q: How long have you lived there?

A: Ten years.

Q: Was it the same residence that you lived at when Fred Tepperman was employed by you?

A: Uh-hum.

193

Q: Mr. Perelman, don't you think I know that address?

A: Then why ask me?

Q: Do you have any residences elsewhere?

A: Yes.

Q: Where are they located?

A: I am not telling you.

Q: Would you tell me the state?

A: No.

Q: Mr. Perelman, do you have a residence in Palm Beach in Florida?

A: I answered you. . . .

Q: How long have you lived at your present residence in Palm Beach?

A: I am not telling you any of my residences, where they are. That's irrelevant . . .

Q: Mr. Perelman, are you a lawyer?

A: No. Are you?

Q: Mr. Perelman, I suggest that we take a break."

It was 10:40 A.M. The deposition had gone on for only 10 minutes. When it finally reconvened, in response to Slotnick's questions Perelman related his education and general background before Slotnick moved the topic on to the purchase of Cohen-Hatfield Industries and subsequently MacAndrews & Forbes. The dueling continued.

Q: Are you aware of a company called MacAndrews & Forbes Group?

A: Yes.

Q: Does that have any relationship to the Cohen-Hatfield Industries?

A: That was the new name for Cohen-Hatfield Industries.

Q: When you say that became the new name for Cohen-Hatfield Industries, are you talking about Cohen-Hatfield Industries does not exist by name at the present moment?

A: I don't understand the question.

Q: Does Cohen-Hatfield Industries exist as a separate entity?

A: Yes.

Q: MacAndrews & Forbes was a successor to Cohen-Hatfield Industries, is that correct?

A: No.

Q: Does MacAndrews & Forbes have anything to do with Cohen-Hatfield?

A: MacAndrews & Forbes is Cohen-Hatfield Industries.

Q: Mr. Perelman, I think if you will try and respond to my question without fencing, we will get done a lot quicker.

A: If I could understand them more easily, I could respond to them more easily.

Q: Okay, I will make them more simple. Are you currently the owner of MacAndrews & Forbes?

A: Yes.

Q: Are there several companies that are called MacAndrews & Forbes, such as Group, Company, Corporation, Limited, etc.?

A: Yes.

Q: Would you list them?

A: MacAndrews Holdings, MacAndrews Group, and MacAndrews Co. I think those are the only three.

Q: How was the name MacAndrews & Forbes derived?

A: I have no idea.

Q: How did you become the sole owner of MacAndrews & Forbes Group, Holdings, Company? If we could do them individually, it would be helpful.

A: MacAndrews & Forbes Group was taken private by MacAndrews & Forbes Holdings.

Q: When did you first own any interest in MacAndrews & Forbes Holdings?

A: At the time it was used as a vehicle to take Group private.

Q: Do you know the year?

A: No.

Q: How did you become involved in MacAndrews & Forbes Holdings?

A: How did I become involved? I don't understand the question.

Q: MacAndrews & Forbes Holdings is a company, is that correct?

A: I answered you. We used that as a vehicle to take Group private.

Q: Perhaps you don't understand my question.

A: Perhaps I don't."

The jockeying for position in the deposition continued for fifteen pages of testimony. Back and forth, hit and dodge. Another half-hour passed and Slotnick knew little more than he had before, other than that Perelman was chairman of MacAndrews & Forbes, and that he also owned Coleman Co., Andrews Group, Revlon, National Health Laboratories, First Madison Bank (the remaining company from the sale of First Gibraltar), and Consolidated Cigar. Refusing to give in, Slotnick continued his attack, yielding significant insight into Perelman's personality.

Q: Do you receive any income from the Andrews Co.?

A: I don't know.

Q: You don't know?

A: No. . . .

Q: What is your position at Revlon?

A: Chairman of the Board.

Q: What is your position at . . . First Madison Bank?

A: I don't think I have a title.

Q: Do you derive any income from the bank?

A: I don't think so.

Q: Do you derive any income from Revlon?

A: I am not sure.

Q: Consolidated Cigar, what is your position with them?

A: I am not sure.

Q: Do you derive any income?

A: I don't know.

Q: Do you sit on the board of any of these companies?

A: Yes.

Q: Which one?

A: Consolidated, Revlon, Coleman, and Andrews.

Q: Do you have an interest in a company called Marvel or something like that?

A: Uh-hum.

Q: How is your interest?

A: Through Andrews.

Q: Do you have a position with regard to that company?

A: I think I am Chairman of the Board.

Q: Is that a public company?

A: Uh-hum.

Q: Do you derive any income from that company?

A: I don't believe so.

Q: Is it that you don't know or you don't believe so?

A: I don't believe I do.

Q: Is there someone in existence that would know the answer to any of these questions?

A: Yes.

Q: Who would that person be?

A: I don't know."

There was a break for lunch, then Slotnick grilled Perelman on his association with his chief financial officer Fred Tepperman, the extent of Howard Gittis's and Donald Drapkin's authority, and the details of the about-to-be famous "breakfast meetings" where all four men would gather at 8:30 A.M. each morning and mix business with pleasure.

Nearly three-quarters of the way through the 169-page deposition, however, the subject reverted to Tepperman's SERP agreement, and Perelman's tone turned accusatory, vehement, and revealing.

"Q: Now, with regard to the SERP, it's your testimony, as you sit here now, that the only person that knew about the benefits that were to go to the individuals who are to receive the SERP benefits, the only individual that knew about the numbers was Fred Tepperman?

A: No, that's not what I am saying. What I am saying to you is that Fred Tepperman knew—I don't know who else knew. I don't know who else knew them, but I tell you this . . . Fred Tepperman, as my chief financial officer, never came to me to tell me of the abusive nature that he was taking, using to take advantage of this plan for his own self-aggrandizements. It was his duty and obligation to come to me and say to me, 'Listen, Mr. Perelman, I want you to be fully aware because I am primary beneficiary of this lark, I want you to be fully aware of what the benefits coming to me are, just so that I am not trying to hide anything from you. I am not trying to steal anything from you.' That is the opposite of what Mr. Tepperman did.

And it is his job, to the extent that he functioned in the job as chief financial offer—chief financial officer, not chief marketing officer, chief financial officer—to bring that to my attention, *my* attention. And he specifically, willfully and fraudulently kept that information from me.

Q: I thought you had indicated earlier that there were other people who made fiscal determinations for MacAndrews & Forbes other than yourself.

A: There was nobody that would have made a determination of—benefit of—this size without my being aware of it. And never once, never once during this whole period, which I say is from 1989 through 1991, did Mr. Tepperman try to make me aware of it.

Never once did he come to me, and I must have spent countless days with him going over numbers, never once did he come in and say, 'Hey, Ronald, I just want you to be aware of what this plan is and what my benefits under this plan are.' Never once.

Q: Is it your understanding that Mr. Tepperman was to receive the greatest number in terms of benefits?

A: I don't know.

Q: Is it your contention that the sums that were to be received by Mr. Tepperman under the SERP were material sums?

A: Yes.

Q: Do you know how much he was supposed to receive under the SERP?

A: In excess of $10 million, as I recall.

Q: At what point?

A: I am not clear.

Q: Would it be at his retirement at age 60?

A: I am not clear.

Q: Well, have you, since the discovery of the SERP, made inquiry?

A: No.

Q: As to what the amounts would be and when?

A: No. All I knew was that they were excessive and far beyond, far beyond, what anybody in their wildest dreams assumed they were.

Q: How did you know that?

A: What do you mean how did I know that?

Q: How did you know?

A: Because they told me the number. And I am the one,

I'm the one that he should have reported it to. If there was an impropriety anywhere within the financial realm of this company, that people were being taken advantage of, it was his duty and job to bring it to my attention, not the senior legal officer's job, not the chief marketing officer's job, not the head of sales, but the head of our financial reporting system, and he didn't do it.

Q: Well, do you remember who reported the numbers to you with regard to the SERP?

A: With regard to Tepperman's SERP?

Q: Yes.

A: Drapkin or Gittis.

Q: Do you remember whether any other numbers were reported to you with regard to other individuals?

A: At that time, no.

Q: And so it was your understanding that at the time you got this information that Fred Tepperman was to get the most amount of money?

A: No, I didn't say that. I said an amount of money that was far beyond what anybody thought he was getting. Maybe there was a guy that joined us when he was 40 years old that would have gotten more.

But the plan—Fred meticulously and deliberately and fraudulently took advantage of the plan that was in existence to make sure that nobody specifically saw what his own benefits were, hid this from every senior executive and went on to perpetuate a fraud against this company.

Q: Who told you that he hid them from every senior executive? How did you come to that conclusion?

A: He hid them from me. He *hid* them from me. He hid them from *me*. As the Chief Executive Officer, he reports to me. And it was his duty to bring to my attention anything that was out of the ordinary. And the benefits that he was reaping under that plan were far out of the ordinary and not only did he *not* bring them to me, he went out of his way to make sure that I *never* found out about them.

Q: Why did he do this, to make sure you never found them out?

A: He never showed me any reports. He never had any discussions with me. He never brought it to my attention. He never highlighted them in the balance sheet. He never highlighted them in a footnote. He never brought to mind what these plans were costing us, did everything out of the ordinary to make sure that I was not aware of it. For one reason. Because he was the major beneficiary. And there is no difference, and it is no different than if the account department or data processing department—instead of giving him $100,000 a month check, gave him $1 million a month check—and he didn't come to me and say, 'Listen, I just want you to know, they are paying me $12 million a year instead of a million, two. He took advantage of that just exactly the same way, exactly the same way.

Q: Well, $12 million a year is an excessive salary, isn't it? You are talking about $12 million. Would that be—

A: I am talking about a fraud, taking advantage of a fraud. And that's what he did. He fraudulently, willfully and wantonly withheld that information from me.

Q: Mr. Perelman, if you could calm down. I know you are upset.

A: Any thief excites me. And he was a thief. He is no different than the goons you represent downtown. It's just another thief, which is precisely why I don't want you to know my address.

Q: Mr. Perelman, I know you are excited.

A: I am not excited. I am not excited. When I get excited, you will know I am excited.''

Excited or not, Perelman was at the very least outraged by what he viewed as a traitor within his ranks. A man whose life no longer revolved solely around work. An executive who would no longer follow the leader and pull his share of the load. As a result, he found himself fired.

"Q: That was your power and authority [to fire Tepperman]?

A: He gave us no choice. He refused to attend serious and important meetings that the company was in the midst of. And when we asked him to by telling him he must attend those meetings, [Tepperman responded] 'well, fire me.' He gave us no choice.

Q: As a result of that statement you fired him?

A: No, as a result of his not performing his duties and functions over a long period of time, not being available to deal with issues over a long period of time, and coming into my office and telling me that specifically he was not going to attend a series of meetings because he wanted to take a vacation in Florida and 'if you want to fire me, fire me.' It was a culmination of months of that one incident in my office, that last incident, not because he told me to fire him, but because he refused to do the duties and obligations that he was hired to do.

. . . He never kept our regular business hours. Our regular business hours go from 8:30 to 7:30."

When pressed by Slotnick about when Tepperman's office attendance began to change, Perelman couldn't offer a specific date, but he nevertheless recalled that once Tepperman began to keep his own hours, the chief financial officer's work suffered as well.

"At some point, and I can't be specific when it occurred, he changed his hours dramatically. We have a breakfast meeting every morning at 8:30 for every senior executive. He missed that. He missed the morning meetings, missed them, came in at 10, 11 every morning, left at 3:30, 4 o'clock in the afternoons, wouldn't be available to handle important meetings late in the afternoon with banks or potential purchasers of assets. Just decide on his own that he was going to keep different hours."

Tepperman's erratic hours and his inattention to business lasted for months, and Perelman no longer could or would function with him drawing a $1.3 million salary but not doing his job as chief financial officer. What mattered to Perelman in the end was that his ability to do business was being affected. Very much affected.

"Q: Do you recall Fred telling you [his wife] had Alzheimer's disease?

A: Yes.

Q: So, therefore, it's your testimony that you noted that he missed morning meetings before he ever had a conversation with you about his wife's illness?

A: Yes. I have answered, that's to the best of my recollection.

Q: Your recollection?

A: Yes.

Q: Did anybody else ever come to you during 1990 and 1991 and tell you Fred's wife, Joan, had Alzheimer's disease or that Fred said she had Alzheimer's disease?

A: I don't know at what point in time. I don't think anybody told me but him, and I don't know when it was.

Q: Did you ever have any conversations with Fred Tepperman about his wife's illness in which you told him that was too bad, but he would have to continue working full time no matter what the situation was or words to that effect?

A: I don't remember how I told him to handle his wife's illness. I am sure I said that I am sorry that she is sick, whatever she has, and just keep in mind that you cannot be her nurse, that if she is functioning with Alzheimer's, that she is going to need proper professional treatment and you should get her professional treatment. You need not be a chauffeur, you need not be her nurse, you should not be her companion. You should be her husband and supporter and provide her the best possible medical services.

Q: Did you ever remember telling him that he should not walk around looking unhappy because that would be a reflection on the fact that the company might not be doing well?

A: No.

Q: Did you ever indicate to him what his outward appearance, that his outward appearance might have some effect upon how others would view the company?

A: No.

Q: For example, if you deal with bankers, don't look sad, don't look unhappy, because they are liable to believe that we are in difficulty?

A: I think bankers look at financials. They don't look at faces."

The verbal bout between Slotnick and Perelman continued until 2:30 P.M. when the financier suddenly had had enough. He wanted out, he had work to do, and the only thing standing between him and the door was a logical excuse why he could no longer continue.

"I am not feeling well right now," Perelman said abruptly. "I will be happy to sit here for a little period of time, but I am not feeling well. I am not going to be able to stay for a long period of time. I would hope that if you felt ill—"

Slotnick said, "Mr. Perelman, if you are ill, I am not going to keep you."

"I do not feel well," Perelman repeated.

"I would like to state for the record, I think you are full of crap; you are fine," Slotnick responded, unmoved. "I think this is a way of ending early. Obviously, if you are not well, and you suggest that you are not well suddenly, you have just told me that you wanted to go back to work, if you are not well, you can leave right now."

"Okay. Thank you very much." And with that Ronald Perelman disappeared into a Manhattan spring afternoon.

It would be another two years before the trial would begin on June 19, 1995. Public relations man Mortimer Matz issued a second release and set the stage.

"FOR IMMEDIATE RELEASE: June 19, 1995

The trial started today in NY Supreme Court, White Plains, where Fred L. Tepperman, the former executive vice-president and chief financial officer of McAndrews [sic] & Forbes, sued the firm privately owned by mega-billionaire Ronald O. Perelman for $25 million for monies due him under his contract.

"Tepperman was fired on December 30, 1991, when he took his wife, who was suffering then from the early stages of Alzheimer's disease, to their Florida home for the holidays. Perelman demanded that he postpone any trips and remain to be totally attentive to the business needs of the empire builder.

"Today, in court, Barry Slotnick, Tepperman's lawyer, sought a postponement of the case because Tepperman's wife, presently in a nursing home in Florida (where Tepperman now lives), was suffering from a 105-degree fever and was removed to a hospital. Perelman's attorney, with their [sic] continual lack of compassion, argued against the postponement. The judge ruled that the postponement was appropriate and postponed opening statements until Monday and allowed the jury selection to proceed on Thursday."

The trial would be in the new court building tower in downtown White Plains. A modern, glass and concrete structure, it was an unemotional design geared toward business. The Supreme Court of the State of New York was located on the eighth floor.

The jury selection phase of the trial began on June 26, and produced an all-female jury—six women of varying socioeconomic backgrounds. In an rare move for a civil case, Judge Fredman had invoked a gag order, silencing the attorneys on both sides.

For Tepperman's lawyer, Barry Slotnick, the move was particularly restricting. Well known in New York for his sensational courtroom delivery and previous successful defense of such clients as subway vigilante Bernhard Goetz; the Godfather of Chinatown, Benny Ong; and mob boss Joseph Colombo, Sr., Slotnick railed in the courtroom in an attempt to get the gag order rescinded.

Before the judge put the order into effect, it was Slotnick who had hired public relations whiz Mortimer Matz to keep the press informed about his client's case. The court of public opinion is a powerful tool for influencing potential jurors, and one which Slotnick had utilized very effectively in the past.

By contrast, media silence would prove helpful to Perelman's attorney Stanley S. Arkin, a Harvard Law School graduate with a client list that included Andrew Crispo, the art dealer accused of a sex-torture-abduction and tax evasion; and Edmund Safra, who had sued American Express, charging the firm spread rumors about money laundering in several Safra institutions.

With the gag rule in place, the New York media were eager for Slotnick's opening statement, certain that what Tepperman's attorney would reveal would become headlines on the hard-fought tabloid circuit. And the flamboyant lawyer did not disappoint them. With fire-and-brimstone enthusiasm, and for a full 100 minutes, Slotnick used broad strokes to paint the foundation of the suit.

In early 1991, Tepperman's fifty-one-year-old wife Joan had been diagnosed with Alzheimer's disease. Slowly, tragically, her personality changed as her memory began to slip into the black nothing of a decaying mind. Concerned for the health of his wife of thirty years, Tepperman became distracted, unfocused, his energy diffused of purpose and intent.

As the executive vice-president and chief financial officer of Perelman's empire, he knew the turf well. In the fast-paced world of corporate mergers and takeovers, Tepperman could ill afford to falter. In the seven years he had been Perelman's financial lieutenant, he had helped orchestrate the billionaire's success.

Tepperman was highly rewarded for his faithful service. Earning $275,000 when he initially signed on with MacAndrews & Forbes Group on June 1, 1984, he saw his salary climb to $1,210,000 a year by the time he was fired, just after Christmas in 1991. In addition, he received millions of dollars in bonuses, a new Mercedes-Benz, membership in a business club, and an apartment in New York City. But his success could have no effect on his wife's mercilessly debilitating disease. As the Alzheimer's advanced, Tepperman began to withdraw into a strange new world of depression.

He came in late to work, missing daily breakfast meetings held in Perelman's opulent Beaux Arts town house on Manhattan's tony East 63rd Street. He delegated more and more work to underlings and left the office in late afternoon to return to his home in Scarsdale, New York. As a result, he incurred the wrath of Perelman—a man well known for his sense of drama and feisty temperament.

Tepperman's attorney Barry Slotnick told the jury that Perelman was "a petulant child" who "wasn't going to honor his commitments because Fred valued Joan above him. Ronald Perelman was not going to play second fiddle to Fred Tepperman's sick wife," Slotnick contended.

Perelman, the lawyer claimed, was "vicious" and revealed his "anger and his evil" through a series of "dirty tricks" in the months that preceded Tepperman's firing. Slotnick painted Perelman as a cantankerous bully who had forced Tepperman to choose between providing care for his ill wife or devoting himself to his boss's demands.

Among the many accusations hurled by Slotnick was that Perelman was "a cheat and a liar, who doesn't pay attention to his commitments." Slotnick, however, did acknowledge that his client was distracted on the job. "I think there were times that he stared out the window," Slotnick admitted. "That's not gross misconduct. That's human."

Randy Whitestone, a former Associated Press business editor who covered the trial for Gannett newspapers, was struck by Slotnick's sense of drama and conviction. "He pounded the lectern in front of him, shouting at the jury as if he were part of a TV melodrama," Whitestone said. "Yet, he was effective in generating sympathy for Tepperman. You felt for this guy, despite his multimillion-dollar salary. In any other courtroom, he would have been the rich, bad guy. In this courtroom, however, a million dollars was pocket change."

But it was Slotnick's portrayal of the daily breakfast meetings, among the very meetings that Perelman insisted were so vital to Tepperman's job performance, that provided the most intriguing tease toward what might lie ahead. "Those meetings," Slotnick vented, seemingly incredulous, "those meetings that were so important. The conversation ran from Mr. Perelman's . . . sexual exploits the night before to lox and bagels and some business."

"He wasn't shirking his duties," Slotnick said. "He worked

well. He worked properly. But he angered and annoyed Mr. Perelman." It didn't matter that a single deal which Tepperman handled for Perelman netted the financier $1 billion in profit," Slotnick said. He was finished as soon as it was obvious that he wasn't willing to devote 100 percent of every waking hour to MacAndrews & Forbes.

Slotnick claimed that Howard Gittis tried to coerce Tepperman into agreeing to move into another position in the company at a reduced salary, telling him that Perelman now wanted him to work exclusively on finding acquisitions for MacAndrews & Forbes. Tepperman refused, and when he did, Slotnick suggested that the wheels of a "conspiracy" were put into motion to remove Tepperman from the picture altogether.

Slotnick said that in 1991 Perelman insisted Tepperman cancel his planned Thanksgiving vacation with his sick wife. Tepperman, however, had no intention of changing his agenda to satisfy Perelman and left town, further aggravating an already tense situation.

When the chief financial officer attempted to leave again the following month, this time for a long Christmas holiday—perhaps his last with his ailing spouse—the writing was boldly on the wall. According to Slotnick, Tepperman announced his plans to leave the office between December 20 and January 6. As the financial officer prepared to travel to Florida, Howard Gittis faxed an ultimatum to Tepperman's office and his homes in Scarsdale and Boca Raton. "Dear Fred," the fax said. "You must return by December 23. If you don't, that's unacceptable."

Slotnick turned pleadingly to the jury. "They let him fly to Florida with his wife, knowing the circumstances and knowing the fax was being sent." Tepperman did not return on December 23 or any other day. On December 30, he was fired.

The saga recounted by Slotnick was one of a corporate America that demanded undivided loyalty in return for multimillion-dollar compensation. It was one in which there was little allowance for a personal life, not even for a tragic family illness. Tepperman's job was not only terminated; so, too, was his health insurance at a time when his wife's medical bills were running $280,000 a year.

Stanley Arkin, in his opening statement, played another set of cards altogether. Basing his case on Tepperman's deliberate failure to perform the duties for which he was hired, Arkin sidestepped the issue of a terminally ill wife as much as possible. Whether it was caused by family disease, laziness, or other outside concerns mattered not. What Arkin wanted the jury to realize was that Tepperman stopped doing his job . . . period.

"As the executive vice-president and chief financial officer of MacAndrews, Tepperman owed MacAndrews fiduciary duties to exercise care and the utmost good faith and undivided loyalty in the performance of his duties," Arkin's court filing had stated. "Tepperman breached his fiduciary duties to Mac-Andrews." Arkin set out to prove the point.

In contrast to Slotnick's dramaturgy, Arkin was calm, precise, reassuring. Facing the jury and speaking in a low voice, Arkin suggested that Tepperman deserved no sympathy.

"This is not about a man who missed a few breakfast meetings," Arkin explained. "This is not about a man who could do his job by fax and telephone. It's about a person who changed his lifestyle and did not want to accept the consequences of his choice. He wanted it both ways."

More than merely doing an unacceptable job in exchange for over a million dollars in salary, Tepperman was insolent, distracted, and ineffective, said Arkin. Ronald Perelman, according to Arkin, gave him latitude to work out his problems. "For over a year, we attempted to get through to Fred Tepperman and explain to him that he was not doing his job. Nobody was saying, 'Don't spend time with your wife.' No one was unsympathetic," added Arkin. "They did what they could for the man. They were patient as can be . . . and decent."

Without giving specifics, Arkin said that Tepperman cost MacAndrews & Forbes "tens of millions of dollars" during the sale of a Revlon subsidiary, because he wasn't paying attention to his job. This was a man, Arkin said, who "took ten weeks vacation when he was entitled to four."

Pointing to the tolerance exhibited by Perelman for over a year, Arkin turned to the jury and asked, "How long can you fly the plane without a navigator? How long can you do this and not risk your company's health?" The firing of Fred Tepperman was "life as it is."

The following day, the New York tabloids bled from the heart for Tepperman. Perelman was depicted as more than just "The King of Mean." The papers implied that he was vulgar, uncaring, condescending, and evil.

His fury at the headlines and news reporting of the trial was intense. He wanted New Yorkers in general and the jury in particular to see Fred Tepperman as Ronald Perelman saw him—an opportunist who took advantage of Perelman's patience and kindness.

The following day, when Fred Tepperman's attorney, Barry Slotnick, petitioned the judge to allow cameras into the courtroom, Arkin made his move. In arguing successfully against the cameras, Perelman's attorney landed a few tough blows of his own.

Slotnick's remarks characterizing Perelman as a "petulant child," among other pejoratives, were "totally inflated, totally inappropriate, and totally wrong," Arkin contended. "I didn't mention that Mr. Tepperman was living with his wife's nurse and had given her half the house in Boca Raton, Florida," he added, needing no other dramatics to make the point.

The courtroom rustled with whispers and muffled gasps. Arkin had shocked everyone with his remarks about the nurse, for much of Tepperman's case was built on his being the loyal, grief-stricken spouse. Slotnick scrambled for the high ground. "If the defense wants to talk about my client's present life, so be it," Slotnick countered. He quickly confirmed that Tepperman had a live-in relationship with his wife Joan's former nurse, a woman named Denese Galban. But he insisted that the relationship was "sanctioned by Joan's parents, by her children, by all who know it's necessary for him to go on with his life."

When Tepperman took the stand, six women jurors sat straight-backed, unmoving as they listened intently to his testimony. Yet no one could look at him in the same way after Arkin's telling revelation. The executive's right hand moved repeatedly to his face, stroking the skin between his nose and his upper lip as he spoke. His manicured fingernails reflected the fluorescent lighting that gave a stark, pale cast to the New York State Supreme Courtroom.

Pensive, reflective, biting his lower lip, and fighting back tears, Tepperman told of his wife's progressive illness. "She became quiet," he said. "I thought maybe it was because of some of the pressures I brought home from work." He made mention of her forgetfulness, the changes in her personality.

At first, Tepperman added, Perelman was understanding. "Both Ronald and Howard [Gittis] expressed sorrow, sympathy, and asked if there was anything they could do," Tepperman testified. It was only later, during the subsequent year, that their concern turned to distrust.

Wiping tears from his eyes, Tepperman added, "He suggested that I do what [auto-sales mogul] Victor Potamkin did—I know he had his wife institutionalized by putting her in a condo with a bunch of nurses in it. I told him I wasn't going to do it."

Portraying Perelman as a corporate monster, Tepperman continued his emotional testimony. "Ronald came into my office one day and he told me to get used to it, in the same way that if my office was painted brown and there was no white paint, I'd have to get used to it." Later, after returning from lunch, Perelman told Tepperman, "Don't look so sad. The bankers will think the company is in trouble."

When Slotnick asked about the breakfast meetings, Tepperman answered that he never considered them "mandatory."

"Did Perelman or Gittis discuss their sexual escapades?" Slotnick asked.

"On occasion," was Tepperman's guarded response. The impeccably groomed accountant pushed at his white hair as if the question itself made him uncomfortable.

Before the day was out, Tepperman also boasted that he had helped fashion a $750 million acquisition war chest for Perelman that was underwritten with the help of Michael Milken, and took credit for personally pushing through the purchase of the Texas savings and loans which resulted in Perelman's multibillion-dollar tax credits. Yet, despite his tears and emotion, and everything he said in his own defense, the next day the New York papers alighted on the scandal of the live-in nurse like flies on compost.

REVLON CASE GETS DIRTY, touted the *Daily News*, while its competition, the *New York Post*, managed to get a photo of the woman and her pudgy fifteen-year-old daughter about to enter Tepperman's Mercedes in Florida.

According to the *Post*, Galban had gone into hiding in an effort to keep from being called as a witness by Perelman's attorneys. The tabloid added, "Directory assistance gives the same Boca phone number for Denese Tepperman and Fred Tepperman," revealing that Galban had begun to use Tepperman's name.

The next day, Tepperman refused to answer questions about the nurse from reporters outside the courthouse and moved quickly to return to the witness stand. There, he continued to portray Perelman as unpredictable and subject to irrational outbursts.

"Is it fair to say Mr. Perelman had a penchant for screaming and yelling?" Slotnick asked his client on the stand.

"That's fair to say," Tepperman testified.

When he recalled his ill-fated Thanksgiving trip to Florida, he lobbed more charges about Perelman's tantrums: "Perelman said, 'You really shouldn't go away next week. Lots of things are happening.' "

"Can you tell me what the crisis is?" Tepperman had said. He told Perelman that to change his plans would be extremely difficult.

"I'm the boss," Perelman supposedly then raged. "I don't have to answer these questions. You have to be here next week because I want you to be here next week."

"Why are you trying to do this to me?" Tepperman said that he argued back. "If you guys are trying to force me to resign, fire me," the financial officer told Perelman, before taking off to Florida in a defiant stance.

The strain between Tepperman and Perelman sometimes seemed matched by the tension between the trial's attorneys and Supreme Court Justice Samuel G. Fredman. After both Slotnick and Arkin argued that the other side was trying to steer press coverage, which by this point had increased to wire service and television reports, the judge reached his limit.

"Don't tempt me to do something I don't want to do," Fredman railed. Afterward, Slotnick made it clear to the press that he knew "a lot about Perelman," suggesting that the truth would come out in one fashion or another.

When Tepperman returned to the stand for a third day, he brazenly charged that Perelman was not above tampering with figures in the game of buy and sell. "I had some differences with [Perelman] concerning the way he'd present numbers," Tepperman testified. Even so, as chief financial officer, it was Tepperman who certified that all accounting was correct.

Worried, and confused over Perelman's behavior during a heated argument about how much he was allowed to reveal to bankers who were considering loan applications for Revlon, Tepperman testified that he even hired an attorney in 1989 to cover all his bases.

Returning to the question of pensions, attorney Slotnick produced notes from a business meeting to show that a special retirement package had been approved by the MacAndrews & Forbes executive committee a full two years before Tepperman was hired.

It was not a good day for Ronald Perelman. Besides the doubts cast on his credibility in the courtroom, he got bad news from the investment community. Standard & Poor's Ratings Group took steps to lower its ratings on certain debts of Marvel Entertainment Group, citing decreased earnings and increased borrowing. According to Standard & Poor's, net profits at Marvel had fallen due to a slip in sales of baseball and hockey cards from its Fleer division.

But the next day in court, the fourth for Tepperman on the stand, Stanley Arkin got a chance to punch back. The lawyer dramatically set Tepperman up with copies of memos and a letter from Tepperman's attorney, handing each to the jury to read. In an internal memo, written to himself, Tepperman wrote, "H [Howard Gittis] came into my office and wanted to know my plans. He said as a friend, if I didn't make an arrangement with ROP [Ronald O. Perelman] and was away for two weeks over Christmas, ROP would go crazy."

Tepperman apparently informed Slotnick of the discussion, because Slotnick fired off a fax to Perelman's attorney, addressing what he labeled as a "veiled threat." He also advised his client to ignore Perelman's demands. When Tepperman testified he knew nothing of Slotnick's faxed letter, Arkin produced notes in Tepperman's own handwriting which clearly stated that he had received a call from his secretary advising him of Slotnick's fax.

Taking a large gulp of water, Tepperman did his best to regroup. "My recollection may be wrong," he confessed. "It is so entrenched in my mind, it is hard to deal with what my notes say. I see what the handwritten notes say, and they conflict with my recollection. I guess the best I can say at the moment is that I'm confused by it."

The confusion didn't stop there. Neither did the controversy. Slotnick was called to the stand and was questioned by Arkin about a meeting he had arranged a month and a half before the trial began with Perelman's general counsel, Barry Schwartz. During the meetings, Slotnick was alleged to have spoken on Tepperman's behalf, and offered to structure a deal between Tepperman and Perelman to take advantage of a business opportunity supposedly as rich as the First Gibraltar purchase.

According to inside sources, Tepperman wanted to encourage Perelman to join him in investing in a high-tech company in Florida. The company was unnamed, but sources suggest it was Bio-Magnetic Therapy Systems, a medical equipment maker in Boca Raton. Despite the animosity between the two men, a $30 million lawsuit, and the name-calling in which Tepperman recently engaged, it appeared he was only too happy to rejoin Perelman in business.

Slotnick testified that when Schwartz passed along the information to Perelman, the financier agreed to consider the deal, saying "business is business." He also asserted, however, that Perelman agreed to Slotnick's request not to reveal any of the details of the deal during the trial. "Dumbfounding" is the way one journalist covering the trial perceived the surprise admission from the Tepperman camp. "But nothing surprises me with this group," he added.

On Tepperman's fifth day of testimony, the focus returned to his retirement package. Arkin unrelentingly tried to break Tepperman's composure. He accused Perelman's former chief financial officer of inserting "a one percent kicker" into his retirement plan in 1989, effectively doubling its benefits. Tepperman denied that such was the case. Pressing the accountant's back further to the wall, Arkin got Tepperman to admit on the stand that he did not specifically inform Howard Gittis of the increase in his SERP proviso.

Additionally, Arkin got Tepperman to recant some of his earlier testimony that Perelman forced him to juggle financial figures. He now confirmed that all information from his office had been correct and true.

Arkin also introduced facts that placed Perelman in a kindlier light. He disclosed that Perelman had not only donated $10,000 to Alzheimer's research after learning of Tepperman's wife's problem but had also provided a chauffeur for the woman when she became too ill to drive.

Nevertheless, Slotnick's revelations from inside the world of MacAndrews & Forbes were becoming more and more damaging, and it came as no great surprise that Perelman wanted to end the court proceedings quickly. He pushed Arkin for a timetable for how long Tepperman would testify, an answer there was no reliable way of predicting.

On day six of Tepperman's testimony, it was clear that there weren't going to be any winners. No one realized this more than Ronald Perelman. On the eve of his own date with the witness stand, Perelman did what he had done so often before—he settled the case in a move that caught many outsiders by surprise.

Exact details of the settlement were sealed by Justice Fredman, although sources inside the Tepperman camp estimated the amount which Perelman paid Tepperman at over $10 million. "It is said about the disposition of all lawsuits that the worst settlement is better than the best litigation," Justice Fredman intoned to the press at the trial's end. He also announced that the gag order on all parties in the litigation would remain in effect. "The matter has been settled in its entirety," he said. "A very special aspect of its disposition is the very specific agreement among all concerned that its details not be made known to anyone other than this court, the participants themselves, and their attorneys."

The settlement freed Perelman from having to face another round of questioning by Slotnick. Inevitably, the questions would have dealt with Tepperman's charges of tantrums and sexual boastings. Thus Tepperman's deposition remained the only clue to what the hostile witness might have said. (It has been revealed here for the first time.)

Prior to the announcement of the settlement, Tepperman was seen smiling as he walked casually around the courtroom, his countenance full of anticipated victory. Yet his reputation as a highly paid, loyal, and competent financial officer had certainly not emerged unscathed. No amount of money could erase that fact.

Jurors leaving the courthouse were overheard to comment

that they thought both men despicable. Their opinions, however, no longer mattered. For Perelman, it was over. For Tepperman, the pain of watching his wife die of an incurable disease was only beginning. Regardless of how much her husband had received in the settlement, Joan Tepperman continued to be the victim, an that was one trial and one life sentence that not even Justice Fredman could end or change. A year later, Joan Tepperman would be dead.

TEN

Laughing All the Way

For all the coverage the Tepperman suit received, ironically it wasn't Perelman's only ongoing court battle. In contrast to what many regarded as the financier's capitulation in the Supreme Court of New York, the Supreme Court of Delaware was handing him an unequivocal and monumental victory.

In a unanimous sixty-one-page decision, the Delaware appellate court decided for Perelman and against Cinerama in the Technicolor case. It vindicated Perelman's actions even though it stated that the board of directors of Technicolor may have short-circuited their responsibilities to their stockholders. Nevertheless, said the decision, the board made a satisfactory deal for the sale of the company, and met the "entire fairness" test required by law.

The case was one of the longest-running in Delaware history and one from which Perelman refused to back down by settling with Cinerama. The outcome meant that while boards of directors must seek the highest price for their company when it is being sold, they cannot be held liable if they haven't explored every possible alternative.

In still a third case, Perelman made out slightly less successfully. In the New York City Supreme Court, he was brought before Justice Lewis Friedman by ex-wife Claudia Cohen when he withheld a $450,000 spousal support payment. Perelman, it seemed, was concerned that Cohen was blabbing details of their divorce settlement to her current beau, Senator Alfonse D'Amato. Pillow talk, so to speak. If Cohen was indeed talking, it violated the confidentiality pact she had signed as part of their divorce settlement. Cohen denied any wrongdoing and entered the case to the Supreme Court claiming harassment.

Justice Friedman sided with Cohen and told Perelman to pay up immediately. The billionaire was not willing to give in so gracefully. Even as he was writing the check, he continued to urge his attorneys to investigate what knowledge D'Amato might have about his private affairs. In addition, he pushed Cohen for a full accounting of her art, cars, and certain belongings in her palatial Park Avenue co-op—items which Perelman figured just might arguably be his.

For his part, D'Amato had his spokesman state that he had "no knowledge of the terms of their agreement and would be happy to state that on the record." He never did.

The very same week, Perelman's bank account rose another $11 million dollars from the sale of his North County Road Palm Beach property. The purchaser was a shell corporation called Oceanic Holdings Estate that was said to be owned by a "prominent German family" interested in maintaining their privacy. Little more than that was known, other than the fact that the buyer asked to have the 2,000-gallon fish tank, complete with fish, included in the deal.

With four houses still left in his name, Mr. Ronald Perelman gave Mrs. Ronald Perelman her choice of which to call home. Her answer, as always, was not predictable. Patricia Duff Perelman wanted a home all her own—and got it. With husband, baby, and real estate broker in tow, she went house hunting in away-from-it-all Southport, Connecticut.

She wanted it to be far from the hustle and bustle of Manhattan, and Malibu East, the Hamptons, as well as the snobbery of Palm Beach. Connecticut, she felt, was the country, and the perfect place for baby Caleigh to grow and run and play without the intrusion of the real world. Mrs. Perelman found a storybook house set among twenty acres of property that included the original Pepperidge Farm of cracked-wheat bread fame.

Three stories of wood siding and dormer windows, the house was called Rock Meadow by its first owner, Broadway composer Richard Rodgers. Patricia Duff Perelman bought Rock Meadow with her own money and set about renovating the place.

The good news was that there weren't any lawsuits connected with the renovation; the bad news was that there was more to be done than her original plan of a little paint, a little wallpaper, and a few new bathrooms. When it was finally completed, however, Patricia Duff Perelman had turned the old house into *her* kind of home: a sink-into-the-sofa and curl-up-your-feet kind of sanctuary that was so totally un–Ron Perelman that visitors were said to have marveled at how at home he seemed there.

Perelman wasn't the only one. Caleigh was said to love crawling through the autumn leaves. And it was at Rock Meadow that she uttered her first word. While rumor had it the word was "cash," it actually sounded more like "goo."

Goo or not, by the time the word was happily cooed, Papa Perelman had a smile on his face for other reasons. His application for a casino license in Atlantic City had been unanimously accepted by the state Casino Control Commission. While speculation remained high as to what, exactly, Perelman intended to do with the license once he officially received it, insiders suggested that he would purchase an ongoing casino rather than build one from the ground up.

In a statement after his final twenty-minute hearing before the commission, Perelman cryptically said that "our plans are to look for opportunities that present themselves." He was surrounded by his normal retinue of bodyguards and advisors. "We like the gaming industry," he added. "And if you're going to be in the gaming industry, you've got to be in Atlantic City."

Seeming to share the sentiment, Stephen A. Wynn, chairman of Mirage Resorts and owner of the Mirage and Treasure Island Hotels in Las Vegas, among others, was also cleared by the commission for a gaming license in the Boardwalk City. He promptly announced plans to build a twin-casino, twin-hotel complex on what was formerly the city dump.

Back in New York, Perelman was seen lunching with his oldest son Steven in a public display of harmony. Steven, of course, was the very same son who had once blocked the construction crew's exit in East Hampton when the workers were attempting to leave the site for a weekend break. After graduating from Brown University and receiving both a Bachelor of Law and Master of Business Administration degree from the University of Pennsylvania, Steven had risen through the ranks at papa's Revlon corporation. He seemed the son that Perelman could control.

Not so with Steve's younger brother Joshua. Josh had followed Steven into the University of Pennsylvania, where he not only maintained an excellent academic record but also became a champion heavyweight wrestler on the varsity team. Despite his frequent matches, his father is said to have never once seen him wrestle. Whether by choice or because Joshua didn't want him there is a matter of speculation. What was very clear was Josh's request of his fraternity brothers, many of whose fathers knew Perelman well. His request was simple. He didn't ever want his father to learn which fraternity he had pledged.

The split between Joshua and his father deepened when the young Perelman announced his engagement to Stacy Kossow, an accountant whom he had met while attending Penn. Perelman insisted that Josh have the girl sign a prenuptial agreement to protect his son's inheritance. (Published reports that Perelman also insisted that Kossow convert to Judaism prior to the ceremony are untrue. She already was Jewish.) When Josh refused to go along with his father's demand, Perelman played hardball, threatening to boycott the wedding if the agreement wasn't signed.

When Stacy Kossow became Mrs. Joshua Perelman, Ronald Perelman kept his word. So did his son. There was no prenuptial agreement, and the older Perelman stayed away from the ceremony. Since that point, his son has stayed away from him.

Steven Perelman received the same ultimatum when he became engaged, inside sources allege. Unlike his brother, however, Steven is said to have ended the relationship to avoid a difficult situation.

If he had difficulty with his sons' romances, Ronald Perelman seemed to be having better luck with his own. While rumors swirled about bickering between Ron and Patricia, there was no sign of it in their public appearances. And in August 1995, they went public in a major way. The pair joined President and Mrs. Clinton on vacation in Jackson Hole, Wyoming.

It was hardly a camp-out for either couple. While the President and First Lady spent two weeks at Senator John D. Rockefeller IV's expansive ranch, Villa House, Ronnie and Pat plunked themselves down next door at investor Ray Minella's home, which he rented to them for $2,500 a day.

The official statement from the White House said that Clinton planned to "hike and camp and raft" (on white water, no doubt). "He's looking forward to horseback riding as well," the statement indicated. Bubba's Bar-B-Que provided the vittles; Ron Perelman, the cigars—the President being a fellow H. Uppman enthusiast.

On the MacAndrews & Forbes home front, Perelman became the subject of a sudden rash of rumors linking him with the now-out-of-prison Michael Milken. Milken was said to have been hired by Perelman to ferret out new entertainment investments for Perelman's Andrews Group. Speculation had it that MGM might be a target.

Having recently performed similar duties for Rupert Murdoch, Milken had no reason to put a lid on the talk. Perelman's official mouthpiece, James Conroy, however, denied any Perelman-Milken connection on any level. At the same time, he put the kibosh on any deal for MGM.

Perelman *was* pursuing another savings and loan. Perelman offered $32 a share to purchase San Francisco Savings & Loan, with its $4.1 billion in assets. Ford was engaged in talks for several months, and the deal was finally concluded in August 1995.

For Perelman, the end of summer meant a period of atypical calm. While wife Patricia spent the season in Connecticut, most days found the financier at his usual 8:30 A.M. breakfast meetings in Manhattan. But weekends saw Perelman spending long stretches of time at The Creeks in East Hampton, enjoying the swans that gently glided past on Georgica Pond and the glow of evening sunsets.

Sea grass edged the five fingers that formed the pond, which more accurately is a backwash from a tide pool that spills in from the Atlantic Ocean. Perelman's neighbors kept their distance, allowing him his privacy while maintaining their own.

Famous names from Hollywood were everywhere in what's now known as Malibu East. Steven Spielberg was across the way in a sprawling postmodern palace. So too were Calvin and Kelly Klein, who took privacy to a new level by importing tons of pine trees to block the curious.

The members-only Georgica Association had their annual get-together, but Perelman did not attend. He wasn't in the socializing mood—more careful now than ever to stay at home and protect the privacy of his family.

The picture-postcard serenity was not to last. Even in the tranquility of East Hampton, reality was only a meeting away—in this case, a meeting requested by Wayne Thompson, head of security at Perelman's Long Island home. The fifty-one-year-old former New York cop had an alleged request: $500,000 in cash in return for his silence. Thompson had called MacAndrews & Forbes vice-president Jaymie Durnin and said that he needed a one-on-one to discuss "bugs and newspapers." When Durnin reported the call to Perelman's vice-president of security, ex-FBI man Floyd Clarke, he wasted no time in bringing the local FBI in on the case.

Thompson and Patrick Ryan, a thirty-nine-year-old handyman on the property, were met at the East Hampton Airport by MacAndrews & Forbes's executive vice-president, Richard Halperin, the next day just after noon. According to Halperin, Thompson demanded the payment of $250,000 each in exchange for the pair's silence. Otherwise, they threatened to go to the New York Bar Association as well as the *East Hampton Star* newspaper with their information: Perelman had had rooms at The Creeks wired for sound and cinema. Bugged, as it were.

At 11 P.M. that evening, both men were met by a pair of MacAndrews & Forbes employees and each was handed a check for $250,000. FBI agents observed the transfer and, accompanied by local police, followed the pair back to Ryan's cabin. As Thompson and Ryan toasted their success with beer, the FBI agents moved in and made their arrests.

As to the bugs? In reality, they turned out to be no more than audiovisual equipment installed in the children's quarters to keep them safe and secure against kidnapping, and to alert adults to falls or other mishaps.

According to Leonard Lato, an assistant U.S. attorney, Thompson and Ryan were grossly misguided. "The security personnel for whatever reasons figured that the purpose of this device was to eavesdrop on guests."

Both men pleaded not guilty, and Ryan in particular claimed total innocence. He claimed he was only trying to tip Perelman off to an extortion attempt and nothing more. The case has yet to go to trial.

The episode did little to help Perelman's reputation as a man in need of intense security, a reputation not softened by his omnipresent bodyguards, who were equipped with high-tech surveillance devices and walkie-talkies. All the fuss was irritating to Patricia Duff, who did not like being watched, even if by her own people.

While Perelman licked his wounds inside his opulent East 63rd Street complex, a piece of his history was fading away in an estate outside of Philadelphia. Samuel Rosenblum died of cancer in his Bala Cynwyd home at the age of 82. Perelman was unaware of the death of this remarkable man who had helped launch his high-yield financial empire by selling shares in a licorice company named MacAndrews & Forbes to the Koffman Brothers in 1978. Had Perelman known, would he have paid his respects?

Perhaps: Perelman had a strong charitable streak. He was about to donate $4.74 million to Princeton University for the creation of a multidisciplinary program of Jewish learning. To be precise: the Ronald O. Perelman Institute for Jewish Studies. He was also endowing a new chairmanship, the Ronald O. Perelman Professor of Jewish Studies, at the university.

Nor had his personal interest in religion lessened. If anything, he was eager to take a more public stand in both academic and political circles to help advance Judaism. The previous June, shortly before the start of the Tepperman trial, Perelman had flown to Washington to chair a dinner at the Grand Hyatt Hotel to posthumously honor the Lubavitchers' deceased leader, Rebbe Menachem Schneerson.

Perelman had been joined on the dais by orthodox bearded rabbis, cloaked in traditional black. They sat in marked contrast to the tailored executive in his silk yarmulke and custom-made suit, attended by his son Steven, a public relations man, and an assistant carrying an attaché case and cellular phone. Regardless of the differences in his dress and lifestyle, Perelman remained deeply devoted to the Lubavitcher sect and its teachings, helping to fund the Lubavitch Center with $3.7 million.

He opened the altruistic side of his wallet once again in October, donating another $10 million to the Guggenheim Museum, this time as its president. Much of this gift was used to repay tax-exempt bonds issued by New York City for the museum's expansion and restoration program.

In November, he again underwrote the fund-raising Fire and Ice Ball in Hollywood. Or, more precisely, in Beverly Hills. In 1995, the $500–$1,000-a-plate dinner-dance was held inside the new Barney's department store on Wilshire Boulevard. Melanie Griffith joined Ron and Patricia Perelman, this time with new boyfriend Antonio Banderas on her arm. The cosmetics counters were dotted with sample Revlon giveaways.

Jack Nicholson came alone and contently watched the

other arriving stars, including Christian Slater escorting Courtney Cox, who wore an original Badgley Mischka gown. Lauren Holly, dripping satin, came with on-again, off-again beau Jim Carrey, while Sharon Stone entered stag, dolled up in a Valentino. No one outshone event co-founder Lilly Tartikoff, however. The former ballet star wore an original Isaac Mizrahi ball gown. "This program is altering the course of medicine," Lilly told the star-studded gathering, who chowed down on a meal prepared by Spago's Wolfgang Puck, drank champagne, and listened to a performance by Lyle Lovett—and all under seventeen crystal chandeliers installed for the occasion.

Suddenly Revlon seemed to be on everyone's lips, not because of the Fire and Ice Ball, but because of its latest product success. The cosmetics giant had scored a hit with its ColorStay lipstick, featuring Cindy Crawford in a series of ads. Since its introduction, the nonsmear lipstick had become the number-one seller in drug and discount stores, pacing Revlon to a banner year. With its slogan, "It won't kiss off on your teeth, your glass, or him," ColorStay LipColors had made its mark at exactly the time Revlon and its leader needed something extremely indelible—for Perelman was quietly preparing a second attempt to go public with Revlon stock in order to reduce the company's staggering $1.47 billion debt.

In recognition of Jerry Levin's success at launching the new line, Perelman promoted the executive to the post of chairman and chief executive officer. Ex-chairman Perelman took the title of chairman of the executive committee of the board of directors. George Fellows replaced Levin as president, moving over from another Revlon division.

By the end of the month, Perelman made the stock offering official and filed plans with the Securities and Exchange Commission. While the filing did not indicate the exact number and price of the issue, it did disclose that Perelman would retain more than 80 percent control for tax purposes.

There were other fascinating details in the filing, including the fact that Revlon paid $2.3 million to a trust benefiting members of Perelman's family for the rent of a warehouse in New Jersey. Among other expenditures listed was $500,000 paid for the use of a private plane to a company owned by three MacAndrews & Forbes executives, including Jerry Levin (who the filing revealed had earned $2.6 million in salary in 1994). Additionally, there was a reference to $600,000 paid by Revlon to Perelman's Consolidated Cigar for assistance in assembling lipstick cases.

With sales rising and losses falling, Revlon seemed well-positioned this time out for a successful initial public offering. Helping fuel such speculation was the enormously positive reception the week of Perelman's filing to the initial public offering of Estée Lauder Companies. It was a dramatic example of a company waiting for the perfect opportunity to strut its stuff along Wall Street, and the payoff was impressive and instantaneous.

Estée Lauder opened its stock sale at $26 a share, and it immediately leaped up $8.50. Yet the jump was more indicative of the strong profit and loss statement of the company than the prospects of cosmetics in general. Lauder carried little long-term debt, in bold contrast to Revlon.

In any case, after his Revlon filing Perelman bided his time. He turned his attention back to Marvel Entertainment, which had taken a nosedive in the market due to the sustained baseball strike. The strike had all but wiped out sales of baseball cards and put an enormous strain on the company due to its Fleer division.

In a joint venture with Planet Hollywood, Perelman announced plans to open restaurants themed around characters from Marvel Comics. While the concept of a Hulketeria left some people wondering whether the Revlon chief was becoming a comic book character himself, it didn't dissuade Perelman from scouting locations in Manhattan, Las Vegas, Orlando, and London—the usual big four for entertainment-themed restaurant launches.

There are many ways to welcome in the new year. Ronald Perelman began 1996 by making *Spy* magazine's list of "The 100 *Worst* People, Places & Things of 1995." Perelman widely missed the top spot (that belonged to fellow New Yorker, Donald Trump). "The Ronald" took a distant 28th place. According to *Spy* magazine, Perelman made the list not for dumping ex-wife Cohen or his treatment of secretaries or even building contractors. Perelman's "misdeed" wasn't even in 1995. The magazine said of him: "Sued by Fred L. Tepperman—Perelman's former CFO who had been instrumental in his amassing a $4.5 billion fortune—for firing him in 1991 after he took a Christmas vacation to spend time with his wife, who was ill with Alzheimer's disease."

He was in celebrated company. Also making *Spy*'s list in their February 1996 issue were #5: "Them Clintons"; #8: "Newty Toot Toot"; #13: "Do Me Moore"; #23: "Bob 'The Tongue' Packwood"; and #30: "Cheese-In-Crust Pizza (for those who feel the usual amount of fat and grease on a slice of pepperoni pizza just isn't enough)."

If the "honor" deflated Perelman, it certainly didn't show. The financier was thriving in the glow of renewed Wall Street interest in Revlon, thanks to his upcoming stock offering. By February, it still hadn't happened but was rumored to be imminent. Like an advertisement teasing a new product, Perelman carefully leaked bits and pieces of the offering's details during the weeks prior to its sale.

He was going to sell 15 percent of the company—some 7.5

million shares. The selling price of the initial offer was still being widely speculated about, with guesses ranging from $19 to $22 a share. At those prices, the company had a value of approximately $2.3 billion (or a net value of $1 billion after subtracting its outstanding debt). More important, Revlon was making money—and Perelman was suggesting that the time was ripe for others to share in his glory.

For the first time in years, Revlon was able to show quarterly earnings. Moments before the expected sale of stock, Revlon announced a $3.3 million net profit for the quarter (compared with a $4.4 million loss during the same period the year before). When the issue finally hit the New York Stock Exchange at the end of February, Ronald Perelman and Jerry Levin, as well as Revlon models Cindy Crawford and Claudia Schiffer, toured the exchange in a publicity stunt that almost matched the excitement generated by the stock. But not quite. At the initial offering price of $24, it was an instant hit, with investors rushing to gobble up all 7.5 million shares. Before the day's end, the stock had risen as high as $29⅝.

When someone invested in Toy Biz or Coleman or Meridian, or for that matter New World, Marvel, or even Revlon, the investment wasn't just in the company whose stock was being purchased. The investment was in Ronald Perelman, and Perelman was riding the crest of a wave in a tide that had begun forming back in Elkins Park, Pennsylvania, and had yet to recede.

With the success of the Revlon offering, rumors about other Perelman-run businesses began to swirl—the biggest of which was the imminent sale of his New World television empire to News Corp.'s Rupert Murdoch. The timing for a Murdoch buyout of New World seemed to be in his favor. With the corporation's twelve TV stations reaching 14.3 percent of the households in the United States, the company was still operating at a dramatic loss. But the bleeding of red ink was said to be nearly over by most stock analysts, and even New World's president and chief operating officer, Art Bilger, was upbeat about the future.

"My view is that 1996 is a real breakthrough year for us," he was quoted as saying. "All three pieces of our business—the stations, programming, and advertising—are starting to hum."

It was true that the company had managed to elicit some positive word-of-mouth about its three first-run syndicated series, "Access Hollywood," "Two," and "Loveline." Additionally, it had moderate success with its prime-time series "Second Noah," picked up for a second season by ABC.

The federal government cooperated as well with the signing in February 1996 of a new Telecommunications Act which saw some dramatic deregulation of the industry. Chief among the new rules was one that limited the number of television stations any single broadcaster could own. The previous maximum was twelve. Under the new rules, a single broadcaster was restricted only to the number of viewers its owned stations could reach—up from the former 25 percent of viewers to a new high of 35 percent.

According to Booz, Allen & Hamilton analyst Michael Wolf, "With the wider ownership rules, the logical merger partner for New World would be News Corp. The question is going to be at what price."

By March, the price that Murdoch was offering for New World was pegged at $21 a share. The price Perelman was asking: in the neighborhood of $28. Two months later, despite a lot of back-and-forth conversation, the deal appeared to be a dead issue, with neither party anxious to move from their price point.

They weren't going to sell New World, and it was apparent that they needed to grow. New World started to look around for new opportunities, and the best that they saw was a company called King World.

King World was one of the largest domestic distributors of syndicated television programming, representing such Top Ten series as "Jeopardy," "Wheel of Fortune," and "The Oprah Winfrey Show." It was also widely known that the company's chairman and president—brothers Roger and Michael King—had been pursuing buyers for over a year. (A $1.8 billion bid for the company by broadcasting entrepreneur Ted Turner had been scuttled by Turner Broadcasting System's board of directors the previous year as being too high.)

The buyout seemed ideal for both companies. King World would receive a ready-made station base from which to launch new programming, and New World would get an influx of cash. At the time of the talks, King World was said to have $529 million in available cash and be generating around $200 million in cash flow per year.

New World, by comparison, found itself with close to a billion dollars in debt, and continuing to lose money. In an effort to improve its financial position, the company had moved to sell its two NBC affiliates—KNSD in San Diego and WVTM in Birmingham, Alabama—for $425 million. With an annual cash flow of about $130 million, New World was struggling under its debt load. A King World deal would not only have taken care of the debt but doubled the company's cash flow as well.

By the week following the July 4 holiday, the King World sale to New World should have been a done deal. Estimates suggest that the selling price was $1.5 billion and that all parties had agreed in principle to the terms of the contract. Despite completion of documents by the New World Communications Group lawyers, King World was still nit-picking.

"There was always some excuse," a party close to the negotiations confided. "Basically, Perelman was eager to close the deal and get on with business. The King brothers moved at a different pace. At one point things were in place, but I understand some of their board was on vacation. Highly unusual for a company that's really interested in selling."

Stock analysts were quick to speculate that the purchase of King World was likely little more than a ruse to force Rupert Murdoch back to the bargaining table before the cost to buy New World became too rich even for the media entrepreneur. It was a charge that Perelman repeatedly denied.

In any case, Perelman was not behind the delays that kept the King World deal from closing, allowing one last window of opportunity for a Murdoch move. It was to come during the week following Independence Day at the annual summer retreat hosted by investment banker Herbert A. Allen. Every day of the week-long outing for executives and their families began with early morning seminars followed by family sporting events and private dinners. And it was at one such dinner that Murdoch approached Perelman and expressed his continuing interest in New World.

For Ronald Perelman, the moment was nirvana. With the pressure from the impending King World deal and the prospect of a Murdoch move, it was a billion-dollar horse race with a finish line only days away. It wasn't until late Sunday afternoon that Murdoch made his move to contact Perelman again, this time with a firm offer for New World minus any King World acquisition.

The final agreement for the King World deal was due to be presented to the two companies' boards of directors two days later on Tuesday, July 16. The King World board was meeting at 9 A.M. to ratify the agreement; the New World board at 2 P.M., same day, same agenda. On July 15 at 5 P.M., however,

Ron Perelman received a call from New World Communications chief William Bevins saying that the King brothers had some new demands—demands that were termed "deal breakers."

"If they are deal breakers, they're deal breakers," came the official MacAndrews & Forbes response. And with that sentence, the King World company went back on the open market, and the way was cleared for Rupert Murdoch to close his own deal for New World Communications.

"It all came down to hours," a source reported. "It could really have gone either way." Unusual perhaps for some companies, but not MacAndrews & Forbes. It was just such last-minute flexibility and the ability to move quickly that had become the hallmark of Ronald Perelman.

The final deal called for Murdoch's News Corp. to pay 1.45 shares of its preferred limited voting stock in exchange for each share of New World common stock. With the deal expected to close early in 1997, the sale price ultimately would be determined by the value of News Corp. stock, but estimates by Bloomberg Business News placed the sale price at near $3 billion ($2.48 billion in stock and the assumption of $590 million in New World debt). Of the total, nearly $1 billion would go directly to Ronald Perelman.

With the addition of New World's ten broadcast outlets, Rupert Murdoch and his Fox network became the world's leading TV station owners—a total of twenty-two stations. Yet it was Perelman who received most of the positive press, due chiefly to the high sale price he received.

"Perelman simply played a better poker game in the final round," according to media analyst Art Rockwell of Yaeger Capital Markets.

As it turned out, it wasn't the only billion-dollar deal that Perelman had on his plate. Only twelve days later, on July 29,

Perelman dropped $1.2 billion to purchase California Federal Bank through his First Nationwide Holdings division of MacAndrews & Forbes. The merger of First Nationwide with CalFed created the fourth-largest S&L in the country with 242 branches in three states—California, Florida, and Texas. The deal was structured by Perelman's partner, Gerald Ford, who commented that "we have almost doubled the size of the company, but more importantly, we've enhanced the franchise of the combined companies."

Indeed the merger seemed a perfect fit, with most of First Nationwide's branches in Northern California, and the majority of CalFed's in the southern half of the state. While Ford suggested that the CalFed logo would hang over the combined companies, sources close to Perelman indicated that he preferred the First Nationwide name. Regardless of the moniker, the deal was looked upon by many analysts as the start of a new merger-mania in the savings and loan industry, with many suggesting that Perelman would be eager to gobble up more.

"He's the consummate businessman," said a former top Revlon executive. "He buys, he sells, he deals. And while he may not be gentle in his ways, he does things legally, if not ethically—which is a lot more than many corporate heads do."

Still, even as he lauded Perelman, this executive voiced a profoundly troubling insight into a man who should, by anyone's standard, have the world by the tail.

"Here is a man who appears to fear nothing. Yet, when you know him, *really* know him, you sense that he fears everything. He hides it well under his success, and impatience, and beautiful wives; his brilliance in negotiating, his limos, his cigars. But it's there—the fear, I mean. It never leaves. Perhaps it's because for all his success on a business level, he has yet to really learn how to deal on a human one. With emotions, and compassion, and discovering that there is something more important than net profit."

The executive went on to describe a working vacation which several top executives of Perelman's companies took to a tropical paradise. "He was never able to relax, to empty his mind of the next deal. Even in the pool, he was on his cellular phone."

As for those who had come and gone (or come and stayed) in Perelman's life, fates have varied widely. Fred Tepperman, the aggrieved chief financial officer, moved permanently to Boca Raton, Florida, where he found little comfort with a new employer. Less than two months after receiving his undisclosed settlement from Perelman, Tepperman was back in court, this time suing Bio-Magnetic Therapy Systems, the medical equipment manufacturer that had hired him after MacAndrews & Forbes dropped its ax.

According to Tepperman, the Florida firm failed to pay him for 347 hours of consulting work he furnished them between February and April. Tepperman alleged that he had agreed in principle to take the job of president of Bio-Magnetic at a salary of $400,000 a year, a considerable drop from his previous high of $1,300,000 under Perelman. He also claimed to have been offered stock options and profit sharing in the suit.

Brandon Tartikoff announced his resignation from New World at the time of the company's sale to News Corp. According to inside sources, he returned to independent production smiling and "a very rich man." He continued to make the commute between New Orleans and Los Angeles.

As for Perelman's triumvirate of lieutenants—Howard Gittis, Bruce Slovin, and Donald Drapkin—they continued to be the boss's best friends, sharing lox and bagels at breakfast, and a power lunch nearly every day. Like Perelman himself, they were always looking forward to the next deal, the next crisis, the next victory, from their command post on East 62nd Street.

Perelman's first wife, Faith Golding, happily married a prominent Manhattan plastic surgeon and still radiated much of the quiet charm that attracted Perelman to her when she was a seventeen-year-old. She continued to live in their original Park Avenue digs, surrounded by luxury and loved by her children.

Steven Perelman rose within the Revlon corporation to run the fragrance division and was said to possess many of his father's business skills.

Joshua Perelman graduated from the University of Pennsylvania and entered the accounting profession, along with his wife Stacy. He remained estranged from his father.

Hope Perelman graduated in 1995 from the University of Pennsylvania and chose a career in teaching.

Deborah Perelman graduated in 1996 from Princeton University and was said to be weighing offers from graduate schools.

Perelman's second wife, Claudia Cohen, after having announced her undying love for Senator Alfonse D'Amato, found the romance too difficult given the demands of their work and family commitments. They officially broke up, as they had started, in front of the press. "We've decided to remain the best of friends and see each other whenever we can," Cohen was quoted in New York's *Daily News*. Cohen's entertainment reports continued to be featured on the syndicated talk show "Live with Regis & Kathie Lee." She was still spotted on the usual circuit of premieres, parties, and black-tie dinners, and in August 1996 filed another suit against her ex-husband for failing to keep up with his alimony payments.

Daughter Samantha Perelman proves precocious, outgoing, and her father's favorite movie date.

Patricia Duff Perelman continued to be active in Democratic Party fund-raisers and independent as ever. Nevertheless, Patricia has managed to leave her imprint on a variety of fields. As the new president of the Revlon Foundation, she was said to be expanding the cosmetics giant's philanthropic focus, which until recently had been largely centered on educational facilities as well as breast and ovarian cancer research. On her own agenda, not surprisingly, were the environment and children.

She was Perelman's proud companion at the Metropolitan Museum of Art's black-tie bash for its Costume Institute and at the Fire and Ice Ball in Beverly Hills. Those around MacAndrews & Forbes's offices have admired her extraordinarily low-key attitude—in comparison to Claudia Cohen, at least. Her penthouse office in MacAndrews & Forbes's East 62nd Street headquarters exuded quiet energy. But not always.

During the 1996 Democratic Convention, Ron Perelman's notoriously short fuse touched the high-octane drive of Patricia Duff. The result: an explosion that threatened to rip wide their home-front harmony. Reports suggest that Duff incited her husband's wrath by attending a party for Vice President Al Gore without Perelman's permission. Rumor has it he'd discovered that Duff had been in contact with her divorce attorneys weeks before the convention. Push came to shove during the couple's limo ride to Chicago's United Center, where they were to hear President Clinton's acceptance speech.

While Duff dug in her high heels and stayed, Perelman took a detour to the airport, where his private jet was waiting to whisk him quietly back to New York. Once there, he called the locksmiths and had the locks on Duff's penthouse office changed, then pink-slipped her two secretaries to further prove exactly who was the boss.

"They're both emotional. What do you expect?" responded sources within the Perelman camp. "They fight, they kiss, they make up."

Despite their personal animosity, daughter Caleigh Sophia remains the love of both of their lives.

And as for Ronald Owen Perelman . . . at press time, he continued to buy and sell properties with the same enthusiasm for doing business he had displayed since childhood. Despite the fact that he had by now made more money than most Third World countries' national budgets, he showed no sign of stopping or even slowing down.

His charitable contributions continued to be far-flung, ranging from the $14,533,834 he gave Machne Israel to the $12,003,383 he awarded the Salvation Army. There was $1.6 million to the Collegiate School, another $1.3 million to Brandeis University, just over a million each to Carnegie Hall and the Metropolitan Opera, an even million to the Survivors of the Shoah and to the Ronald Reagan Presidential Foundation, plus lesser amounts to the National Multiple Sclerosis Society, the United Way of Tri State, the United Negro College Fund, Camp Gan Israel, and the New York City Outward Bound Center.

Still surrounded by security guards, Perelman continued to enjoy private walks. But, even more, he preferred being in bed by 10 P.M. The cigar remained, the arrogance remained, as did the impatience.

According to Donald Drapkin, "Ronald is pretty simple. He wants to be happy, he wants to enjoy his companies, and he wants to have a few laughs." Not much to ask, when money is king.

SOURCE NOTES

Much of this book is based on interviews conducted with a variety of individuals whose lives have been intertwined with Ronald Owen Perelman and his family. From company executives to classmates, business competitors to family friends, they all share two things in common—knowledge of the behavior of Ron Perelman and a desire to remain anonymous because of it. For that reason alone, many credible sources remain uncredited to protect their identity.

In addition, the following articles and references were used extensively to piece together many of the facts relating to the life of Ronald Perelman, who, despite his stated wish to live his life away from the scrutiny of the press, managed to be chronicled in over 600 news reports and stories. Articles appearing without bylines carried no author refcrence. Page numbers refer to East Coast late editions. Page numbers in other editions may vary. Sources of direct quotations within the text are generally not included, for to do so would have become tedious within the structure of the work.

"4 Top Execs at Revlon Get New Duties," *Women's Wear Daily*, November 17, 1995, page 2.

"$10 Million Donation to Penn," *New York Times*, November 6, 1988, page 41.

Daniel Akst, "Compact Video Seeks Chain of Drugstores," *Los Angeles Times*, February 8, 1986, page IV, 3.

John Anderson, "Venturesome Capital," *Texas Monthly*, November 1990, page 42.

Kevin Anderson, "Perelman In on Transworld," *USA Today*, October 27, 1986, page 2B.

"Andrews Group Inc.," *New York Times*, June 6, 1989, page D4.

"Andrews Group Inc.," *New York Times*, May 27, 1989, page A33.

"Andrews Group Inc.," *New York Times*, May 10, 1989, page D4.

"Another Perelman Coup?" *New York*, March 31, 1986, page 22.

"Another Stab at Gillette," *Time*, August 31, 1987, page 41.

Susan Antilla, "Off Hours, a Man of Society," *USA Today*, April 17, 1989, page 5B.

Susan Antilla, "Perelman's Latest Tack: Friendly Deals," *USA Today*, April 17, 1989, page 5B.

Associated Press, "Settle Reached in Perelman Lawsuit," *Newsday*, July 19, 1995, page A35.

Associated Press, "Clinton Defends Accepting 'Soft-money' Donations," *Philadelphia Inquirer*, June 23, 1994, page A3.

Associated Press, "Cruel Portrait of Perelman in Suite by Fired Executive," *Newsday*, July 6, 1995, page A37.

Associated Press, "Revlon Tender Bid by Perelman Group," *New York Times*, April 2, 1987, page D5.

Associated Press, "Takeover Studied for MacAndrews," *New York Times*, May 17, 1983, page D4.

Associated Press, "Tartikoff Is Moving to New World," *Philadelphia Inquirer*, June 15, 1994, page F3.

Associated Press, "U.S. Spends $890 Million on S&L Sold to Perelman Firm," *Los Angeles Times*, March 10, 1990, page D2.

"Attracting Large Canvases," *Art News*, March 1994, page 36.

Blake Bailey, "Dream-house Confidential: The Renovatin' Perelmans—They're Back!" *Spy*, May 1991, page 78.

Malcolm Balfour, "Billionaire Sells Palm Beach Home," *New York Post*, July 13, 1995, page 14.

"Bankruptcy Judge Gives Perelman Control of SCI TV," *New York Times*, May 7, 1993, page D3.

Al Barker, S. C. Michael, and Claffey and Corkey Siemaszko, "Ron Aides Held in Extort Try," *New York Daily News*, August 30, 1995, page E14.

Geraldine Baum, "New Video on Women's Cancers," *Philadelphia Inquirer*, November 15, 1990, page D11.

Leslie Baum, "Buying Off One Raider—and Getting Ready for Another," *Business Week*, November 17, 1986, page 68.

Lisa Belkin, "Perelman: Moving Up Quietly," *New York Times*, November 18, 1986, page D1.

Lisa Belkin, "The Prisoner of Seventh Avenue," *New York Times*, March 15, 1987, page D16.

Lisa Belkin, "Restoring the Magic at Revlon," *New York Times*, January 7, 1986, page D1.

"Belmont Industries Holding Talks on Sale of Ironworks," *Wall Street Journal*, May 27, 1970, page 6.

"Belmont Iron Holders Vote 3-for-1 Split, Rise in Shares," *Wall Street Journal*, September 3, 1968, page 16.

"Belmont Iron Works Plans to Buy P&C Holding Corp.," *Wall Street Journal*, September 13, 1967, page 28.

Anthony Bianco, "Salomon and Revlon: What Really Happened," *Business Week*, October 12, 1987, page 156.

"Billionaire, Former Aide Settle Dispute," *Los Angeles Times*, July 19, 1995, page D2.

Fred R. Bleakley, "Buying Back, and Buying Off," *New York Times*, November 13, 1986, page D2.

Sandra Block, "Buffett's Wealth Hits $16.6 Billion," *USA Today*, February 29, 1996, page 1B.

Sandra Block, "Offering Puts Revlon in New Light," *USA Today*, March 1, 1996, page 3B.

Bloomberg Business News, "Ex-Perelman Aide Sues New Employer," *New York Times*, September 8, 1995, page D6.

Bloomberg Business News, "Perelman Seeks Casino License," *New York Times*, December 24, 1994, page 42.

David Blum, "The Shy Stripper," *New York*, November 18, 1985, page 38.

"Boat People," *Esquire*, March 1994, page 28.

"Borghese and Halston Lines Are Sold to Saudi Investors," *Wall Street Journal*, January 21, 1992, page A4.

Chris Boulding, "Advertising Challenge to Power of the Press," *Independent*, October 9, 1994, page 17.

Harriet Johnson Brackey, "Perelman Buys New World Studio," *USA Today*, April 11, 1989, page 1B.

Rhonda Brammer, "Thing of Beauty? A Hard Look at Revlon's Proposed Offering," *Barron's,* June 1, 1992, page 14.

Steve Brennan and Lisa de Moraes, "Tartikoff's Out: More to Follow," *Hollywood Reporter,* July 18, 1996, page 1.

Leslie Brody with Alan Farnham, David Kirkpatrick, et al., "Big Investors on Wall Street," *Fortune,* October 26, 1987, page 8.

Nancy Rivera Brooks, "Revlon Drops Takeover Bid for Gillette, Sells Back Shares," *Los Angeles Times,* November 25, 1986, page IV,1.

Nadine Brozan, "Ronald O. Perelman," *New York Times,* September 22, 1995, page B6.

Connie Bruck, *The Predators Ball: The Junk-bond Raiders and the Man Who Stalked Them.* New York: Simon and Schuster, 1985.

Neil Budde, "Merger Raids Run Rampant in Stock Rally," *USA Today,* March 9, 1987, page 1B.

Elisabeth Bumiller, "Amore D'Amato: The Senator, the Rich Guy & His 2 Wives," *Washington Post,* February 28, 1995, page D1.

Graham Button, "Perelman Moves Up," *Forbes,* October 19, 1992, page 16.

Graham Button, "Tough Transition," *Forbes,* January 3, 1994, page 14.

Christopher Byron, "Happily Ever After," *Esquire,* April 1995, page 58.

Christopher Byron, "Pressure on Perelman," *New York,* November 26, 1990, page 22.

Mariann Caprino, "Revlon Inc. Arranging $500 Million Line of Credit," *Philadelphia Inquirer,* April 21, 1992, page D18.

Mariann Caprino, "Revlon Will Sell Stock to Cut Its Debt Burden," *Philadelphia Inquirer,* May 27, 1992, page B5.

David Carey, "Can Raiders Run What They Raid?" *Fortune,* June 4, 1990, page 193.

Bill Carter, "Fox Will Sign Up 12 New Stations; Takes 8 From CBS," *New York Times,* May 24, 1994, page A1.

Dennis Cauchon, "High Rollers Could Reap Big Profits," *USA Today,* December 30, 1988, page 1B.

Dennis Cauchon, "Perelman, Bass Take Over 2 S&Ls," *USA Today,* December 29, 1988, page 1B.

Kenneth Chang, "Splaaaaaaat! Comic Books No Longer Reaping Big Sales in Single Bound," *Los Angeles Times,* March 2, 1996, page D1.

"Chase Manhattan Corp.," *Wall Street Journal,* March 16, 1993, page A3.

"Checkmate for the King of Junk Bonds," *U.S. News and World Report*, February 6, 1989, page 44.

Christopher Chipello and Ann Hagedorn, "Revlon Proposes to Buy Gillette and Is Rebuffed," *Wall Street Journal*, June 19, 1987, page 3.

Alan Citron and John Lippman, "Barry Diller: Up to What, With Whom?" *Los Angeles Times*, March 18, 1992, page D5.

Marjorie Coeyman, "Perelman Plans a Marvel-ous New Chain," *Restaurant Business*, October 10, 1995, page 2.

Laurie P. Cohen, "TV Deal Propels Ron Perelman Onto the Hollywood Firmament," *Wall Street Journal*, May 25, 1994, page B1.

Robert J. Cole, "Bergerac's Retreat Discussed," *New York Times*, October 15, 1985, page D21.

Robert J. Cole, "Family Clash on MacAndrews," *New York Times*, June 18, 1983, page D32.

Robert J. Cole, "A Fight to Acquire Revlon Is Expected," *New York Times*, August 17, 1985, page 37.

Robert J. Cole, "High-stakes Drama at Revlon," *New York Times*, November 11, 1985, page D1.

Robert J. Cole, "Pantry Bid Is Opposed by Revlon," *New York Times*, August 20, 1985, page D1.

Robert J. Cole, "Pantry Pride Revlon Bid Raised by $1.75 a Share," *New York Times*, October 19, 1985, page 34.

Robert J. Cole, "Perelman Is Said to Sell CPC Stock," *New York Times*, November 7, 1986, page D1.

Robert J. Cole, "Perelman Seeks Stake in Salomon," *New York Times*, September 29, 1987, page D1.

Robert J. Cole, "Perelman Stock Sale Fuels Takeover Talk," *New York Times*, September 14, 1988, page D1.

Robert J. Cole, "Perelman Trademark: An Ability to Act Fast," *New York Times*, December 29, 1988, page D2.

Robert J. Cole, "Revlon Loses a Takeover Ruling," *New York Times*, October 24, 1985, page D1.

Robert J. Cole, "Revlon Off in Absence of Bid," *New York Times*, August 16, 1985, page D3.

Robert J. Cole, "Revlon Reportedly Protests Bank's Role in Bid," *New York Times*, August 21, 1985, page D2.

Robert J. Cole, "Revlon Yields Its Right Early," *New York Times*, September 15, 1987, page D1.

Robert J. Cole, "Salomon Reassured on Revlon," *New York Times*, September 30, 1987, page D1.

Robert J. Cole, "Speculation Centers on Jacobs in Gillette Buying," *New York Times*, July 13, 1987, page D5.

Robert J. Cole, "Takeover Accepted by Revlon," *New York Times*, November 2, 1985, page 35.

Robert J. Cole, "A Victory by Revlon Seen Near," *New York Times*, August 28, 1985, page D1.

Glenn Collins, "Revlon Pushes an Offering at as Much as $22 a Share," *New York Times*, February 6, 1996, page D1.

Mark M. Colodny, "LBO Man," *Fortune*, July 15, 1991, page 12.

Jennet Conant, "On Golden Pond," *Vanity Fair*, August 1995, page 60.

Jennet Conant, "The Good Life: Star Reporter," *Harper's Bazaar*, November 1989, page 146.

Jennet Conant, "Working Girl," *Esquire*, September 1994, page 144.

Chuck Conconi, "Personalities," *Washington Post*, June 2, 1989, page D3.

Michael Connor, "Seagram Considers Sale of Time Warner Stock," *Philadelphia Inquirer*, April 11, 1995, page C1.

"Contenders for Rich List," *New York Times*, May 11, 1989, page D5.

James Cook, "Back to Business," *Forbes*, October 5, 1987, page 40.

"Cooper Industries Plans Purchase and Merger," *New York Times*, November 22, 1994, page D5.

Erica Copulsky, "Perelman's New World—the Next Paramount," *Portfolio Newsletter*, April 25, 1994, page 1.

"Corrections & Amplifications," *Wall Street Journal*, April 9, 1982, page 4.

"Couples," *Philadelphia Inquirer*, April 13, 1994, page C2.

"Couples," *Philadelphia Inquirer*, December 1, 1993, page C4.

"Court Gives Revlon a Stay," *New York Times*, October 25, 1985, page D5.

Alison Leigh Cowan, "Perelman Says Quest for Gillette Isn't Over," *New York Times*, April 15, 1988, page D3.

Alison Leigh Cowan, "Revlon Asks to Bid for Gillette," *New York Times*, August 18, 1987, page D1.

"CPC Stock Sold," *New York Times*, November 6, 1986, page D3.

"The Credible Perelman," *Forbes*, May 15, 1989, page 164.

Gregory Crouch, "Perelman Puts Video Unit to Work," *Los Angeles Times*, March 3, 1988, page IV,6.

John Crudele, "A Buyout of Revlon Is Studied," *New York Times*, March 7, 1987, page A35.

John Crudele, "CPC Seeks Corporate Reshaping," *New York Times*, November 5, 1986, page D1.

John Crudele, "Forstmann in Buyout of Revlon," *New York Times*, October 14, 1985, page D1.

John Crudele, "New Bid, as Revlon Hints at Buyout," *New York Times*, October 3, 1985, page D1.

John Crudele, "Pantry Bid for Revlon up to $56.25," *New York Times*, October 8, 1985, page D1.

John Crudele, "Pantry Pride Cuts Revlon Bid," *New York Times*, September 14, 1985, page 33.

John Crudele, "Pantry Pride Raises Revlon Bid to $50," *New York Times*, September 28, 1985, page 37.

John Crudele, "Revlon Buyout Held Workable," *New York Times*, October 2, 1985, page D1.

John Crudele, "Rorer Buys Drug Unit of Revlon," *New York Times*, November 30, 1985, page 29.

John Curran, "2nd Billionaire, Perelman This Time, Bets on Atlantic City," *Philadelphia Inquirer*, December 23, 1994, page S2.

"D'Amato and Wife Granted a Divorce," *New York Times*, April 8, 1995, page 27.

Jeffrey Daniels, "It's Payday for Perelman," *Hollywood Reporter*, July 18, 1996, page 8.

Jeffrey Daniels, "Murdoch Has the Whole New World in His Hands," *Hollywood Reporter*, July 18, 1996, page 1.

Mark Davis, "The Financier Didn't Say if He Is After a Particular One," *Philadelphia Inquirer*, July 27, 1995, page C1.

Kathleen Day, "A Look at One Investor's S&L Bargain," *Washington Post*, March 12, 1989, page H1.

Francis X. Dealy, Jr., "Pearlstine Before Swine," *Spy*, June 1993, page 44.

Al Delugach, "British Concern Agrees to Buy Technicolor, Inc.," *Los Angeles Times*, September 10, 1988, page V,1.

Al Delugach, "Jilting Parretti, New World Sells Out to Perelman for $145 Million," *Los Angeles Times*, April 11, 1989, page IV,1.

Kathleen Deveny, "Perelman's Vaunted Marketing Skills Produce Only Mixed Results at Revlon," *Wall Street Journal*, March 4, 1991, page B1.

Dan Dorfman, "Newsletter: Raider Might Launch Bid for Philip Morris," *USA Today*, October 17, 1988, page 2B.

Dan Dorfman, "Perelman Rumor Boosts Sears Stock," *USA Today*, October 6, 1988, page 1B.

Dow Jones, "Perelman Stake of 2.6 Million Shares in BankAmerica Is Going on Market," *American Banker*, February 1, 1993, page 13.

Dow Jones, "Soros Group Buys a Stake," *New York Times*, January 27, 1995, page D5.

Georgia Dullea, "Chronicle: Cigar Bands Are Pink for Ronald Perelman and Patricia Duff," *New York Times*, December 16, 1994, page B9.

Brian Dumaine, "Earning More by Moving Faster," *Fortune*, October 7, 1991, page 89.

Amy Dunkin, with Laurie Baum and Lois Therrien, "This Takeover Artist Wants to Be Makeover Artist, Too," *Business Week*, December 1, 1986, page 106.

"Editorial: Hearst Not Only Loser," *Advertising Age*, August 29, 1994, page 19.

Jack Egan, "White-Knight Time on Wall Street," *U.S. News & World Report*, October 12, 1987, page 60.

Kurt Eichenwald, "$250 Million Stake Seen in Shearson by Investor," *New York Times*, December 7, 1989, page D2.

Kurt Eichenwald, "Market Place: Maneuvering at Marvel Comics Vanquishes the Short-sellers," *New York Times*, March 26, 1993, page D4.

Kurt Eichenwald, "Revlon Head Reported in Shearson Talks," *New York Times*, December 6, 1989, page D1.

Judith Evans, "Company Secret No More: Fired Aide Alleges More Perelman Foibles in Testimony," *Newsday*, July 11, 1995, page A25.

Judith Evans, "Perelman Aide Recounts Quarrel," *Newsday*, July 8, 1995, page A13.

"Eye Scoop," *Women's Wear Daily*, June 6, 1995, page 3.

"Eye Scoop: Ronald Perelman," *Women's Wear Daily*, December 16, 1993, page 16.

"Eye Scoop: Ronald Perelman," *Women's Wear Daily*, August 31, 1993, page 4.

"Eye: Hollywood Dresses Up," *Women's Wear Daily*, November 16, 1995, page 4.

"The Fab Parties," *Premiere*, June 1996, page 101.

Geraldine Fabrikant, "King World Said to Be in Talks Over Acquisition by New World," *New York Times*, June 15, 1996, page C1.

Geraldine Fabrikant, "Perelman Agrees to Acquire Control of SCI Television," *New York Times*, February 18, 1993, page D22.

Geraldine Fabrikant and Shelby White, "Noblesse Oblige . . . with Strings," *New York Times*, April 30, 1995, page C1.

Fairchild News Service, "Perelman Fined for Exceeding Limit in Political Contributions," *Women's Wear Daily*, March 18, 1993, page 11.

Fairchild News Service, "Revlon's Perelman May Testify in Tepperman Suit," *Women's Wear Daily*, June 23, 1995, page 15.

Esther B. Fein, "Latter-day Celebrities," *New York Times*, November 4, 1992, page C21.

Andrew Feinberg, "Fanciful Theories on Perelman's Obsession with Gillette," *New York Times*, August 23, 1987, page C8.

James Feron, "Proxy Firm Founder Pleads Guilty to Theft and Fraud," *New York Times*, March 21, 1990, page D5.

"Financier Ronald Perelman," *Television Digest*, February 22, 1993, page 7.

"First Nationwide to Get San Francisco S&L," *New York Times*, August 29, 1995, page D5.

Daniel Fischel, *Payback: The Conspiracy to Destroy Michael Milken and His Financial Revolution.* New York: HarperBusiness, 1995.

Alison Fitzgerald, "Bally's Park Place Announces a Plan to Become A.C.'s Largest," *Philadelphia Inquirer*, February 8, 1995, page S1.

Alison Fitzgerald and Thomas Turcol, "A Casino Land Sale Reveals How A.C. Prices Have Sunk," *Philadelphia Inquirer*, December 30, 1994, page A1.

James Flanigan, "Appeasement's Price," *Financial World*, October 6, 1987, page 16.

Geoffrey Foisie, "Battle of the Billionaires," *Broadcasting & Cable*, March 15, 1993, page 48.

Geoffrey Foisie, "It's a New World for Ronald Perelman," *Broadcasting & Cable*, January 3, 1994, page 46.

Geoffrey Foisie, "SCI-TV Gets a Makeover," *Broadcasting & Cable*, February 22, 1993, page 47.

Geoffrey Foisie, "SCI-TV Readies for 'Vertical Integration,'" *Broadcasting & Cable*, July 19, 1993, page 46.

"The Forbes Four Hundred: Ronald Owen Perelman," *Forbes*, October 17, 1994, page 107.

Michael Freeman, "The Genesis of Perelman," *Mediaweek*, March 28, 1994, page 9.

Michael Freeman, "NBC, New World Near Affiliation, Program Pact," *Mediaweek*, July 10, 1995, page 7.

Mike Freeman, "New 'Mini-studio' Rumored," *Broadcasting & Cable*, August 2, 1993, page 15.

Brett Duval Fromson, "The Screwiest S&L Bailout Ever," *Fortune*, June 19, 1989, page 114.

Charles Gandee, "Holding Her Own," *Vogue*, April 1996, page 308.

Juliann Garey, "A Tristar Is Reborn," *Entertainment Weekly*, April 16, 1993, page 12.

Charles Gasparino and Pamela Mendels, "$30M Suit Raises Compassion Issue," *Newsday*, July 7, 1995, page A33.

Robert Gearty, "Perelman Settles Ex-Aide's $38M Suit," *New York Daily News*, July 19, 1995, page 2.

Robert Gearty and Jane Furse, "Ex-Aide Sez Revlon Big Misled Banks," *New York Daily News*, July 11, 1995, page 10.

Robert Gearty and Jane Furse, "Explosive Charges: Former Top Aide Was a Thief, Perelman Says in Statement," *New York Daily News*, July 8, 1995, page 3.

Robert Gearty and Jane Furse, "I'm No Cheater, Sez Perelman Foe," *New York Daily News*, July 13, 1995, page 24.

Robert Gearty and Jane Furse, "Vacation Note Trips Fired Exec," *New York Daily News*, July 12, 1995, page 10.

Robert Gearty and Jane Furse with George Rush, "Perelman Returns Fire: Mogul's Lawyer Tells Court of Axed Exec's Mistress," *New York Daily News*, July 7, 1995, page 1.

Debra Gendel, "People Who Need Stylish People," *Los Angeles Times*, March 13, 1995, page V,5.

William Giese, "Gillette Pays, Revlon Scrams; Greenmail Is In," *USA Today*, November 25, 1986, page 1B.

"Gillette Accused Perelman of Insider Trading," *Los Angeles Times*, November 20, 1986, page IV,2.

"Gillette Greenmail Has Traders Peeved," *USA Today*, November 26, 1986, page 2B.

"Gillette Sued to Block Revlon's Takeover Bid," *Los Angeles Times*, November 18, 1986, page IV,2.

"Gillette Wins Court Test," *New York Times*, June 27, 1987, page D1.

Kenneth N. Gilpin, "Gillette Rejects Revlon Bid," *New York Times*, August 25, 1987, page D1.

"Good Friend for Gutfreund," *Economist (London)*, October 3, 1987, page 88.

Howard Goodman, "$69 Million Face-lift Set for Penn," *Philadelphia Inquirer*, April 21, 1995, page B1.

William Goodwin, "New Load to Revlon Group Goes Into Syndication," *American Banker*, May 2, 1990, page 10.

Cynthia Green, "25 Executives to Watch in 1986," *Business Week*, April 18, 1986, page 230.

Jay Greene, "Perelman: Deep Pockets and Big Showbiz Ambitions," *Variety*, January 24, 1994, page 39.

Steven Greenhouse, "New Ways to Stop a Corporate Raider," *New York Times*, August 22, 1985, page D4.

John Greenwald, "Predator's Fall," *Time*, February 26, 1990, page 46.

Alex Gregory and Peter Huyck, "The Spy 100," *Spy*, February 1996, page 54.

Joe Haberstroh, "Confusion Seen in Perelman Extortion," *Newsday*, August 31, 1995, page A26.

Haligoluk. Haverford, Pennsylvania: Haverford School Press, 1960.

Keith H. Hammonds, "Gillette Inches Closer to the Razor's Edge," *Business Week*, February 29, 1988, page 36.

Keith H. Hammonds, "Gillette May Be Getting Closer to the Blade," *Business Week*, April 25, 1988, page 84.

Amy Harmon, "Deals: Studios," *New York Times*, August 18, 1995, page D4.

Amanda Harris with Kevin Flynn and Michael Weber, "A Contest With Deep Pockets," *Newsday*, October 28, 1994, page A7.

Kathryn Harris, "Broadcasting's Creators of a New World," *Los Angeles Times*, June 18, 1994, page D1.

Kathryn Harris, "Tri-Star Sells 9% of Its Stock to Perelman," *Los Angeles Times*, November 20, 1986, page IV,2.

Jennifer Havilah, "Asec Exec Says Perelman Inflated Number$," *New York Post*, July 11, 1995, page 3.

Jennifer Havilah, "Axed Aide Tells of Testy Tycoon's Temper Tantrums," *New York Post*, July 8, 1995, page 2.

Jennifer Havilah, "Ex-Perelman Exec Tripped Up by Own Diary," *New York Post*, July 12, 1995, page 10.

Jennifer Havilah, "Perelman & Fired Top Exec Settle for at Least $10M," *New York Post,* July 19, 1995, page 2.

Jennifer Havilah, "Perelman Case Gets Down and Dirtier," *New York Post,* July 7, 1995, page 3.

Jennifer Havilah, "Perelman: Fired Exec Was Out to Cheat Me," *New York Post,* July 13, 1995, page 14.

Jennifer Havilah, "Xmas Vacation Spelled End for Perelman Exec," *New York Post,* July 14, 1995, page 12.

Thomas C. Hayes, "Perelman Group Wins Bidding for San Antonio Savings," *New York Times,* March 10, 1990, page A32.

Thomas C. Hayes, "Talking Deals: A Veil of Secrecy in Texas Rescues," *New York Times,* December 29, 1988, page D2.

Kevin Helliker, "Coleman to Offer Public a Stake of 16%," *Wall Street Journal,* February 26, 1992, page 4.

Daniel Heneghan, "Perelman Seeks A.C. Casino License," *Atlantic City Press,* December 22, 1994, page C5.

Diana B. Henriques, "Acquisition of Technicolor Under Court Scrutiny Again," *New York Times,* May 24, 1995, page D3.

Diana B. Henriques, "Cinerama V. Technicolor: A Suit That Has Wall Street's Attention," *New York Times,* May 23, 1995, page D8.

Diana B. Henriques, "Nation's Business Court Under Fire," *New York Times,* May 23, 1995, page D1.

Diana B. Henriques, "Perelman Wins Victory in Delaware in Technicolor Purchase Suit," *New York Times,* July 18, 1995, page D1.

Daniel Hertzberg and Hank Bilman with Roger Lownstein, "Pantry Pride Could Finance Cash Bid of $2 Billion for Revlon, Analysts Say," *Wall Street Journal,* August 16, 1985, page 18.

Jonathan Hicks, "MacAndrews to Acquire Coleman," *New York Times,* March 21, 1989, page D4.

Bill Hoffmann, "Revlon King Leaves Gossip-Queen Wife," *New York Post,* August 18, 1991, page E14.

Sallie Hofmeister, "It's Not Easy Being a Brave New World," *Los Angeles Times,* February 6, 1996, page D6.

Sallie Hofmeister, "NBC and New World Strike Deal," *Los Angeles Times,* July 11, 1995, page D4.

David Holmberg, "Power Dinner in Palm Beach Plays Up Perelman's Status," *Palm Beach Post,* March 30, 1995, page 4A.

Jenny Hontz, "When Worlds Collide," *Daily Variety*, June 14, 1996, page 1.

Peter Hood, "Ron Cohn Called Them the Perfect Couple," *Spy*, February 1988, page 55.

Craig Horowitz, "Dream Team Jr.," *New York*, November 21, 1994, page 30.

Craig Horowitz, "The Richest Guy in Town," *New York*, September 6, 1993, page 46.

"How a Buy-out Works," *USA Today*, October 17, 1985, page 1B.

"How the Rich Do It," *Philadelphia Inquirer*, April 11, 1991, page C2.

Mary Huhn, "HFM, Perelman Green-Light 'Premiere,'" *Mediaweek*, May 22, 1995, page 6.

Mary Huzinec, "Passages," *People Weekly*, February 6, 1995, page 69.

Suein L. Hwang, "Perelman Plans Public Offering for Cigar Firm," *Wall Street Journal*, June 27, 1996, page B14.

James C. Hyatt, "Perelman Plans Sweet Cash Dividend After Licorice Maker's Stock Offering," *Wall Street Journal*, June 29, 1992, page B8C.

Nina Hyde, "From Palm Beach," *Washington Post*, January 8, 1989, page F3.

"In Brief," *Broadcasting & Cable*, June 14, 1993, page 104.

"Investor Ronald Perelman," *Television Digest*, February 21, 1994, page 71.

Margaret A. Jacobs, "Perelman Settles Dispute With Fired Aide," *Wall Street Journal*, July 19, 1995, page B10.

Thomas Jaffe, "Ron Perelman's Nonlinear Math," *Forbes*, February 14, 1994, page 60.

Don Jeffrey, "Perelman Mulls Second TW Takeover Attempt," *Nation's Restaurant News*, January 11, 1988, page 3.

Douglas Jehl, "An Ill Wife, a Tough Boss and a Lawsuit," *New York Times*, June 28, 1995, page D1.

Harriet C. Johnson, "Takeover Lockouts Get Harder," *USA Today*, November 4, 1985, page 6B.

Harriet C. Johnson, "Revlon Battle Engages 'Media-shy' Perelman," *USA Today*, August 28, 1985, page 2B.

Harriet C. Johnson, "Revlon Makeup Unsure in Deal," *USA Today*, November 4, 1985, page 6B.

David Johnston, "No. 2 Man at F.B.I. to Quit for Job with Financier," *New York Times*, November 25, 1993, page B16.

Dave Kansa and Laura Bird, "Inside Track," *Wall Street Journal,* June 21, 1995, page C1.

Daniel Kaplan, "Six Claim No. 1 Spot in First Nationwide Deal," *American Banker,* October 11, 1994, page 32.

Anne Kates, "$4.7B Revlon Offer Spurned by Gillette," *USA Today,* June 19, 1987, page 2B.

Shawn G. Kennedy, "Modern Opulence: A Return to One-Family Use on the Upper East Side," *New York Times,* December 2, 1990, page J7.

James Ketelsen, "Mr. Fixit," *Forbes,* May 22, 1995, page 66.

James Kim, "Slam! Marvel Stock Takes 17% Plunge," *USA Today,* February 19, 1992, page 1B.

Ralph T. King, Jr., "BankAmerica, in Texas Push, to Buy Branches of Perelman's First Gibraltar," *Wall Street Journal,* September 22, 1992, page A3.

Ralph T. King, Jr., "Ron Perelman's $640 Million Unsure Thing," *Forbes,* October 30, 1989, page 42.

Steve Klinkerman, "Perelman Sale Illustrates Agency's Dilemma," *American Banker,* March 13, 1990, page 10.

Steve Klinkerman, "Perelman Thrift Sells Its Unit in Oklahoma," *American Banker,* August 11, 1992, page 1.

Steve Klinkerman, "Perelman's Texas S&L Put on Block in Pieces," *American Banker,* August 10, 1992, page 1.

Steve Klinkerman, "Tax Breaks, Guarantees Spurred 1st Texas Deal," *American Banker,* January 10, 1989, page 2.

Jerry Knight, "A Tale of Two Billionaires," *Washington Post,* June 3, 1990, page H1.

Jerry Knight, "U.S. Halts $2.5 Billion in Tax Breaks for S&L Buyers," *Philadelphia Inquirer,* March 8, 1991, page C10.

Elizabeth Kolbert, "Tartikoff Sings On at TV Upstart," *New York Times,* June 15, 1994, page D19.

Jesse Kornbluth, *Highly Confident: The Crime and Punishment of Michael Milken.* New York: Morrow, 1992.

Jeffrey Kutler, "Acquirers May Brush Elbows in Texas," *American Banker,* January 3, 1989, page 10.

Wade Lambert and Randell Smith, "Perelman Didn't Overpay," *Wall Street Journal,* October 22, 1990, page B2.

Hal Lancaster, "Perelman Sells Oklahoma Unit of S&L Purchased Amid Controversy," *Wall Street Journal,* August 11, 1992, page A4.

Mark Landler, "Citizen Ron," *Business Week,* December 13, 1993, page 52.

Mark Landler, "How Time Warner May Calm Its Investors," *New York Times,* May 18, 1995, page D6.

Mark Landler with Laura Zinn, "The Makeup Maker Who Would Be Media Mogul," *Business Week,* June 14, 1993, page 95.

Calvin Lawrence, Jr., "Perelman Putting Coleman in Corporate Chest," *USA Today,* March 21, 1989, page 2B.

James Ledbetter, "Clipboard," *Village Voice,* August 30, 1994, page 7.

David Leibowitz, "Ron Perelman's Other Company," *Financial World,* November 3, 1987, page 133.

David Leonhardt, "Perelman Firm to Buy Boston Whaler for $20M," *Boston Globe,* June 25, 1993, page 61.

David Leonhardt, "What Evil Lurks in the Heart of Ron?" *Business Week,* January 22, 1996, page 44.

Harriet Lessy, "At Perelman Home, New Family Makeup," *Philadelphia Daily News,* December 16, 1994, page 52.

Gary Levin, "Revlon's Perelman Buys Into Infomercials," *Advertising Age,* November 15, 1993, page 3.

Kate Bohner Lewis, "How Not to Marry a Billionaire," *Forbes,* July 31, 1995, page 16.

Larry Light, "Perelman Is No Superhero to Investors at Andrews," *Business Week,* July 23, 1990, page 57.

Larry Light and Laura Zinn, "Painting a New Face on Revlon," *Business Week,* April 6, 1992, page 26.

Larry Light with Monica Roman, "Why Perelman Faces Life Without Makeup," *Business Week,* April 1, 1991, page 71.

Jennifer Lin, "Drexel Falls Victim to the Junk-bond Market It Created," *Philadelphia Inquirer,* February 15, 1990, page D1.

Steven Lipin, "Perelman Said to Pull a Revlon Unit Off Block, Dissatisfied With Offer," *American Banker,* November 30, 1990, page 14.

John Lippman, "Fox Network's Historic Raid Rewrites Affiliates Rulebook," *Los Angeles Times,* May 25, 1994, page D1.

John Lippman, "Tartikoff to Head Unit of New World," *Los Angeles Times,* June 15, 1994, page D1.

John Lippman and Richard Turner, "New World Communications Is

Said to Be in Talks to Buy Cannell Studios," *Wall Street Journal*, January 9, 1995, page B2.

"Liza Solos in Revlon Campaign," *USA Today*, September 1, 1987, page 2B.

Joe Logan, "Another Big Deal for Ronald Perelman," *Philadelphia Inquirer*, May 26, 1994, page G1.

Joe Logan, "Revlon Chairman Perelman Cuts Another Massive Deal," *Orlando Sentinel*, May 29, 1994, page D1.

Elaine Louie, "Perelman Gift to Penn," *New York Times*, April 28, 1995, page B2.

Roger Lowenstein, "Note-holders, Perelman Clash Over a Pledge," *Wall Street Journal*, January 26, 1990, page C1.

Tom Lowry, "Suit: He's King of Mean," *New York Daily News*, July 6, 1995, page 4.

"MacAndrews & Forbes Co.," *Wall Street Journal*, April 21, 1980, page 33.

"MacAndrews & Forbes Group Inc.," *Wall Street Journal*, July 7, 1987, page 47.

"MacAndrews & Forbes Group Inc.," *Wall Street Journal*, November 2, 1983, page 47.

"MacAndrews & Forbes Group Inc.," *Wall Street Journal*, May 10, 1983, page 14.

"MacAndrews & Forbes Holdings Inc.," *Wall Street Journal*, November 24, 1993, page C25.

"MacAndrews & Forbes Holdings Inc.," *Wall Street Journal*, June 15, 1984, page 40.

Carl MacDonald, "Mr. and Mrs. Perelman Build Their Dream House(s)," *Spy*, April 1989, page 150.

Jamie Malanowski, "Naked City: The Usual Suspects," *Spy*, May 1989, page 40.

Jamie Malanowski, "Naked City: The Usual Suspects," *Spy*, November 1988, page 18.

Joe Mandese, "Fox Jolts Nets Into New Era," *Advertising Age*, May 30, 1994, page 34.

Kevin Maney, "Perelman Is Cutting a Deal With Gillette," *USA Today*, November 17, 1986, page 1B.

Kevin Maney, "Perelman's Sharp Deals," *USA Today*, August 18, 1987, page 3B.

Gene G. Marcial, "Has Perelman Taken a Shine to Sterling Drugs?" *Business Week*, July 13, 1987, page 10.

Gene G. Marcial, "Has Perelman Won His Proxy Fight?" *Business Week*, September 9, 1985, page 72.

Gene G. Marcial, "Has Ron Perelman Spotted a Pearl?" *Business Week*, June 26, 1995, page 126.

Gene G. Marcial, "The Heavy Hitters May Be Swinging at Salomon Again," *Business Week*, March 14, 1988, page 109.

Gene G. Marcial, "High Rollers Heap Chips on Aztar," *Business Week*, July 17, 1995, page 90.

Gene G. Marcial, "Is That Ron Perelman Come a Courtin'?" *Business Week*, November 30, 1992, page 91.

Gene G. Marcial, "Ron Perelman: Vegas or Bust?" *Business Week*, January 16, 1995, page 72.

Gene G. Marcial, "With Perelman on the Prowl, Even P&G Isn't Safe," *Business Week*, December 12, 1988, page 106.

"Marketline: Perelman Said to Sell TW Services Stake," *USA Today*, September 14, 1988, page 3B.

"Marvel Entertainment Group," *Wall Street Journal*, May 10, 1993, page C19.

"Marvel Entertainment Plans to Offer 3.5 Million Shares," *Wall Street Journal*, May 15, 1991, page A3.

Andrew Maykuth, "Mystery Investor Purchases 6.3 Percent of Resorts' Share Yesterday," *Philadelphia Inquirer*, January 7, 1995, page D1.

Steve McClellan, "Perelman Didn't Mean to Start a Revolution," *Broadcasting & Cable*, April 17, 1995, page 49.

Karen McCormack, "What's Up: The Mogul's Wine," *Money*, May 1995, page 22.

Craig R. McCoy, "Rendell War Chest Holds $2.3 Million," *Philadelphia Inquirer*, January 31, 1995, page B2.

Robert McGough, "The Joys of Being an Insider," *Forbes*, December 31, 1984, page 33.

Jim McTague, "Break S&L Deals, Congress Urges," *USA Today*, September 17, 1990, page 2B.

Jim McTague, "Congress and S&L Deals: More Bite or Bark?" *American Banker*, March 10, 1989, page 6.

Jim McTague, "Perelman, Bass, Ford Motor Saved Total of $2.8 Billion in Taxes," *American Banker*, January 11, 1989, page 2.

William Mehlman, "TW Services Finds Support as Bargain Price/Value Play," *Insider's Chronicle*, March 30, 1987, page 1.

R. H. Melton, "Dole's Think Tank to Return Leftover Funds," *Philadelphia Inquirer*, June 21, 1995, page A7.

Robert Metz, "The Perils of Perelman: Obscure Lawsuit Could Hurt Raider," *Boston Globe*, December 18, 1990, page 46.

William Meyers, "How Ron Perelman Became the Richest Man in America," *Institutional Investor*, May 1989, page 140.

James W. Michaels, "Side Lines: The Assets Shrink but the Debts Don't," *Forbes*, December 10, 1990, page 8.

James W. Michaels with Phyllis Berman, "My Story—Michael Milken," *Forbes*, March 16, 1992, page 78.

Laureen Miles, "Stations: Ronald Perelman," *Mediaweek*, May 9, 1994, page 8B.

Lauren Miles and Michael Freeman, "NATPE '95 Q&A: Ron Perelman," *Mediaweek*, January 23, 1995, page 22.

Alan Mirabella, "Hard Charger Leads Ron to New Land," *Crain's New York Business*, May 30, 1994, page 1.

"Mockler Alienates Gillette Investors," *USA Today*, June 19, 1987, page 2B.

Mike Mokrzycki, "Fired Executive Fires Back With Suit Against Perelman," *Philadelphia Inquirer*, July 6, 1995, page C1.

Joanna Molloy, "Time Demands," *New York Daily News*, February 23, 1996, page 3.

John Moody with Barbara Rudolph, "Corporate Creep Show," *Time*, July 17, 1995, page 39.

"More Than Just Another Raider?" *U.S. News & World Report*, December 29, 1986, page 70.

Gretchen Morgenson, "The Perils of Perelman," *Forbes*, December 10, 1990, page 218.

Allen R. Myerson, "Cigar-loving Perelman Buys Quite a Big Supply," *New York Times*, December 15, 1992, page D6.

Allen R. Myerson, "A New Ford in California's Future," *New York Times*, April 18, 1994, page D1.

Allan Nadler, "King of Kings County: The Messiah Dies—and Lives," *New Republic*, July 11, 1994, page 16.

Gautam Naik, "Perelman Consolidates Some Properties as Part of His

Plans for Media Empire," *Wall Street Journal*, February 18, 1994, page D5.

"Nailing Down a Victory at Revlon," *Business Week*, November 18, 1985, page 52.

Nathaniel C. Nash, "$5 Billion Rescue of 5 Savings Units Is Planned by U.S.," *New York Times*, December 28, 1988, page A1.

Nathaniel C. Nash, "2 Savings Bailouts Costing $7 Billion Confirmed by U.S.," *New York Times*, December 29, 1988, page D2.

Enid Nemy, "Charles Revson of the Revlon Empire Dies," *New York Times*, August 25, 1975, page 30.

William Neuman, "Sex, Lox, Bagels & Biz," *New York Post*, July 6, 1995, page 3.

"The New Acquirers: What Can the Business Expect to See?" *Savings Institutions*, February 1989, page 40.

"A New Face at Revlon?" *Time*, March 18, 1991, page 69.

"New World Accepts Offer by Pathé," *New York Times*, February 25, 1989, page A35.

"New World Buyout Set," *New York Times*, April 11, 1989, page D17.

"New World Communications Group," *TV Digest*, September 19, 1994, page 8.

"New World Entertainment," *New York Times*, January 26, 1989, page D4.

"New World Seeks a Backer," *New York Times*, January 31, 1989, page D4.

John Newberry, "FSLIC's S&L Bailouts a Bonanza for Lawyers," *USA Today*, December 29, 1988, page 2B.

Edith Newhall, "Perelman's $10 Million," *Art News*, April 1995, page 29.

Anne Newman, "Marvel Sees Net Rising Sharply Over 2 Years," *Wall Street Journal*, March 29, 1993, page 9L.

Anne Newman, "Perelman Is Pressured to Raise Offer for Marvel Entertainment to $30 a Share," *Wall Street Journal*, April 26, 1993, page A9a.

"Newslines: Perelman Gets Tender for Marvel," *Variety*, May 10, 1993, page 258.

"Newsmakers: Chest Pains Send Penny Marshall to the Hospital," *Philadelphia Inquirer*, May 31, 1994, page E2.

"Newsmakers: Queen Bumped by a Couple of Rich, Uh, Milk Men," *Philadelphia Inquirer*, April 11, 1994, page C2.

"Newsmakers: Who's Who at Tonight's Trump-Maples Wedding," *Philadelphia Inquirer*, December 20, 1993, page F2.

Floyd Norris, "Boom in Comic Books Lifts New Marvel Stock Offering," *New York Times,* July 15, 1991, page D1.

Bob O'Brien, "Ronald O. Perelman," *Variety,* September 26, 1994, page NY-8.

"Offer Raises Marvel Stock," *Philadelphia Inquirer,* March 23, 1993, page IV,1.

"Officers Back Sale of Pantry Pride," *New York Times,* February 27, 1985, page 5.

Yumiko Ono, " 'Nonsmearing' Lipstick Makes a Vivid Imprint on Revlon," *Wall Street Journal,* November 16, 1995, page B1.

Yumiko Ono, "Revlon Files Initial Public Offering That Keeps Perelman in Control," *Wall Street Journal,* November 20, 1995, page B4.

Yumiko Ono, "Revlon Inc. Details Its IPO, Reports a Quarterly Profit," *Wall Street Journal,* February 6, 1996, page B12.

Jack Otter, "New Home for Revlon Chairman," *Newsday,* June 10, 1993, page 27.

"Pantry Pride Fills Key Post," *New York Times,* July 9, 1985, page 2.

"Pantry Pride's Plan for Revlon," *New York Times,* August 24, 1985, page D1.

"Pantry Pride," *New York Times,* October 12, 1985, page 43.

"Pantry Revlon Suit Cites Plan," *New York Times,* October 9, 1985, page D10.

Ellen Paris, "The Perils of Perelman," *Forbes,* December 11, 1989, page 65.

Alexandra Peers, "Perelman Scoops Up Marvel's Depressed Shares," *Wall Street Journal,* August 17, 1994, page C1.

Martin Peers, "Perelman Playing Cool on Time-Warner Buy," *Variety,* May 29, 1995, page 4.

Martin Peers, "Perelman Seeks License to Operate Casino," *Daily Variety,* December 23, 1994, page 4.

"People to Watch in 1986," *USA Today,* December 31, 1985, page 2B.

"People: Ronald Perelman," *U.S. News & World Report,* April 22, 1991, page 13.

"Perelman Acquires Leading U.S. Cigar Company," *New York Times,* March 5, 1993, page D3.

"Perelman Confirmed the Sale of His CPC Stake," *Los Angeles Times,* November 7, 1986, page IV,1.

"Perelman Group Buying Reebok Boat Unit," *New York Times*, June 25, 1993, page D3.

"Perelman Invests in TV Infomercial Producer," *Los Angeles Times*, November 18, 1993, page D2.

"Perelman Ousts Coleman Chief," *USA Today*, May 3, 1989, page 2B.

"Perelman Outfit May Bid $714M for Revlon," *USA Today*, March 9, 1987, page 2B.

"The Perelman Papers," *Forbes*, October 23, 1989, page 360.

"Perelman's Casino Application," *Wall Street Journal*, July 27, 1995, page B3.

"Perelman's Gift," *Crain's New York Business*, January 24, 1994, page 50.

Chuck Philips, "Pop Shopping: Booming Music Business Has Investors Drooling," *Los Angeles Times*, June 2, 1995, page D1.

Edward T. Pound, "Ten Political Donors Hit With Fincs for Violations of Contribution Limits," *Wall Street Journal*, March 18, 1993, page 14.

Bill Powell with Carolyn Friday, "A White Knight Saves Salomon," *Newsweek*, October 12, 1987, page 66.

"Power Plays: Ron Perelman—How Green Was His S&L?" *Philadelphia Magazine*, September 1990, page 16.

Terry Pristin, "Financier Gets a Casino License," *New York Times*, July 27, 1995, page B1.

Steven E. Prokesch, "Bergerac's Sudden Reversal," *New York Times*, October 5, 1985, page D1.

Steven E. Prokesch, "Pantry Pride Chairman Hunts Biggest Prey Yet," *New York Times*, August 28, 1985, page D1.

Steven E. Prokesch, "Revlon's New Alluring Look," *New York Times*, August 22, 1985, page D1.

"Property Values," *Philadelphia Inquirer*, May 11, 1993, page IV,3.

Todd S. Purdum, "Forstmann Raises Bid for Revlon," *New York Times*, October 14, 1985, page D1.

Todd S. Purdum, "A Reviving Cosmetics Line," *New York Times*, October 5, 1985, page D1.

Todd S. Purdum, " 'Tired' Clinton in Tetons for a 17-Day Vacation," *New York Times*, August 16, 1995, page B10.

"Raider Unwelcome," *USA Today*, January 11, 1988, page 2B.

Anthony Ramirez, "The Raider Who Runs Revlon," *Fortune*, September 14, 1987, page 56.

Anthony Ramirez, "Revlon's Striving Makeover Man," *Fortune*, January 5, 1987, page 54.

Barbara Rehm, "RTC Prepays Notes Used in Perelman Thrift Deal," *American Banker*, February–April 1992, page 1.

Larry Reibstein with Carolyn Friday and Nonny Abbott, "The Smart Money in S&L's," *Newsweek*, January 9, 1989, page 40.

Rita Reif, "Thomas Ammann, Modern Art Dealer and Collector, 43," *New York Times*, June 11, 1993, page A28.

Patrick M. Reilly, "Perelman, Hachette Gaze Starry-eyed at Big for K-III's Premiere Magazine," *Wall Street Journal*, May 22, 1995, page B3.

Patrick M. Reilly, "Perelman, Irate, Pulls His Ads Out of Hearst," *Wall Street Journal*, August 22, 1994, page B1.

Paul Reuiter, "Texas Bailout Leader Built Empire on Challenges," *Los Angeles Times*, December 29, 1988, page IV,1.

Reuters, "Marvel-MCA Deal Is Seen," *New York Times*, June 15, 1994, page 19.

Reuters, "Revlon Shares in the Pink With IPO," *Los Angeles Times*, March 1, 1996, page D2.

"Revlon Boss Ron Perelman's Tiff with Hearst Magazines," *Cosmetic Insider's Report*, September 5, 1994, page 1.

"Revlon Debt to Double," *New York Times*, August 30, 1985, page D4.

"Revlon Files Debt Comment," *New York Times*, September 11, 1985, page 18.

"Revlon Fund Shift Is Barred," *New York Times*, October 16, 1985, page D26.

"Revlon Inc. Agrees to Pay Forstmann," *New York Times*, December 3, 1985, page D4.

"Revlon Is Sued," *New York Times*, August 23, 1985, page D4.

"Revlon Plan for Bond Deal," *New York Times*, June 29, 1991, page A36.

"Revlon Regroup," *Delaney Report*, February 28, 1994, page 1.

"Revlon Rejects Reduced Offer," *New York Times*, September 25, 1985, page D5.

"Revlon Says Unit's Sale Is Off," *New York Times*, December 27, 1985, page D4.

"Revlon to Sell Max Factor Unit to Trim Debt," *Philadelphia Inquirer*, April 11, 1991, page D10.

"Revlon Tries Again," *USA Today*, February 6, 1996, page 1B.

James Risen, "Investor Is Still Reaping Big Benefits From 1988 S&L Deal," *Philadelphia Inquirer*, September 20, 1994, page C1.

James Risen, "Investor Perelman Still Benefits from '88 Deal," *Los Angeles Times*, September 20, 1994, page D1.

James Risen, "Washington Watch: Love Those Loopholes," *Financial World*, November 22, 1984, page 16.

J. Max Robins, "New World, Perelman Get With the Program," *Variety*, June 20, 1994, page 19.

Monica Roman, "The Changes at Revlon Are More Than Just Cosmetic," *Business Week*, November 20, 1989, page 74.

Monica Roman, "New Tune for Perelman?" *Hollywood Reporter*, February 28, 1996, page 1.

Lois Romano, "The Reliable Source," *Washington Post*, August 10, 1994, page D3.

Peter Romeo, "Transworld Weighs Options to Block Hostile Takeover," *Nation's Restaurant News*, November 10, 1986, page 2.

"Ronald Perelman Donates $10 Million," *New York Times*, December 12, 1991, page B12.

Robert A. Rosenblatt, "Subsidized Sale of Failing Thrift Is Under Attack," *Los Angeles Times*, May 2, 1990, page D1.

Tracie Rozhon with N. R. Kleinfield, "Getting Into Co-ops: The Money Bias," *New York Times*, October 31, 1995, page 1.

"Ruffles and Flourishes," *New York Times*, December 4, 1994, page 63.

George Rush and Joanna Molloy, "Perelman Losing Sleep Over Al & Claudia's Pillow Talk," *New York Daily News*, July 14, 1995, page 21.

"Sam, Make Way for Ron," *Time*, May 22, 1989, page 87.

Jesus Sanchez, "Perelman Gives Revlon Makeover," *USA Today*, November 25, 1986, page 1B.

Linda Sandler, "Investors Weigh Price of Following Perelman," *Wall Street Journal*, June 5, 1995, page C2.

Linda Sandler, "Marvel Entertainment's Disarray Is a Study in the Ups and Downs of Betting on Perelman," *Wall Street Journal*, November 21, 1995, page C2.

Linda Sandler, "Revlon Share Offering Is a Chance to Prove Perelman's Persuasive Power with Investors," *Wall Street Journal*, November 27, 1995, page C2.

Suzanne Sataline, "Samuel Rosenblum, 1982, a Giant of Business in Post-war Phila.," *Philadelphia Inquirer*, September 15, 1995, page D11.

"Savings Plan by Perelman," *New York Times*, December 15, 1988, page D18.

Sydney H. Schanberg, "Why Cut Al Slack? Because He's in Love!" *Newsday*, March 7, 1995, page A27.

Susan Schmidt, "Sale of First Gibraltar Bank May Triple Investor's Money," *Washington Post*, September 23, 1992, page C1.

Richard B. Schmitt, "Court Holds Directors to Higher Standard," *Wall Street Journal*, November 1, 1993, page B6.

"SCI Says It Has Creditors' Approval for Chapter 11 Reorganization Plan," *Wall Street Journal*, March 5, 1993, page B3.

Marvin R. Shanken, "Ron Perelman," *Cigar Aficionado*, Spring 1995, page 54.

Eben Shapiro, "New World Shares Rise: Soros Firm Acquires Stake," *Wall Street Journal*, January 25, 1995, page B7.

Dan Shaw, "Even for Party-boy Painter, 3 Nights of Celebrating Are a Lot," *New York Times*, March 5, 1995, page 39.

Gail Shister, "Channel 3 Could Be Subject to Affiliation Switch by Group W," *Philadelphia Inquirer*, July 8, 1994, page F9.

Gail Shister, "Channel 3 in Fox's Lair? It'd Be a Match Made in Pro-football Heaven," *Philadelphia Inquirer*, June 8, 1994, page F6.

Gail Shister, "Fox Move Takes Toll on CBS," *Philadelphia Inquirer*, May 25, 1994, page A1.

Gail Shister, "Murdoch Expects More Stations, Affiliates to Join Fox Network," *Philadelphia Inquirer*, July 14, 1994, page E6.

Gail Shister, "NBC's Dawn Patrol Unveils Its 'Window on the World' Studio Today," *Philadelphia Inquirer*, June 20, 1994, page C5.

"Shy Perelman Is in Limelight," *USA Today*, November 17, 1986, page 2B.

"Sick-Bay Report," *Philadelphia Inquirer*, August 22, 1991, page C2.

"Signals: Revlon Group," *Fortune*, December 8, 1986, page 14.

Allan Sloan, "Citizens Beware: High Taxes Bounce Right Off Loophole Man!" *Los Angeles Times*, April 4, 1993, page D5.

Allan Sloan, "Comic Deal May See Perelman Laughing All the Way to the Bank," *Los Angeles Times*, June 3, 1991, page D5.

Allan Sloan, "Deal to Switch CBS Affiliates Appears to Create Value Out of Thin Air," *Washington Post*, May 31, 1994, page C3.

Allan Sloan, "Everyone Into the Blind Pool," *Forbes*, April 4, 1988, page 36.

Allan Sloan, "Fitzgerald Would Have Appreciated Perelman and His Pending Purchase," *Los Angeles Times*, September 25, 1994, page D2.

Allan Sloan, "How Perelman Pocketed a Cool $1.2 Billion on Sale of S&Ls," *Los Angeles Times*, September 27, 1992, page D5.

Allan Sloan, "How to Make $2 Billion," *Financial Weekly*, February 6, 1990, page 36.

Allan Sloan, "How You Can Invest with Revlon's Ron Perelman," *Money*, July 1994, page 19.

Allan Sloan, "Musical Chairs With TV Stations a Master Stroke by Master Moneymakers," *Los Angeles Times*, May 29, 1994, page D2.

Allan Sloan, "Perelman Deal on Andrews Is for Brave Only," *Los Angeles Times*, May 28, 1990, page D5.

Allan Sloan, "Pyramid Power," *Forbes*, January 27, 1986, page 30.

Allan Sloan, "What Color Is Your Mail?" *Forbes*, October 19, 1987, page 36.

Allan Sloan and Laura Jereski, "A Tale of Our Times," *Forbes*, May 18, 1987, page 180.

Pat Sloan, "Perelman Eager to Snare Gillette," *Advertising Age*, November 17, 1986, page 1.

Jack Smith, "In Your Face: Nothing Seems So Out of Step as a Cigar Smoker," *Philadelphia Inquirer*, August 7, 1994, page 12.

Liz Smith, "Peopletalk," *Philadelphia Inquirer*, March 9, 1995, page G2.

Liz Smith, "Peopletalk," *Philadelphia Inquirer*, December 19, 1994, page G2.

Liz Smith, "Peopletalk," *Philadelphia Inquirer*, June 29, 1993, page F2.

Liz Smith, "Peopletalk," *Philadelphia Inquirer*, December 9, 1992, page F2.

Liz Smith, "Peopletalk," *Philadelphia Inquirer*, November 10, 1992, page B2.

Liz Smith, "Peopletalk," *Philadelphia Inquirer*, July 14, 1992, page D2.

Liz Smith, "Peopletalk," *Philadelphia Inquirer*, November 9, 1991, page C2.

Liz Smith, "Peopletalk," *Philadelphia Inquirer*, October 14, 1991, page D2.

Liz Smith, "Peopletalk," *Philadelphia Inquirer*, August 19, 1991, page D2.

Liz Smith, "Peopletalk," *Philadelphia Inquirer*, January 15, 1985, page F3.

Liz Smith, "Peopletalk," *Philadelphia Inquirer*, January 11, 1985, page D2.

Liz Smith, "Peopletalk," *Philadelphia Inquirer,* December 24, 1984, page C2.

Liz Smith, "Perelmans: So Civilized," *Newsday,* August 19, 1991, page 11.

Randall Smith, "Can Perelman's Future IPOs Be as Good as Marvel's?" *Wall Street Journal,* October 24, 1991, page C1.

Randall Smith, "Perelman Plans to Sell Stock of Revlon Unit," *Wall Street Journal,* July 10, 1990, page A2.

Randall Smith and Laura Landro, "Perelman Bids for SCI Television Inc., May Ally With Another Station Group," *Wall Street Journal,* February 17, 1993, page A2.

Randall Smith and Jeffrey A. Trachtenberg, "Initial Offering of Revlon Stock Is Withdrawn," *Wall Street Journal,* July 31, 1992, page A3.

Randall Smith and Jeffrey A. Trachtenberg, "New Revlon Offering: Will the Latest Makeover Dazzle?" *Wall Street Journal,* May 27, 1992, page B4.

Randall Smith and Jeffrey A. Trachtenberg, "Perelman Is Said to Again Delay IPO for Revlon," *Wall Street Journal,* February 11, 1993, page A4.

Randall Smith and David Wessel, "New Look: The 80s Are Over, and Ron Perelman Now Is a 'Builder,'" *Wall Street Journal,* March 27, 1990, page 1.

Randall Smith and Kathleen Deveny with Alecia Swasy, "Perelman Launches Sale of Revlon Units to Procter & Gamble for $1.14 Billion," *Wall Street Journal,* April 11, 1991, page A4.

Randall Smith and Kathleen Deveny with Alecia Swasy, "Sale of Revlon Beauty Line Considered by Perelman," *Wall Street Journal,* March 1, 1991, page A3.

Robert Sobel, *Dangerous Dreamers: The Financial Innovators from Charles Merrill to Michael Milken.* New York: Wiley, 1993.

William H. Sokolic, "Atlantic City's Oasis of Affordable Housing," *Philadelphia Inquirer,* March 17, 1991, page I,1.

W. Speers, "Newsmakers: Celebrity Docket," *Philadelphia Inquirer,* June 17, 1995, page C2.

W. Speers, "Newsmakers: Couples," *Philadelphia Inquirer,* April 14, 1995, page C2.

W. Speers, "Newsmakers: Couples," *Philadelphia Inquirer,* January 31, 1995, page F2.

W. Speers, "Newsmakers: Couples," *Philadelphia Inquirer*, December 17, 1994, page D16.

W. Speers, "Newsmakers: Couples," *Philadelphia Inquirer*, November 25, 1994, page C2.

W. Speers, "Newsmakers: Couples," *Philadelphia Inquirer*, June 7, 1994, page C2.

W. Speers, "Newsmakers: Big Bucks," *Philadelphia Inquirer*, June 4, 1994, page D13.

W. Speers, "Newsmakers: Couples," *Philadelphia Inquirer*, March 28, 1992, page D2.

W. Speers, "Newsmakers: Living Space," *Philadelphia Inquirer*, January 1, 1994, page D13.

W. Speers, "Newsmakers: Locally Connected," *Philadelphia Inquirer*, August 13, 1994, page F2.

W. Speers, "Newsmakers: Markings," *Philadelphia Inquirer*, July 14, 1995, page E2.

W. Speers, "Newsmakers: Markings," *Philadelphia Inquirer*, February 18, 1995, page F2.

W. Speers, "Newsmakers: No 'Touchy-Feely,' says Peter Jennings of His Dinner with Barbra Streisand," *Philadelphia Inquirer*, January 21, 1995, page D11.

W. Speers, "Newsmakers: Revlon Owner Said to Take a Powder," *Philadelphia Inquirer*, August 17, 1991, page D2.

Leah Nathans Spiro with Ronald Grover, "The Operator," *Business Week*, August 21, 1995, page 54.

Elizabeth Sporlan, "Claudia Cohen: How to Reach for the Stars and Settle for a Stellar Bank Account," *People Weekly*, May 7, 1990, page 157.

Benjamin Stein, *A License to Steal: The Untold Story of Michael Milken and the Conspiracy to Bilk the Nation.* New York: Simon & Schuster, 1992.

Greg Steinmetz and Ralph T. King, Jr., "Perelman Wins Bidding for Ford's Struggling Thrift," *Wall Street Journal*, April 15, 1994, page B4.

Richard Stengel, "Free Mike Milken," *Spy*, February 1990, page 44.

"Sterling National Bank and Trust Co.," *New York Times*, March 25, 1982, page D2.

Christopher Stern, "Deal in Works for Interest in Guthy-Renker," *Broadcasting & Cable*, November 15, 1993, page 81.

Amy Stevens, "Denny's Agrees to Alter Practices in Bias Settlement," *Wall Street Journal*, March 29, 1993, page 9C.

Richard W. Stevenson, "Bergerac Quits Revlon Posts," *New York Times*, November 6, 1985, page D4.

Richard W. Stevenson, "Decisions for Owner of Revlon," *New York Times*, November 4, 1985, page D1.

Richard W. Stevenson, "Pantry Pride Control of Revlon Board Seen Near," *New York Times*, November 5, 1985, page D5.

David Stipp, "Abex Agrees to Shed Operations, Merge Its Assets With MacAndrews & Forbes," *Wall Street Journal*, November 22, 1994, page 5.

"Stockholder Meeting Briefs," *Wall Street Journal*, March 7, 1984, page 51.

Jonathan Storm, "As Fox Scrambles Network World, Viewers Wonder: What's On?" *Philadelphia Inquirer*, May 29, 1994, page D1.

Gary Strauss, "Marketline: TW Shares Rise on Coniston Offer," *USA Today*, October 7, 1988, page 3B.

Stephanie Strom, "Revlon Bond Slide Raises Questions," *New York Times*, June 8, 1994, page C1.

Stephanie Strom, "Stock Sale Postponed by Revlon," *New York Times*, July 31, 1992, page C1.

"Suit Filed on Revlon Contract," *New York Times*, November 22, 1985, page D4.

"Summering in Avalon," *Philadelphia Inquirer*, July 29, 1990, page D2.

"Surreal City," *Philadelphia Inquirer*, January 10, 1991, page D1.

"Survivor Found After 9½ Days," *Newsday*, July 9, 1995, page A16.

Alecia Swasy, "Procter & Gamble Is to Buy Some of Revlon Inc.'s Lines," *Wall Street Journal*, April 10, 1991, page 6.

"Talking Deals: Gillette Testing Standstill Pact," *New York Times*, June 25, 1987, page D2.

"Technicolor Inc.," *New York Times*, March 8, 1983, page D2.

Rick Telberg, "Junk-bond Scare Imperils Transworld, Perelman Truce," *Nation's Restaurant News*, December 1, 1986, page 82.

David Tobenkin, "New World, NBC Near Shows-for-Stations Deal," *Broadcasting & Cable*, July 10, 1995, page 15.

Craig Torren, "When Are 7 TV Stations a Media Play?" *Wall Street Journal*, October 25, 1993, page C1.

Mark Tran, "Debt-troubled Revlon for Sale," *Guardian* (London), March 2, 1991, page 11.

"Transworld Fights Back," *USA Today*, October 28, 1986, page 1B.

"TV Stations Sold," *New York Times*, March 7, 1986, page 4.

University of Pennsylvania Record, Philadelphia: University of Pennsylvania Press, 1964.

Vartanig G. Vartan, "Revlon Plans Buyback Worth $57.50 a Share," *New York Times*, August 27, 1985, page D1.

Lawrence Ven Gelder, "Fire at the Four Seasons: Everyone Who's In Is Out," *New York Times*, March 16, 1995, page B3.

"Video Corp. Of America," *Wall Street Journal*, October 8, 1984, page 37.

Carol Vogel, "Inside Art: Big Gifts at the Guggenheim," *New York Times*, October 20, 1995, page C30.

Carol Vogel, "Revlon's Chairman Donates $10 Million to the Guggenheim," *New York Times*, January 20, 1994, page C15.

Wall Street Journal Staff Reporter, "Chief Executive to Buy Remainder of MacAndrews," *Wall Street Journal*, September 26, 1983, page 18.

Wall Street Journal Staff Reporter, "Cohen-Hatfield Says Investor Bought 40% of Outstanding Shares," *Wall Street Journal*, May 25, 1978, page 40.

Wall Street Journal Staff Reporter, "Cohen-Hatfield Buys About 22% of the Stock of a Candy Producer," *Wall Street Journal*, October 29, 1979, page 28.

Wall Street Journal Staff Reporter, "Cohen-Hatfield Offers $24 a Share to Acquire MacAndrews & Forbes," *Wall Street Journal*, December 24, 1979, page 13.

Wall Street Journal Staff Reporter, "Compact Video Elects Aides of MacAndrews Unit to Management," *Wall Street Journal*, March 29, 1984, page 51.

Wall Street Journal Staff Reporter, "Court Dismisses Holder Suit," *Wall Street Journal*, October 10, 1994, page B6.

Wall Street Journal Staff Reporter, "Divorce Clouds Plans by Perelman to Buy All of MacAndrews," *Wall Street Journal*, June 20, 1983, page 16.

Wall Street Journal Staff Reporter, "G&W Talks Terminated on Sale of Cigar Unit," *Wall Street Journal*, August 18, 1982, page 33.

Wall Street Journal Staff Reporter, "MacAndrews & Forbes Approves

Transaction to Take Firm Private," *Wall Street Journal,* October 12, 1983, page 5.

Wall Street Journal Staff Reporter, "MacAndrews & Forbes Chief May Acquire Rest of Firm's Shares," *Wall Street Journal,* May 17, 1983, page 2.

Wall Street Journal Staff Reporter, "MacAndrews & Forbes, Cohen-Hatfield Sign Definitive Merger Pact," *Wall Street Journal,* January 28, 1980, page 14.

Wall Street Journal Staff Reporter, "MacAndrews & Forbes Ends Richardson Bid," *Wall Street Journal,* December 4, 1981, page 4.

Wall Street Journal Staff Reporter, "MacAndrews & Forbes Faces 9 Suits Over Plan to Take Firm Private," *Wall Street Journal,* December 19, 1983, page 38.

Wall Street Journal Staff Reporter, "MacAndrews & Forbes Increases Its Stake in Technicolor to 81%," *Wall Street Journal,* December 7, 1982, page 19.

Wall Street Journal Staff Reporter, "MacAndrews & Forbes Says Group of Holders Suing Cohen-Hatfield," *Wall Street Journal,* February 25, 1980, page 12.

Wall Street Journal Staff Reporter, "MacAndrews & Forbes Slates Debt Offering, Drops Stock Proposal," *Wall Street Journal,* September 29, 1992, page C23.

Wall Street Journal Staff Reporter, "MacAndrews & Forbes to Begin Negotiating Terms of Merger Offer," *Wall Street Journal,* January 9, 1980, page 18.

Wall Street Journal Staff Reporter, "MacAndrews Officer, Wife Settle Dispute Over Control of Stock," *Wall Street Journal,* July 18, 1983, page 5.

Wall Street Journal Staff Reporter, "Perelman Plans Merger, New Multimedia Company," *Wall Street Journal,* November 29, 1993, page A4.

Wall Street Journal Staff Reporter, "Perelman Plans to Sell National Health Labs' Shares for $357 Million," *Wall Street Journal,* February 4, 1992, page C20.

Wall Street Journal Staff Reporter, "Perelman Seeks Permit for New Jersey Casino," *Wall Street Journal,* December 22, 1994, page A6.

Wall Street Journal Staff Reporter, "Perelman to Acquire, for a Higher Price, Cigar Firm He Sold," *Wall Street Journal,* December 15, 1992, page A12.

Wall Street Journal Staff Reporter, "Revlon Inc.'s Levin Gets Additional Title of Chief Executive," *Wall Street Journal*, August 12, 1992, page B2.

Wall Street Journal Staff Reporter, "Richardson Co. Attempt to Block MacAndrews' Tender Offer Is Denied," *Wall Street Journal*, November 5, 1981, page 24.

Wall Street Journal Staff Reporter, "Richardson Co. Gets Friendly Witco Offer of $27.50 a Share to Rebuff MacAndrews," *Wall Street Journal*, November 23, 1981, page 23.

Wall Street Journal Staff Reporter, "Richardson Rejects MacAndrews & Forbes Proposed Takeover," *Wall Street Journal*, November 3, 1981, page 23.

Wall Street Journal Staff Reporter, "S&P Lowers Ratings on Debt of 3 Entities Perelman Controls," *Wall Street Journal*, July 12, 1995, page C15.

Wall Street Journal Staff Reporter, "Video Corp. Accepts Offer of $33.3 Million by Closely Held Firm," *Wall Street Journal*, October 15, 1984, page 12.

Jeannette Walls, "Perelman-Simmons: The Synergy," *New York*, March 8, 1993, page 13.

Sharon Waxman, "Top Editors Quit Movie Magazine," *Washington Post*, May 18, 1996, page D1.

Leslie Wayne, "Regulators Are Seeking to Revise Some Sales of Savings and Loans," *New York Times*, August 5, 1990, page A1.

Pat Wechsler and Roger D. Friedman with Beth Landman, "Bill and Hillary's Revlon Retreat," *New York*, August 21, 1995, page 11.

Pat Wechsler with David Feld, "Perelman, Diller Talk Takeover," *New York*, January 3, 1994, page 9.

Judith Weinraub, "Four Named Trustees of Kennedy Center," *Washington Post*, January 12, 1995, page C3.

Linda Wells, "Returning to Revlon's Glory Days," *New York Times*, October 2, 1988, page C1.

Debra West, "Executive Testifies to Many Clashes with Perelman," *New York Times*, July 13, 1995, page D3.

Debra West, "Ousted Official Settles Suit Against Perelman's Company," *New York Times*, July 19, 1995, page D4.

James A. White, "Technicolor Pays a Director $150,000 for Aiding

Takeover Bid by MacAndrews," *Wall Street Journal*, November 8, 1982, page 10.

Randy Whitestone, "Executive Tells Court of Clashes with Perelman," *Gannett Suburban Newspapers*, July 11, 1995, page 5A.

Randy Whitestone, "Financier Drove Man From Job After Wife's Illness, Lawyer States," *Gannett Suburban Newspapers*, July 6, 1995, page 4.

Randy Whitestone, "Judge Warns Lawyers," *Gannett Suburban Newspapers*, July 8, 1995, page 5A.

Randy Whitestone, "Perelman's S&L Deal Smartly Sized," *USA Today*, December 15, 1988, page 2B.

"Who's News," *Wall Street Journal*, March 8, 1993, page B1.

R. Foster Winans, "Merger Mania Seems to Be Staging a Comeback Despite High Interest and Stock Prices," *Wall Street Journal*, December 20, 1983, page 55.

Chris Wloszczyna, "Perelman Cashing In With IPOs," *USA Today*, February 28, 1992, page 3B.

Wilton Woods, "How the 12 Top Raiders Rate," *Fortune*, September 28, 1987, page 52.

"Workplace: The 24-hour-a-day Fast Track," *New York Times*, July 2, 1995, page C2.

Catherine Yang with Leah Nathans and Todd Vogel, "It's the End of an Era for S&L Rescues—but What an End," *Business Week*, January 9, 1989, page 40.

Laura Zinn with Sunita Wadekar Bhargava and Elizabeth A. Lesly, "The New Ron Perelman Has an Old Problem," *Business Week*, June 14, 1993, page 94.

Sam Zuckerman, "B of A to Buy Texas Offices of Gibraltar," *American Banker*, September 22, 1992, page 1.

Sam Zuckerman, "A Deal as Solid as Gibraltar," *American Banker*, October 13, 1994, page 4.

Sam Zuckerman, "First Nationwide Acquisition to Test Texan's Profitability," *American Banker*, April 18, 1994, page 25.

Sam Zuckerman, "Perelman Aids Texan's Bid for Ford Unit," *American Banker*, April 12, 1994, page 1.

Sam Zuckerman, "Texan to Pay $1 Billion for Ford's Big Thrift," *American Banker*, April 15, 1994, page 1.

INDEX

275